UNCHARTED WATERS

OTHER BOOKS BY
JIM MCDOWELL

*Peace Conspiracy: The Story of Warrior-Businessman
Yoshiro Fujimura* (1993)

*Hamatsa: The Enigma of Cannibalism on the
Pacific Northwest Coast* (1997)

José María Narváez: The Forgotten Explorer (1998)

The Story of Sidney Island's Three Names (2011)

Father August Brabant: Saviour or Scourge? (2012)

Uncharted Waters

The Explorations of José Narváez
(1768–1840)

JIM McDOWELL

RONSDALE PRESS

UNCHARTED WATERS
Copyright © 2015 Jim McDowell

RONSDALE PRESS
3350 West 21st Avenue, Vancouver, B.C. Canada V6S 1G7
www.ronsdalepress.com

Typesetting: Julie Cochrane, in Granjon 11.5 pt on 15
Cover Design: Julie Cochrane
Cover Art: Gordon Miller's watercolour painting of the *Santa Saturnina* entering the Salish Sea
Paper: Ancient Forest Friendly Lynx 60 lb. Opaque, FSC Recycled, 100% post-consumer waste, totally chlorine-free and acid-free.

Ronsdale Press wishes to thank the following for their support of its publishing program: the Canada Council for the Arts, the Government of Canada through the Canada Book Fund, the British Columbia Arts Council, and the Province of British Columbia through the British Columbia Book Publishing Tax Credit program.

Library and Archives Canada Cataloguing in Publication

McDowell, Jim, 1934–, author
    Uncharted waters: the explorations of José Narváez (1768-1840) / Jim McDowell.

Includes bibliographical references and index.
Issued in print and electronic formats.
ISBN 978-1-55380-434-5 (print)
ISBN 978-1-55380-435-2 (ebook) / ISBN 978-1-55380-436-9 (pdf)

    1. Narváez, José, 1768?–. 2. Pacific Coast (North America) — Discovery and exploration. 3. Pacific Coast (B.C.) — Discovery and exploration. 4. Salish Sea (B.C. and Wash.) — Discovery and exploration. 5. Explorers — Spain — Biography. I. Title.

F851.5.M29 201   917.11'1042   C2015-902990-2   C2015-902991-0

At Ronsdale Press we are committed to protecting the environment. To this end we are working with Canopy and printers to phase out our use of paper produced from ancient forests. This book is one step towards that goal.

Printed in Canada by Marquis Book Printing, Quebec

to the memory of
John Crosse

ACKNOWLEDGEMENTS

First, I want to thank Alan Twigg, editor of *BC BookWorld*, for suggesting this project. Secondly, I am grateful to the University of Oklahoma Press, Norman, Oklahoma, for granting me permission to write a new biography of José María Narváez, which will, for the first time, present a complete account of his life.

I appreciate the assistance of personnel at the following libraries, archives, museums, and institutions: Provincial Archives of British Columbia, Victoria; Vancouver Public Library, Special Collections; Rare Books and Special Collections Library, University of British Columbia, Vancouver, British Columbia; Koerner Library, University of British Columbia, Vancouver; Vancouver Maritime History Museum; University of Victoria Library, Special Collections, Victoria; National Archives of Canada; University of Washington Library, Seattle; Seattle Public Library, Seattle; Bancroft Library, University of California, Berkeley; California History Section, California State Library, Sacramento; William Andrews Clark Library, University of California, Los Angeles; Honnold/Mudd Library, Special Collections, Claremont University Consortium, Claremont, California; Library of Congress, Geography and Map Division, Washington, D.C.; National Archives of U.K.; Biblioteca Nacional, Mexico City; Archivo General de la Nación, Mexico City; Museo Histórico Naval, Mexico City; Instituto de Antropología e Historia, Tepic; Museo Naval, Puerto Vallarta, Mexico; Museo Naval, Madrid; Museo de América, Madrid.

I gratefully acknowledge the information, advice, and encouragement provided by local maritime history enthusiasts Captain Steve Mayo of Bellingham, Washington, and British Columbians: Gordon Miller of Vancouver, Kim Davies and Gary Little of Sechelt, and Brad Morrison of Sidney. I greatly appreciate the enthusiastic assistance that San Jose, California-based Luis Marmolejo (a direct descendant of José Narváez) has contributed about the Spanish language, Narváez genealogy, and his collection of Narváez's charts and maps. Translation assistance with the first edition from Rose Esparza and with this edition from Norma Institoriz and Estefania Navarro Estévez has been essential.

I am also indebted to John Crosse, an independent historian whom I met in the late 1980s while I was researching my first book about José Narváez. At that time, John had started a similar project which he said would involve visiting several foreign archives and collecting considerable first-hand information from personal sailing ventures in British Columbia waterways. John's unpublished manuscript, *In the Wake of Narvaez*, is on file in the Special Collections Library at the University of British Columbia. He was an enthusiastic researcher, a helpful critic, a memorable character, and a good friend.

Finally, it is a privilege to once again acknowledge the invaluable, meticulous editorial assistance and advice provided by Ronald Hatch, who helped me transform a fact-heavy manuscript into a narrative that may finally give José Narváez the place in Pacific Northwest Coast history that he deserves.

CONTENTS

⁀

PART I

Spain Strives to Control the Pacific Northwest Coast

⁀

PART II

The Key Expedition

⌒

PART III

New Spain Changes Course

⌒

MAPS

AUTHOR'S NOTE

In 1998, the Arthur H. Clark Company, which was then based in Spokane, Washington, published my book *José Narváez: The Forgotten Explorer*, as number fifteen in its comprehensive "Spain in the West" series of important historical texts. It consisted of two parts: a partial overview of the life story of the Spanish-Mexican mariner and cartographer José María Narváez, and the first English translation of Narváez's journal of March 8 to October 23, 1788. This detailed seafarer's log, along with the author's notes, described New Spain's earliest comprehensive exploration of Alaskan waters above 60° north latitude, the Gulf of Alaska islands beyond 152° west longitude, and the Aleutian Island chain as far as 166° west longitude. Although this primary document remains of interest to scholars and historians, general readers deserve a more complete, stimulating narrative that illuminates all of Narváez's important activities and accomplishments. The need for such a revision has been highlighted by new interest in this explorer, which the original version has generated in the last sixteen years among historians, local history buffs, regional media, general readers, and online contributors. It is gratifying to see that Narváez's overlooked, yet significant, place in Pacific Northwest Coast history is gaining recognition. In the process, however, considerable misinformation about this individual has been circulated in print by journalists and historians.

To ensure that Narváez's role in the history of what is now British Columbia remains accurately recorded, I believe it is essential to set the record straight by clarifying and correcting such mistakes. To accomplish that objective, without interrupting the following narrative, I have placed specific corrections of other authors' errors in the endnotes, and cited these entries accordingly in the index. This second edition also gives me the opportunity to correct my own mistakes and expand on three aspects of Narváez's activities on the Pacific Northwest Coast that were barely mentioned in the first edition, because of its different focus.

Until now, Narváez's significant supporting role in Pacific Northwest Coast maritime history has been obscured by the attention given to celebrated explorers such as Alejandro Malaspina, Juan Francisco de la Bodega y Quadra, Dionisio Alcalá-Galiano, Cayetano Valdés, and George Vancouver. In reality, during the first phase of eighteenth-century Spanish explorations of the Northwest Pacific Ocean and its coastal waters (prior to the comprehensive Malaspina expedition of 1791–1792), it was *pilotos* (a naval rank that was equivalent to a captain's mate on European and American vessels) such as Narváez who performed most of the day-to-day navigation, reconnaissance, surveying, sounding, and chart work.[1] Although these *pilotos* often did not sign their charts, these documents provided the cartographic foundation for all of Spain's intensive exploration in the region. Recognition and examination of Narváez's accomplishments as an explorer is the primary reason why his story merits a fresh, more complete treatment, which can be readily accessed, understood, and appreciated by readers.

As the first complete biography of Narváez's life and achievements, this book includes new information about the man based on the author's recent findings, updated details concerning Narváez's explorations and activities during some of the most historically important events that occurred along the West Coast of North America and Mexico during his lifetime, and more accurate geographical descriptions. In an effort to view Narváez's experiences from his perspective, to the limited extent that this is possible, I have used Spanish place names throughout the book with either English translations or present-day names in parentheses to clarify various locations as well as generate a greater appreciation for our multi-ethnic history.

An Overlooked Explorer

THE VOYAGES OF EARLY European mariners in wooden sailing vessels, their quests for new trade routes, and their encounters with strangers in unknown lands remain a touchstone of identity for North Americans. Even in our complex era of high technology, global markets, and multicultural interaction, the exploits of these voyagers still capture our imagination. This book is about one of those men — José María Narváez y Gervete, a Spanish-Mexican seafarer. Most of José Narváez's maritime career involved serving as a non-commissioned *piloto* in the Spanish Navy. Nevertheless, he navigated and/or skippered numerous vessels; made several significant discoveries during the age of European exploration on what is now Canada's Pacific Northwest Coast; participated in many of the most important events that occurred there between 1788 and 1795; sailed to other places in the Pacific Ocean and engaged directly in the political upheaval that transformed New Spain into Mexico between 1796 and his death in 1840.

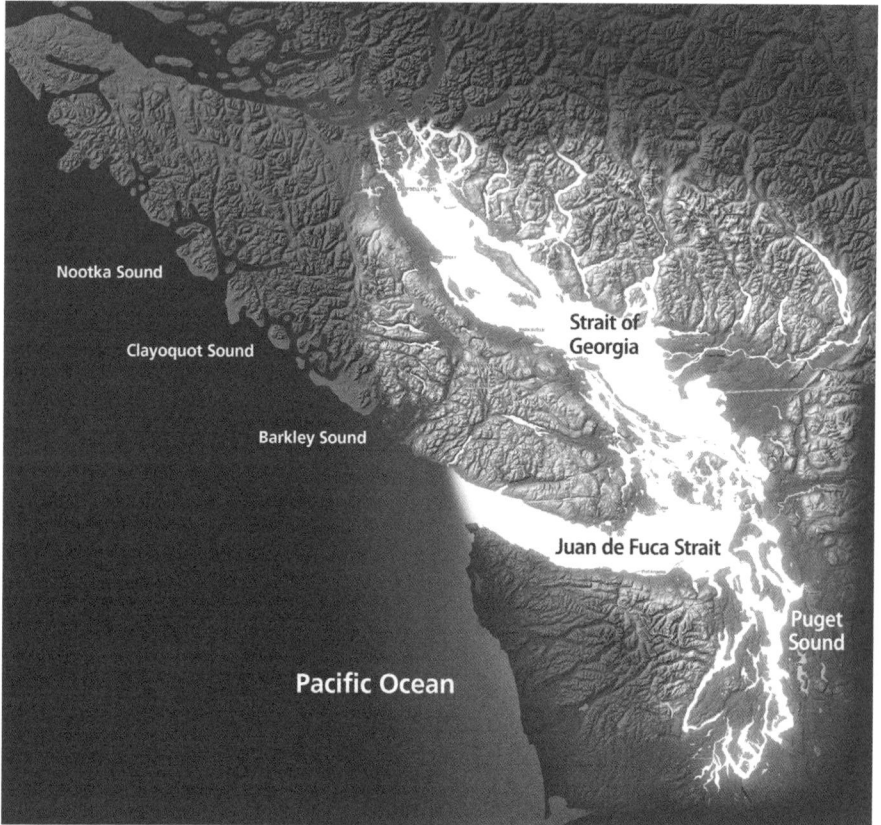

The Salish Sea, comprising the Strait of Georgia, Juan de Fuca Strait, and Puget Sound.

In Pacific Northwest Coast history, Narváez deserves special recognition for three particularly significant explorations. In 1788, the young navigator was the first Spaniard to contact and investigate a functioning Russian fur-trading outpost west of the Gulf of Alaska. The following year, Narváez became the first European to reconnoitre the interior of Juan de Fuca Strait — the long, wide throat of what is now known as the Salish Sea. Extending that exploration in 1791, he became the first European to sail across the large inland gulf that forms the northern part of today's Salish Sea, map the waterway extensively, sight its numerous islands, make brief contact with the people of a few First Nations, and discover the site of what is now western Canada's largest city — Vancouver, British Columbia.

The Salish Sea

In 2009 and 2010, the Province of British Columbia Geographic Names Office, the Geographical Names Board of Canada, the Washington State Board on Geographic Names, and the U.S. Board on Geographic Names each approved the name "Salish Sea" as an official designation for the inland marine waters of southern British Columbia, Canada, and northern Washington, USA. The Salish Sea extends from the north end of the Strait of Georgia and Desolation Sound to the south end of Puget Sound and west to the mouth of Juan de Fuca Strait where it meets the Pacific Ocean. These separately named, interconnected bodies of water form a single estuarine ecosystem, which covers approximately 18,000 square kilometres of inland marine waters.[1] It constitutes one of the world's great inland seas.

Prior to formal governmental adoption of this geographical designation, "Salish Sea" had been used commonly as a name for these waterways by citizens on both sides of the border for years, including Coast Salish people who lived around its shores and spoke one of the dialects of the ancient Salishan language. The Salish Sea is connected to the Pacific Ocean primarily via Juan de Fuca Strait (with comparatively slight tidal influence from the north around Vancouver Island at Point Chatham where Discovery Passage meets Johnstone Strait), and it is bordered by continental shores in the east, Vancouver Island in the northwest, and the Olympic Peninsula in the southwest. The saltwater area of this inland sea contains numerous channels in the North Gulf Islands, the South Gulf Islands, and the San Juan Islands; the large lower Fraser River Delta; the Puget Sound lowlands, Hood Canal, Tacoma Narrows, and Deception Pass.

Until my earlier book, *José Narváez: The Forgotten Explorer*, was published in 1998, other mariners tended to receive credit for these three achievements. In the first instance, most historians had recognized the controversial Captain Esteban José Martínez as having made New Spain's first contact with the Russians when he led the expedition to Alaskan waters in 1788. But Narváez's journal of that voyage, which the author translated into English for the first time,[2] showed they were incorrect. Although Martínez was in charge of the espionage mission, it was Narváez who went ashore first and accomplished a face-to-face encounter.

Regarding Juan de Fuca Strait — thought to be the long-sought western entrance to a legendary Northwest Passage trade route that would supposedly link the Atlantic and Pacific Oceans — it is surprising that it went unexplored by Europeans for as long as it did. Fascination with that hiatus has inspired some imaginative writers to generate fantastic, yet temptingly believable theories which disintegrate when common sense is applied. To place Narváez's actual exploration of Juan de Fuca Strait and one of its extensions in perspective, two of these legends require mention.

One incredible, hypothetical theory was advanced in 2003 by a British Columbia bureaucrat-turned-historian who alleged that it was the colourful English navigator Sir Francis Drake who first sailed *unarmed* through most of the Salish Sea, travelling from *north to south* in 1579 during a *secret* voyage of exploration that somehow was kept hidden from the public for more than four hundred years. The author of this implausible tale also asserted that Drake, continuing south along the Pacific Northwest Coast, probably careened his rotting *Golden Hind* on a small beach inside the miniscule bay now known as Whale Cove, Oregon. No archeological evidence has been found to support this supposition. Furthermore, Whale Cove is a treacherous little recess in the steep rocky shore along an extremely dangerous section of the Oregon coast. Even the skipper of a modern powerboat would hesitate to enter these choppy, churning, unprotected waters. Today, boaters are advised to remain 500 to 600 metres offshore for a distance of 1.6 kilometres north to 1.6 kilometres south of the cove. This author's notion was inspired in part by a crude chart of a tiny cove named Portus Novae Albionis — allegedly drawn by an ancient Greek mariner — which resembles the shape of the vastly larger Drake's Bay north of San Francisco. It is not surprising that this incongruous conjecture has failed to gain any serious support among responsible historians.[3] In reality, sailing *north* along the Pacific Northwest Coast in 1579, Drake failed to sight Juan de Fuca Strait and concluded that "either there is no passage at all through these

Northerne coasts, which is most likely, or if there be, that [it] is unnavigable."[4]

A much more fascinating legend suggests that it was the late sixteenth-century Greek seafarer — commonly known as Apóstolos Valerianos by Euro-American historians and as Ioannis Phokas (or Focus) by Hellenic historians[5] — who claimed to have led an expedition into the Salish Sea as early as 1592, while he was serving as a *piloto* for New Spain, using the name Juan de Fuca. According to Valerianos' tall tale, he supposedly was ordered by Luis de Velasco II, the eighth viceroy, to find the fabled Strait of Anian, an alleged northern waterway that connected the Atlantic and Pacific Oceans. On the Pacific Northwest Coast, Valerianos ostensibly discovered a broad strait between 47° and 48° north latitude and sailed through it between lands that were "rich in gold, silver and pearls" and inhabited by people clad in furs. According to Valerianos's story, he reached the Atlantic Ocean after a voyage of more than twenty days.[6] Although this myth inspired numerous European explorers to search for the Northwest Passage for centuries, it eventually became common knowledge that no such transcontinental waterway existed at this latitude. Furthermore, researchers have never been able to find a single record in the Spanish colonial archives about any part of the fanciful voyage.

Turning from fable to fact, one finds that the historical record documents three aspects of European exploration of Juan de Fuca Strait: the first sighting, probes of its mouth, and penetration of its throat. The renowned Captain James Cook, who investigated so much of the Pacific Ocean for England, sailed right past the fog-shrouded strait in 1778. The first recorded sighting was made in 1787 by a woman: Mrs. Charles William Barkley (Frances Hornby Trevor), wife of the English fur trader who captained the *Imperial Eagle*.[7] Subsequently, three other merchant mariners examined the strait's mouth, but exploration of its interior was left to Narváez. In 1789, he became the first European to chart what is now the Salish Sea's throat.

Narváez's most noteworthy accomplishment, however, was his exploration of a large interior arm of the Salish Sea — unknown to European mariners of the era — which reached northward a great distance. In the summer of 1791, the uncelebrated, twenty-three-year-old Spanish *piloto* became the first European to sail this broad inland sea in command of a small schooner and longboat. Nevertheless, the mariner who is commonly given credit for exploring this waterway and locating the site of the city that now bears his name is Britain's ace surveyor, Captain George Vancouver, who arrived one year later aboard the large square-rigged HMS *Discovery*.

Today, Narváez's remarkable achievements are almost unknown, barely recognized, or generally overlooked, and his biography remains unfamiliar to most North Americans. The fame attained by the British captains Cook and Vancouver for their explorations of the Pacific Northwest Coast in the late 1700s has overshadowed the accomplishments of Spanish mariners during the same period. And few of them have been disregarded more than Narváez. England trumpeted the extremely important voyages of its two famous explorers. Yet the Spanish seafarers and their largely Mexican crews, who did far more work, won little recognition outside Madrid. Spain had no interest in supplying the world with information about the distant area her explorers had found and exploited. The Spanish throne was more intent on trying to retain the entire Pacific coast of North America as its exclusive territory and possibly becoming the first to find the fabled Northwest Passage.

This book is not intended to minimize Captain Vancouver's meticulous hydrographic work in 1792 along the Pacific Northwest Coast, including the Salish Sea. However, he was not the first European to explore most of those waters, to anchor along those shores, to view the majestic mountains, to trade with the Indigenous peoples, nor to name many of the landmarks. The Spaniards preceded him and their stories deserve equal attention. One of them was Narváez, a particularly noteworthy mariner from New Spain and then Mexico. This book recounts the roles he played during four critical periods of Spanish-Mexican maritime history: Spain's eighteenth-century efforts to regain its position as a naval power, compete for control of trade in the Pacific Ocean, and continue geopolitical expansion in New Spain; the escalation in European voyages of exploration in the Pacific during the late eighteenth century; the Mexican revolt from 1810 to 1820; and the controversial administration of Agustín de Iturbide, who ruled the new nation of Mexico for a short time in the early 1820s.

PART I

Spain Strives to Control the Pacific Northwest Coast

CHAPTER 1

A Young Mariner's Journey
from Cadiz to New Spain

JOSÉ MARÍA NARVÁEZ was born in 1768 in Cadiz,[1] a bustling port city in southwestern Spain, located about eighty kilometres northwest of the entrance to the Mediterranean Sea. His parents, Antonio Narváez and Úrsula Gervete, had lived in the clean, attractive, picturesque town all their lives. It was situated at the tip of Isla de León (now San Fernando) — a narrow peninsula joined to the mainland by the small Suazo Bridge. (Today, that short span has been replaced by a four-lane highway and rail line which cross a wide sand spit.)

Because of its cleanliness, the residents called Cadiz, *Tacita de Plata* ("Little Cup of Silver"). Tracing its history back 3,000 years to a Phoenician trading settlement in 1100 BCE, Cadiz now lays claim to being Western Europe's oldest continually inhabited city. The development of trade with the Indies brought prosperity to Cadiz, which reached its

Cadiz and surrounding area, 1813: Cadiz at harbour entrance; San Fernando on east side of Isla de Leon; La Carraca on nearby island; Matagorda on long point east of Cadiz; Puerto de Santa Maria on river east of Cadiz; Viga on shore NE of Cadiz; Rota on shore NNE of Cadiz.

zenith during the eighteenth century, supplanting Seville as Spain's chief port and its most important naval base. With three-quarters of all Spanish trade coming from the Americas, Cadiz became one of the country's greatest, most cosmopolitan cities.

By the time José Narváez was born, the thriving port city had also become a major target of Spain's enemies, and the decimated Royal Navy had already been rendered almost non-existent. Although Spain remained the world's largest imperial and maritime power, with colonies and convoys to be protected, the nation had stopped constructing warships. According to one foreign affairs analyst, "There was no national navy, only several ineffectual 'regional fleets.'"[2] In the age of sail and imperial expansion, no other major maritime nation had let its navy wither away as much as Spain. Both in Europe and overseas, Spain's vast empire had become vulnerable. Determined to regain its position as a naval power, the Spanish crown concentrated a significant portion of its expenditures between 1700 and 1790 on rebuilding a modern navy from scratch — one that could again assert its capability for national defence, colonial growth, and scientific achievement. A comprehensive development plan was formulated that included improved training of officers, stronger naval institutions, and an intensive shipbuilding effort.

Between 1717 and 1772, Cadiz saw the establishment of the Academy of Midshipmen (1717), the Naval College of Surgery (1748), the Astronomical Observatory (1753), the Hydrographic Depot (1770) — precursor of the Hydrographic Bureau (1797) — and the School of Naval Engineers (1772). Hydrographic surveying would soon become a top priority as Spain engaged in charting the entire Pacific coast of the American continents and the major archipelagos of the vast ocean that it still viewed as Spanish territory.

To renew its shipbuilding capacity, Spain started construction of La Carraca royal shipyard in Cadiz in 1720. Along with fully integrated facilities at Santander and Cartagena, La Carraca became one of the nation's first three large shipbuilding sites on the European mainland. In 1732, La Carraca launched its first of seven three-masted, square-sailed *navíos* ("line-of-battle" ships, or battleships).

The line of battle is a military tactic that became widely used in the late seventeenth century. Previous naval tactics involved huge fleets of almost a hundred vessels of various sizes, which closed on each other for chaotic individual combat. Forming a much smaller fleet of large, more heavily armed ships end-to-end in a line created three advantages: each vessel was able to fire its broadside without hitting a friendly ship; in any given length of time, more shots could be fired by the entire fleet; and fire could be concentrated systematically by moving the line in relation to the opposing fleet. Since both lines of sailing ships depended on the wind, they typically sailed along each other or on opposite tacks. A vessel that was powerful enough to stand in the line of battle came to be known as a "ship of the line."

By 1790, Spain's three homeland yards would construct sixty-four such ships of the line. The largest producer, surprisingly, was Havana, Cuba, which turned out seventy-four *navíos* during the period. Altogether, Spain built or acquired 227 ships of the line by the turn of the century. The nation's shipyards also turned out scores of smaller vessels. Consequently, the Spanish Navy reached its apogee between 1780 and 1800, as Narváez became a young adult. During this period, Spain was recognized for having built some of the best *navíos* of the entire century.[3] Despite this buildup, Spain was still trying to catch up with ship production in England and France. Madrid was also dispersing many of its larger vessels far and wide to extend its imperial ambitions, which caused its navy to become thinly spread out. Consequently, naval commanders often found themselves at a disadvantage in European sea battles because they had fewer first-rate battleships and too many older vessels, some of which were in poor condition.

As a child, Narváez played on Cadiz's sandy shores, where he enjoyed long hours watching sailing vessels of all types come and go along the fish-hook curve of Cadiz Bay. On a stormy day, the Atlantic Ocean sent waves crashing over the seawall in great surges of white power, soaking anyone who ventured too close. He was also fascinated by the ancient walled-city's narrow, winding streets. The boy's greatest thrill, however, was seeing one of the new three-decked wooden warships leave port under full sail, flags flying, with hundreds of sailors on board.

Another exciting occasion that captured the youngster's interest was the annual *almadraba* (tuna fishery) — the most important commercial event along the Coast of Light. In late spring, Atlantic tuna fish heading for the Mediterranean swung close inshore just south of Cadiz. For ages, the annual event was conducted in two stages. In the first, fishermen in boats drove the tuna toward the beach and shallow lagoons of Conil, about forty kilometres south of Cadiz. There trumpeters in a tower summoned other men who waded into the water hauling large nets, which they formed into pens to trap the fish. In the second phase, the trapped tuna were speared, hauled ashore with gaffs, and loaded on carts. It often took four or five men to beach a flailing tuna. On shore, the fish were butchered and prepared for sale. Some were sold fresh, but most were salted, dried, and barreled.

Navío *Santa Ana*, 1784.

Narváez was a bright youngster, who became increasingly eager to pursue a naval career. On April 23, 1782, at the age of fourteen, he won acceptance to the Royal (Naval) Academy for Midshipmen at San Fernando on nearby Isla de León. At that time, the midshipmen's school concentrated on a short four-month course of practical instruction that was aimed at turning out trained *pilotos*, not senior officers. These young men learned how to navigate a vessel; estimate geographic locations from visual sightings of the sun, moon, and various landmarks;

and make rudimentary, hand-drawn charts. Because maps were not yet being drawn using the positions of stars and planets, these novice midshipmen lacked scientific training in nautical astronomy. To supplement the limited skills of these *pilotos*, the navy also needed to improve its supply of young cadet officers, because Spain's heightened military activities were taking an increasingly heavy toll on the lives of sailors and midshipmen. In 1783, Vicente Tofiño developed another four-month course of advanced studies that was aimed at training an elite corps of officers who would become expert astronomers and scientists. However, because Narváez had attended only the former program, he would learn most of his advanced hydrographic skills on the job.

In August 1782, Narváez went to sea as an unpaid apprentice,[4] aboard the 70- to 74-gun *navío, Triunfante*.[5] He saw his first combat on October 20, 1782, during the battle of Cape Spartel, which took place about twenty-nine kilometres off the northwest coast of Morocco at the entrance to the Strait of Gibraltar. The territory of Gibraltar, located on the opposite coast of the strait, had been a source of friction between Spain and Britain since 1704, when an Anglo-Dutch fleet captured it from Spain. In 1713 it was handed to Britain "in perpetuity" by the Treaty of Utrecht. When Spain entered the American War of Independence in 1779, it joined forces with France and launched the "Great Siege of Gibraltar." A combined Spanish and French squadron had been engaged in striving to capture the strategically located fortress from Great Britain for three years before Narváez saw action. Britain had successfully resupplied its garrison at Gibraltar in both 1780 and 1781, and was determined to do it again.[6]

The Spanish–French fleet, with Narváez on board the *Triunfante*, anchored inside the Strait of Gibraltar in Algeciras Bay, immediately west of Gibraltar. It consisted of forty-nine ships of the line under the command of Admiral of the Fleet, Luis de Córdova y Córdova, one of Spain's most aggressive naval commanders of that era. However, several of Spain's thirty-five ships were in poor condition, and some of its older, heavier vessels were slow.

The British fleet of thirty-five ships of the line was commanded by Admiral Richard Earl Howe. After sailing from England, it had gathered at Cape St. Vincent, Portugal, to prepare for its entrance into the Strait of Gibraltar. Subsequently, Admiral Howe was heralded for his brilliant effort to escort the large supply convoy of reinforcements to the hard-pressed military base, which had been under siege for three years. Howe's allegedly brilliant tactics won the day.

Actually, he was lucky to manage an awkward, fortuitous departure. When the admiral started to leave the Strait of Gibraltar and return to England, he found his thirty-three remaining vessels poorly equipped, undermanned, and leeward of forty-six battle-ready enemy ships, which had him outgunned. Instead of attacking Howe from their windward position, the Spaniards inexplicably only fired some shots from long range. Howe sailed off without damage. Known popularly as "Black Dick" because of his swarthy complexion, the British admiral served as First Lord of the Admiralty from 1783 to 1788.

Because there is no record of Narváez's experiences during this famous battle, we can only imagine the emotional impact that it had on the youth, the lessons he learned, the memories it imprinted in his mind, and how it helped shape his character. We do know, however, that nine years later, he would be the first European to discover a major fjord along the Pacific Northwest Coast, which he named Bocas del Carmelo (Carmelo's Bay) after the Carmelite monastery founded in the twelfth century on Mount Carmel in Israel, which was dedicated to the Virgin Mary in her aspect as Star of the Sea. Ironically, the English Captain George Vancouver would subsequently rename the glacially-carved inlet Howe Sound in honour of "Black Dick."

From the fall of 1782 to the following spring, Admiral Córdova's fleet battled the English Navy between the Straits of Gibraltar and Cape Saint Vincent in Portugal. During this period, Narváez not only managed to survive military conflict, but he also must have demonstrated certain navigational skills. On January 2, 1783, he was appointed *tercer piloto havilitado* (qualified third mate). The rank of *piloto* (mate) in the Spanish Armada was junior to an *alférez* (ensign), which in turn was junior to a *teniente* (lieutenant) — usually considered the lowest rank of *oficial del mar* (commissioned officer). Narváez had begun his slow climb up the long promotional ladder.[7]

Promoted again on October 1, 1783, this time to a *tercer piloto de número* (third mate), Narváez sailed to Constantinople (now Istanbul) and Cartagena. In 1784, he journeyed to New Spain. His first assignment was the port city of Havana, Cuba — founded in 1514 by the famous, but unrelated, Basque conquistador Pánfilo de Narváez.[8] Sailing from there during the next three years, the young mariner served aboard supply vessels to the ports of New Orleans, Matanzas (Cuba), Veracruz and Campeche (Mexico), and Roatan and Trujillo (Honduras). At sea almost continuously, he went without the standard fifteen-day annual vacation for three years.[9] On November 1, 1787, Narváez was promoted to *segundo piloto havilitado* (qualified second mate) and assigned, along with four other *pilotos*,[10] to the small, remote, but strategically located San Blas Naval Station about 120 kilometres north of what is now Puerto Vallarta on Mexico's west coast. The commandant at San Blas was Esteban José Martínez, an impetuous, hot-tempered, forty-six-year-old lieutenant commander who had been in charge of the outpost for about five years.

After sailing from Havana to Veracruz on the packetboat *Borgoña*, Narváez travelled overland and arrived in San Blas on February 4, 1788.[11] The busy port, which played a key role in the early history of Spain's Baja (Lower) and Alta (Upper) California colonies and the Pacific Northwest Coast, owed its importance to the naval station and supply base that had been established there twenty years before Narváez's arrival.[12]

From its inception, San Blas had seen men of Basque heritage involved in key roles. The first three head shipbuilders — Manuel de Bastarrechea, Francisco Segurola, and Pedro de Yzaguirre — would institute high construction standards that would produce quality vessels for more than three decades. These sailing ships would play essential roles in supplying Spain's colonial missions to the north, maintaining its naval outposts, and extending its military-political authority in North Pacific waters.

Spain had sent its first expedition northward to explore the Pacific Northwest Coast in 1774, with Captain Juan José Pérez in command. Unfortunately, adverse winds and strong currents forced Pérez to

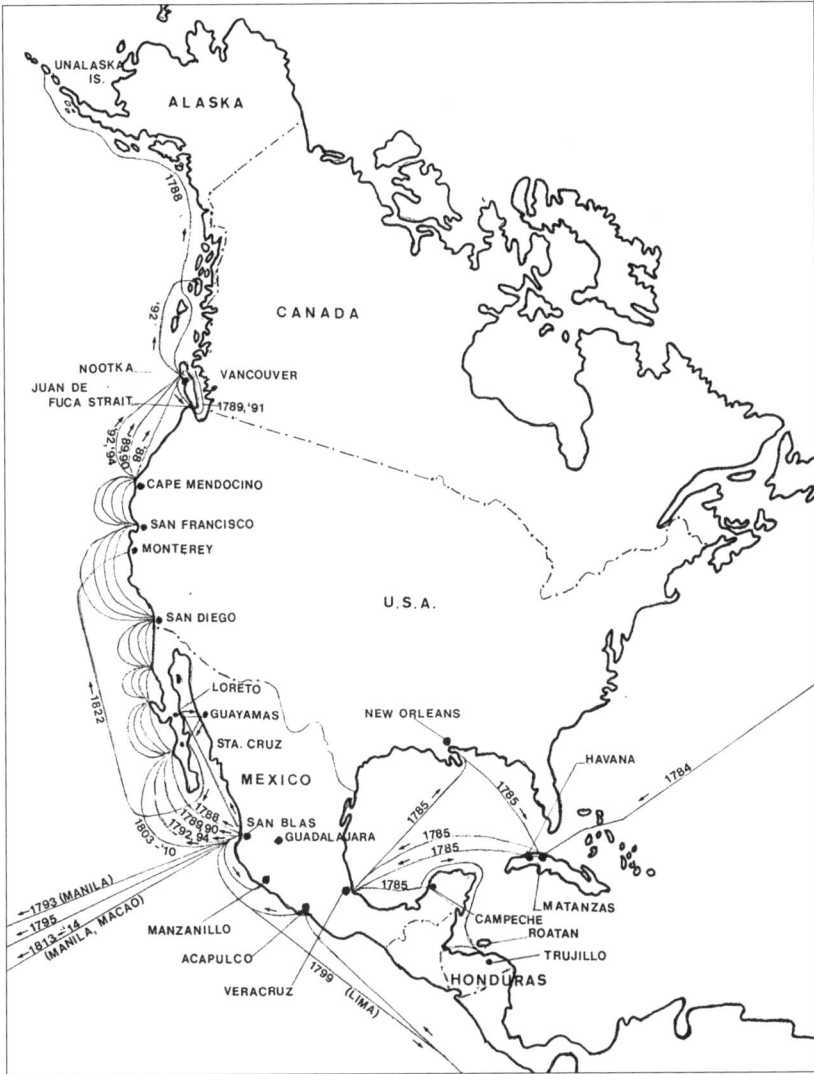

Narváez's voyages, 1784–1822, depicted on a modern map.

reverse course when he reached a latitude of 55°30' minutes north (somewhere west of today's tiny Noyes Island, which is at approximately the same latitude as Ketchikan, Alaska).

Meanwhile, Julián de Arriaga, Minister of the Indies, had sent six new officials to San Blas. Three of them were Basques: Bruno de Hezeta y Dudagoitia, Ignacio de Arteaga, and Juan Francisco de la Bodega y Quadra.[13] In 1775, Hezeta and Bodega made Spain's second voyage northward above Alta California to reinforce Spain's claim of sovereignty on the Pacific Northwest Coast and thwart Russian and English expansion. At about 55°14' north, a landing party went ashore in what became known as Bucareli Sound and took formal possession for the crown. Then the expedition continued north as far as 58°30' north latitude (approximately where the foot of Alaska's La Perouse Glacier meets the ocean in today's Glacier Bay National Park) before foul weather forced them to turn back.

The third Spanish voyage to Alaskan waters was undertaken in 1779 by Arteaga and Bodega. After revisiting Bucareli Bay, they resumed their northward course to the western entrance of what became known as Prince William Sound. There Arteaga went ashore in a bay that he named El Puerto de Santiago on La Isla de la Magdalena (today's Port Etches on Hinchinbrook Island) and declared possession by Spain. Located at 60°18' north latitude,[14] this site would become the basis for Madrid's subsequent claims of sovereignty as far as 61° north latitude. From there, the expedition struggled southwest in stormy weather until they reached the southern end of what is now the Kenai Peninsula, where another possession ceremony was held. Continuing southwest, the explorers reached a protected bay on Afognak Island at about 58°19' north latitude and 152°39' west longitude. At this point, just north of Kodiak Island, Arteaga and Bodega decided it was time to end the mission.

In March 1788, one month after his arrival in San Blas, Narváez would be involved directly in a fourth voyage of exploration of the North Pacific, which would venture farther north in Alaskan waters and southeast along the Aleutian Islands. Dispatched as an espionage mission, it would bring back New Spain's first hard evidence about the extent and objectives of Russian encroachment in the region.

～

Before Spain's imperial expansion reached the west coast of what is now Mexico, the region around Nayarit had been occupied for at least seven thousand years by Huichol people who called themselves Wixárika. Living in small, scattered settlements, they had formed a complex, rich, and highly developed culture that was grounded in a sophisticated psycho-spiritual belief system. By 1528, however, the entire Huichol society was nearly eliminated by the ruthless conquest that was led by Nuño Beltrán Guzmán, President of the First Audiencia in New Spain. Guzmán's tactics of brutality, slavery, and outright genocide sowed seeds of resentment and anger among Aboriginal people that ignited one uprising after another for three centuries.

Those resilient Wixárika who managed to survive the onslaught preserved their ancient sacred spiritual sites and visited them secretly. One of these was on a small, white rock formation offshore which they called Tatéi Haramara (now Piedra Blanca near San Blas). The Wixárika made annual pilgrimages to the isle, from which they still believe the goddess of the sea emerged from the water-covered planet and created the land.

When Spanish Franciscans prepared to set up a mission near the harbour in 1531, they named the area's small port San Blas, in honour of the Roman Catholic martyr known in Europe as Saint Blais.[15] During 1767 and early 1768, New Spain established San Blas as a west coast military base to transport soldiers, weapons, and supplies by sea to carry out a campaign to subdue the Indigenous Seri peoples in Sonora.[16] The government sent out a group of 116 Spanish families who settled below a promontory about forty-six metres high, which rose out of a low swampy plain at the mouth of the meandering San Pedro River. Each year from November to April, the area's briny waters, sandy beaches, marsh grasses, and brackish mangrove swamps attracted about 80 percent of North America's migratory bird population. (Today, it is considered one of the world's most important natural bird refuges.) However, from May to August, the tropical climate could become oppressive as torrential rains, stifling humidity, and clouds of insects — including insatiable mosquitoes — hit the area.

In May 1768, this port was designated as a new naval base for Spanish vessels operating in the Pacific Ocean. A hillside fort was built in 1770 to defend the town's extensive sea trade with the Philippines. The fortification's front wall featured stone carvings of Spain's kings. On the slope behind the fort stood the one-year-older church known locally as Nuestra Señora del Rosario la Marinera ("Our Seafaring Lady of the Rosary").[17] Almost a century later, a newspaper report about removal of the chapel's bronze bells apparently inspired the romantic American poet Henry Wadsworth Longfellow to write his last poem. The first three stanzas painted a nostalgic picture of what were actually a rather grim outpost and a mediocre harbour.

THE BELLS OF SAN BLAS

What say the Bells of San Blas
To the ships that southward pass
    From the harbor of Mazatlán?
To them it is nothing more
Than the sound of surf on the shore, —
    Nothing more to master or man.

But to me, a dreamer of dreams,
To whom what is and what seems
    Are often one and the same, —
The Bells of San Blas to me
Have a strange, wild melody,
And are something more than a name.

· · ·

They are a voice of the Past,
Of an age that is fading fast,
    Of a power austere and grand,
When the flag of Spain unfurled
Its folds o'er this western world,
    And the Priest was lord of the land.

By the time Narváez arrived at San Blas in 1788, the port had reached peak activity as a supply base for all Spanish vessels in the North Pacific,

Restored ruins of chapel, San Blas.

including those making exploration voyages. It also supplied Spain's Franciscan missions in Baja and Alta California, and naval bases at San Diego and Monterey, which had been set up as safe havens for treasure-laden galleons returning annually from Manila to Acapulco, the eastern terminus of the trans-Pacific route. About thirty thousand people lived around the harbour, which was so small it could never accommodate more than four vessels at once. Nevertheless, at that time, it was the second-busiest port and shipbuilding centre on the Pacific coast of North America. Lush forests in the surrounding area provided a plenti-ful supply of hardwoods for vessel construction and repair. Near the

shipyard, a large *corchadero* (rope-making operation) converted hene-
quen fibre from agave plants into threads that were used to make all the
different lengths and sizes of ropes required by sailing vessels. Two batteries of cannon guarded the harbour, which included a marine station,
arsenal, warehouses, and offices.

Despite its increasing profile, the underfunded naval department at
San Blas faced several difficulties: chronic shortages of suitable vessels
and officers; physical isolation from major population centres; a harm-
ful, destructive climate; a variety of endemic sicknesses; and a dearth of
readily available marine equipment. Although the base was costly to

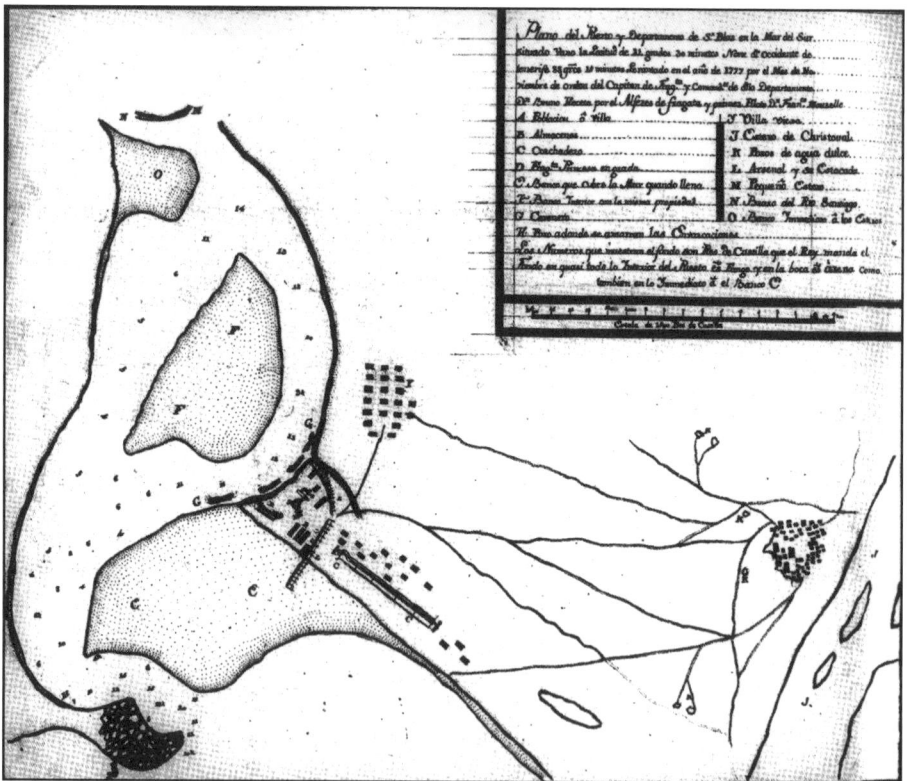

Plan of San Blas, by Capt. Francisco Mourelle, 1777. FROM LEFT: arm of
Santiago River, shoals, four careened vessels along shore, frigate *Princesa* in
construction, naval buildings, long rope factory, old town (upper centre),
main town (far right), Christoval River. (MUSEO NAVAL, MADRID)

Restored ruins of naval headquarters, San Blas.

maintain, it would become strategically essential for launching Spain's major expansion in America — the maritime exploration, exploitation, and settlement of the ocean frontier from Alta California to Alaska.[18]

Geographically, the harbour was a logical choice because it provided the most direct route from the central government in Mexico City to the supply and manpower centre of Guadalajara, and to the two Californias. It was not, however, an ideal deep-sea anchorage. By 1779, it had started to fill up with sand from two waterways: the San Pedro River, which emptied directly into the harbour, and the much larger Santiago River, which sent huge volumes of sediment into the ocean about thirty kilometres north. Consequently, the naval department had been thinking for years about moving its headquarters south to the excellent, larger, extremely active, but more distant port of Acapulco. Unfortunately, that harbour lacked immediate sources of lumber.

"It [San Blas] has the great defect of not being more than an estuary, incapable of receiving boats that are more than twelve feet [draft]," Narváez would write thirty-four years later, when the Mexican Navy finally commissioned him to find a better location.[19] Most large vessels were forced to anchor just outside the estuary, where they had some protection from mild northeasterly winds during the summer. "But it doesn't happen that way when the season of the rains comes in, which make it indispensably necessary to abandon [the harbour] and go [more than one thousand kilometres northwest] to the port of Guaymas on the coast of Sonora," wrote Narváez. "But [San Blas] has the advantage of the exquisite and abundant trees for construction that are produced nearby and can be transported very easily at a small cost on the Santiago River."

In 1788, Lieutenant Commander Martínez handed young Narváez the first of a series of challenging assignments that would make him navigator on voyages of discovery and mapping along the northern coast above Baja and Alta California — a region that Madrid called New Spain, which extended from the southern tip of today's Baja California into what was then becoming known as Oregon Country. This vast, vaguely defined territory would be claimed by Spain, Russia, Great Britain, and France.

Esteban José Martínez.
(HABRON)

Madrid's claim would be based on a papal bull of 1493 and the Treaty of Tordesillas in 1494,[20] as well as explorations of the Pacific coast by Spanish captains, which began in the late eighteenth century. From 1788 to 1795, Narváez would be involved directly and indirectly as a junior officer in most of New Spain's explorations on the Pacific Northwest Coast.

Narváez began his first voyage northward just one month after his arrival in San Blas. From early March to late October of 1788, he sailed to North America's northwest coast as first mate under Gonzalo López de Haro aboard the 196-ton snow-rigged *paquebote* (packetboat) *San Carlos* (alias *El Filipino*). (Two-masted vessels of this size with square sails were said to be snow-rigged or "snows" if they had a third, smaller mast installed immediately behind the mainmast, which could carry a trisail with a boom.) This was the fourth voyage by Spaniards to the northern waters and the first of two important but imprudent expeditions led by Esteban José Martínez. For the next two years, Narváez's destiny would be tied to this contentious, second-rate explorer. Beyond middle age, Martínez had not even achieved the rank of a commissioned officer, and his behaviour displayed a bewildering array of contradictions. As the most experienced *piloto* left at San Blas after all the first-rank officers had been assigned elsewhere, Martínez was prone to abuse his authority and make arbitrary decisions. He hated being stationed in such an unpleasant outpost halfway around the world from his native land and from his wife who wanted his return. To his credit, Martínez was a dedicated, patriotic navy man, who was enthusiastic about extending Spain's settlement northward. However, the impulsive actions that he took to achieve this objective repeatedly backfired. He was prone to erratic, violent, and irresponsible escapades. He was short-tempered, imprudent, and not above using deception to achieve personal and political ends. As a fledgling naval officer, Narváez would find his sense of responsibility, his respect for military discipline, and his diplomatic skills severely tested by Martínez's intimidation and deceit.

CHAPTER 2

Investigating the Russian Threat, 1788

WHAT IMPELLED THE viceroy of New Spain to send Martínez, López de Haro, Narváez, and three other non-commissioned officers on what constituted a poorly disguised spy mission to the Gulf of Alaska and the Aleutian Islands in 1788? The answer was grounded in Madrid's geo-political anxieties concerning eight decades of Russian activity and aspi-rations in the area.

In the early 1700s, Russian expansion across Siberia led Tsar Peter the Great to order an urgent maritime expedition. It was commanded by the Danish navigator Vitus Bering, who was assisted by the Russian Captain Aleksei Chirikov. In 1728, the two men explored the Kamchatka Peninsula and the open sea between Asia and North America, which subsequently would carry Bering's name. In 1741, Bering and Chirikov investigated the Aleutian Islands and the Alaskan coast, confirming the absence of a temperate passage between the Pacific and the Atlantic oceans at those latitudes. Bering also saw what the Spanish later named Mount Saint Elías (another name for Mount Carmel), the second-highest mountain in North America (5,489 metres elevation). It was located on what would become the border of Alaska and the Yukon Territory. This was the first verified sighting by Europeans of what is now western Canada. These Russian explorations also opened this remote area of the North Pacific Ocean to the lucrative fur trade, which the Russians exploited to supply the markets of China with the pelts of sea otters, fur seals, and blue foxes as well as walrus tusks. By 1763, Russian traders reached Kodiak, where the Aleuts (now called Alutiiq) drove them away. Twenty-one years later, the Russians returned under the command of the famous fur trader Grigorii Shelikhov, who established the first European settlement in Alaska at Three Saints Bay.

About twenty thousand Aleuts lived on Kodiak when the foreigners arrived. A few months after landing at Three Saints Bay in two ships, Shelikhov decided to subdue the Indigenous people and force them to hunt sea otters for his company. The commander led seventy armed men in Aboriginal kayaks east from Kodiak to a large headland on what is now Sitkalidak Island, where about two thousand Aleuts had sought safety. Steep cliffs made what would be called Refuge Rock inaccessible from the seaward side. On the other side, the promontory was connected to Sitkalidak Island at the head of Partition Cove by a narrow land bridge, which was underwater most of the time. At low tide, the Russians crossed the narrow reef, charged the headland, killed hundreds of Aleuts, and took five hundred of them as hostages or slaves. The massacre broke the back of Aleut resistance.[1]

Shelikhov also intended to push farther south along the Pacific Northwest Coast into territory where Spain, for more than a century, had assumed it had exclusive control by virtue of Vasco Núñez de Balboa and Ferdinand Magellan having "discovered" the Pacific Ocean in 1513 and 1521 respectively. The Spanish, however, had left the northernmost part of this vast region unexplored.

It was rumours about these potential Russian intrusions into what Spain called its Alta California territory, which had spurred the

Grigorii Ivanovich Shelikhov.

authorities in New Spain to set up the San Blas Naval Station and supply base in May 1768. Determined to reassert its increasingly feeble
claim to sovereignty by "right of discovery," Madrid aimed to control
the entire Pacific Coast using vessels built and manned at San Blas.

During the next eighteen years, two developments escalated the
Spanish government's concern to serious alarm. First, it received reports
of four Russian outposts in Alaska and one allegedly in Puerto de Nuca
(Nootka Harbour). More ominous, Britain's famous voyager Captain
James Cook had met with the Russians at Unalaska. To find out what
was going on, Madrid ordered two vessels dispatched from San Blas on
March 8, 1788: the frigate *Princesa* and the supply vessel *San Carlos*.
Martínez led the expedition in command of the former vessel with as-

sistance from first mate Esteban Mondofia and junior mate (apprentice *piloto*) Antonio Serantes. As second officer of the expedition, López de Haro skippered the latter vessel, assisted by Narváez as first mate, Juan Martínez y Zayas as second mate, and (*pilotín*) José Antonio Verdía as junior mate. The expedition's objective was reconnaissance and espionage, not settlement, of the coasts of Alaska between 60° and 61° north latitude. Narváez kept a succinct journal of the voyage, recording in his stylish handwriting elementary navigational information, some interesting personal observations, and considerable valuable intelligence about Russian activities. Along with the explanations that accompany it, Narváez's log constitutes, in certain respects, a first contact document which reveals some unappreciated discoveries made by this *piloto*.[2]

Despite persistent disputes among Commander Martínez and López de Haro, Serantes, Martínez y Zayas, and Narváez over actual locations, the explorers managed to reach the Alaskan coast. On May 16, Narváez sighted Montague Island to his north along with what he believed was the eastern entrance to Prince William Sound, located by Arteaga nine years earlier. After surveying the southern shore of Montague Island, the expedition entered the western entrance to Prince William Sound (the present Montague Strait) on May 25, and anchored inside. Two days later, the *Princesa* and the *San Carlos* moved farther into this strait to an anchorage at what Narváez "believed" was at 60°08' north latitude, between the Islas Vertis (Green Islands) and the larger Montague Island. (The actual location would appear to be 60°18' north latitude — the same latitude reached by Arteaga in 1779.) In accordance with Martínez's orders, on Sunday June 1, López de Haro, his fellow officers, and a priest, Don José María Díaz, went ashore in a cove on the big island, where they performed an elaborate ceremony of possession (at approximately the same latitude as the Arteaga expedition's earlier ceremony), named their landing place Puerto Flórez in honour of the viceroy of New Spain, declared that the name Prince William Sound was thereby changed to "Prince Carlos Sound," and conducted a Mass. According to Narváez, it was "the first one said between 55° and 60° N [latitude] on these coasts." (Apparently, Martínez remained on board the *Princesa*.)[3]

Six days later Martínez and his officers held a meeting to discuss

Diario de Navegacion q.e espera hazer el 2.° Piloto de la R.l armada D.n Jose Maria Narbaez en el Paquebot de S. M. nombrado el San Carlos (alias el fili pino) al mando del primer Piloto de dha. D.n Gonzalo Lopez de Haro, vajo las Ord.s de la fragata de S. M. nombra da la Princesa su comandante el Alferez de Navio y primer Piloto de la armada D.n Estevan Jose Martinez con desti no ambos Buques de Explorar la Costa Septemptrional de Californias hasta los 61 g. de lat. Norte.

Nota

El Puerto de la Salida es el de S.n Blaz situado en la lat. Norte de 21.° 30 y long. de 00 contada desde el referido Puerto. y el punto de arrivada ó reunion en la Entrada del Principe Guillermo por los 60.° 26 lat. N. y 41° 30 al ori.te del meridiano de S. Blaz la medida de la Cordera consta de 42 pies Ingleses y la Am polleta de 28. seg. vale este Buque es ranco y completo de su pendiente y respeto.

Sabado 8, de Marzo de 1788 âlas 12 del dia remando le van este p.a dar la Vela lo q.e se executo alas 11, de la Noche que aui endo entrado el V.to muy flojo por el N dimos la vela a imitacion del Com.te de la Pag.s Zarretes y Remolg.o âlas 14 L lo que executamos immediatam.te con el Ancla de Bavor cargando todo aparejo y asi nos mantubimos hasta las S de la mañana.

Domingo 9 de Marzo de 1788 al Lunes 10 del mismo Al ponerse el Sol se Dem.Co la piedra Blanca al N. de la Aguja dist.a de dos Leg. y se observo 6,° 41 de Variacion ne alas 6 L havriendose q.e dado el V.to Casi Calma caringando todo aparejo, y dimos fondo al Ancla de Bavor en 10 bra quedando distante de la Costa del tra ves como dos Leg.

First page of Narváez's journal of his voyage to the Gulf of Alaska and Aleutian Islands, 1788. (WILLIAM ANDREWS CLARK LIBRARY) fulfillment of their first assignment: exploration of "Prince Carlos Sound" to 61° north latitude. Martínez proposed that the task should *not* be undertaken unless the winds were favourable. If that happened, all the officers agreed to meet at about 60°44' north latitude, where Narváez said "we could see the continental shore [to the northeast] with the naked eye." It would appear, however, that the rendezvous never occurred, because only longboats were dispatched to make limited surveys.[4]

Ordered (probably by López de Haro) on June 10 to make an independent survey of Montague Island in a fully armed longboat, Narváez headed northwest around the northernmost point of Montague Island at 60°23' north latitude (at least five minutes farther north than the Arteaga voyage went in 1779). From there he sighted Valdéz Arm, which Captain Cook had placed at 61° north latitude. Crossing this entrance to "Prince Carlos Sound," Narváez entered Puerto de Santiago — the northernmost point reached by Arteaga. The next day, Narváez found a large building on Montague Island (probably in what is now Zaikov Bay), which he soon would learn was a Russian outpost. This was Spain's first physical indication of Russia's probable presence in the area.[5]

Although the Martínez expedition was the first Spanish voyage to the Gulf of Alaska that penetrated *both* entrances to Prince William Sound, and it spent considerably more time (nineteen days) in those waters than any previous voyage, it did not achieve its first objective: to fully explore Prince William Sound as far as Valdéz Arm. That effort was aborted because Martínez had wasted too much time on a stormy and prolonged quarrel with his subordinates regarding his insistence that they alter their logs to conform with his records.[6] Martínez became so abusive toward his *pilotos* and so contemptuous of López de Haro's opinions, that the latter, as the expedition's second officer and captain of the *San Carlos*, headed westward on his own — accompanied by Narváez — toward the previously determined rendezvous at what the Spaniards had been calling Isla Trinidad (the small pair of Trinity Islands, southwest of Kodiak Island, which now compose Sitkinak Island).[7]

On June 28, the *San Carlos* approached the southeast shore of Kodiak Island, where López de Haro and Narváez conducted trade with Indigenous people paddling twelve canoes. It became obvious that the Aboriginal people had been trading with Europeans from somewhere. They also carried several small scraps of paper bearing Russian writing, one of which was dated 1784. López de Haro gained the impression that these were vouchers for payment of tribute.[8] Eager to obtain these first indisputable signs of Russian presence, the Spanish captain cleverly swapped trinkets with the Aboriginal people in exchange for their vouchers.[9]

On June 30, López de Haro sent Narváez in an armed longboat to reconnoitre the Russian trading post at Three Saints Bay, Kodiak Island, which was located at 57°09' north latitude and 153°29' west longitude. Thus, Narváez became the first Spaniard to make face-to-face contact

Original location of Shelikhov's fur-trading base on Kodiak Island, 1790.
(SPECIAL COLLECTIONS, UNIVERSITY OF WASHINGTON LIBRARIES)

with a large contingent of Russians[10] when he met Evstrat Delarov, commander of the settlement, which had been established in 1784 by Shelikhov.

Narváez brought Delarov and three other Russians back to the *San Carlos*. In his journal, Narváez wrote: "Captain López de Haro gave them a barrel of wine, some chocolate and other things to get them to tell us more [about the extent of their occupation]. Captain [Delarov] was most appreciative, and he invited us to come to their establishment inside the port. We accepted the invitation and pulled out our chart of these coasts to see if they would either point out some other establishments or give another name to the Port of Nootka or Prince William Sound. When Captain [Delarov] saw it, he took a pencil and drew a very wide and navigable canal ... [west of Kodiak]."[11]

On July 1, Narváez became the first Spanish officer who actually inspected a working Russian outpost. At the end of his visit, Captain Delarov gave Narváez a map of the Alaskan coast. Later, Delarov marked seven Russian outposts on the chart, which he indicated contained a total of 462 men and several sloops. He also said his country was sending two supply vessels to Nootka Sound in 1789 to occupy the port there. In addition, Delarov gave the Spanish mariners a letter dated June 25, 1788, from Cook's River (Cook Inlet), which contained both English and Russian words. Although the Spaniards were unable to read it, they made a copy.[12] It turned out to be a letter from William Douglas, a Scottish ship captain and maritime fur trader, to Horeman Sycoff (Potap Zaikov). Douglas had sailed as an officer with the British Captain John Meares on his first trading voyage to the Pacific Northwest Coast from 1786 to 1787. In 1788, Douglas assisted Meares again by commanding the 200-ton snow-brig *Iphigenia Nubiana* on an independent expedition to explore the Aleutian Islands and collect furs. He entered Cook Inlet and Prince William Sound, and then cruised south along the coast to Nootka Sound, where he joined Meares.

Meanwhile, Martínez had sailed from the entrance of Prince William Sound directly to Isla Trinidad (the Trinity Islands) at 56°32' north latitude and 154°24' west longitude, where, on June 27, 1887, he encountered a lone Russian lookout manning an isolated watchtower. Using

Indigenous couriers, the Russian sent a message to Delarov at Three Saints Bay about the frigate's arrival, and it was handed to Narváez there on July 1. Having obtained a great deal of vital information from Delarov, López de Haro and Narváez set sail on July 2 and, according to plan, rendezvoused with Martínez the next day at the pair of Trinity Islands (today's Sitkinak Island).

Armed with the information supplied by Delarov, the expedition sailed southwestward to investigate the large establishment that the Russians said they maintained on Unalaska Island in the eastern Aleutians. Sailing together on July 5, the two vessels worked their way southeast along the Alaskan Peninsula and the northeastern part of the Aleutian Islands, but — as had happened earlier — they frequently lost contact with each other. On July 21, Martínez sailed south into Unalaska Bay and anchored the *Princesa* off the west shore of Amaknak Island near the head of Iliuliuk Bay at about 53°54' north latitude and 166°30' west longitude — the farthest west in the Gulf of Alaska that any Spanish vessels had ventured. The Russian outpost was located about sixteen kilometres to the south.[13] (The *San Carlos*, with Narváez on board, would not anchor there until August 4, when he would note that today's Needle Rock was to his northwest and Second Priest Rock was southeast.)[14]

Although no armed conflict ensued when Martínez arrived, his warship reportedly took the outmanned and outgunned Russians by surprise. Nevertheless, Potap Kuzmich Zaikov, commander of the vessel *Sv. Aleksandr Nevskii* countered by bluffing about the trading post's military strength. While Zaikov actually had fewer than fifty men under him, he boasted of commanding five hundred and greatly exaggerated the number of Russian outposts in Alaska.[15]

The two parties communicated through Martínez's first mate, Esteban Mondofia, a native of Raguza (today's Dubrovnik, Croatia), whose limited knowledge of Russian was evidently better than the fur traders' understanding of his Serbo-Croatian dialect.[16] Nevertheless, the Russians were pleased that the Croatian read the Lord's Prayer and other prayers with them. Because of the language gap, the Spanish would bring back little information about the Russian colonies.[17] It would, however, constitute the first solid intelligence received by the viceroy of New Spain, Manuel Antonio Flórez.

When López de Haro and Narváez finally arrived at Unalaska, they found Martínez living on shore with Zaikov. The Spaniard had given the Russians ham, raisins, almonds, cheese, and wine.[18] According to López de Haro, the two commanders held long, friendly drinking bouts. Forty-four years later, Narváez recalled the encounter "with pleasure, praised the manners of the Russians at Unalaska, and said that commandant Kuzmich [Zaikov] was a very kind and fine person."[19] Zaikov gave Martínez three maps that covered the Aleutian Islands and the southern tip of Alaska. He also confirmed the alarming information that López de Haro and Narváez had picked up from Delarov — Zaikov and four Russian frigates were scheduled to take possession of Nootka Sound the following year to forestall fur trading and settlement by the English.

In December 1786, Empress Catherine II of Russia had ordered a naval squadron dispatched from the Baltic to the "Eastern Sea" via the Cape of Good Hope and Japan. She stated that the expedition's aim was to "safeguard our rights to the lands discovered by Russian seafarers." Captain Grigorii Ivanovich Mulovskii, age twenty-nine, was selected to command the voyage. His sailing orders included instructions "to take that coast from the harbour of Nootka to the point where Chirikov's discovery [of 1741] begins as possession of the Russian State if no other State is occupying it." However, Mulovskii's expedition would never reach North Pacific waters.

For ten years, the British had been acting as if they had first rights to Nootka Sound because of Cook's discovery of the inlet in 1778, but it was primarily a wide-open fur-trading centre. Indigenous people came to the harbour from the surrounding area to barter their fine sea otter pelts for pocket knives, fish hooks, and other items with vessels from several nations. By the fall of 1788, however, Martínez, López de Haro, Narváez and other *pilotos* on the expedition became convinced that the Russians were about to intervene and might pose an even greater threat to Spain's precarious sovereignty along the Pacific Northwest Coast. The viceroy had to be informed immediately.

Although Martínez may have been a skilled mariner, he was, as noted earlier, an unpredictable commander. During the expedition of 1788, he would be friendly, alert and attentive one day, and then turn sullen, depressed, and abusive the next day. He insulted his subordinates and even attacked one of them physically during the quarrel over log records that occurred early in the voyage.[20] These temper tantrums alienated Narváez and his fellow *pilotos*, at least one of whom was exiled to López de Haro's vessel by the intolerant captain. The ongoing dispute broke out again when the two vessels met at Unalaska. Martínez censured López de Haro for collecting allegedly useless intelligence from Delarov, arrested him, and placed Narváez temporarily in command of the *San Carlos*.[21] Throughout the Alaskan expedition, the heavy-drinking Martínez allowed the *Princesa* and the *San Carlos* to become separated. On the return voyage, both vessels left Unalaska on August 18 and, three days later, broke off contact. López de Haro had specific instructions to meet Martínez in Monterey, California. However, some 550 kilometres off what is now San Francisco, he withdrew his vessel from Martínez's command and, supported by Narváez and the other *pilotos*, headed back to San Blas on his own. He arrived October 22.

After waiting nearly a month in Monterey for the *San Carlos* to show up from the north, Martínez finally gave up and set sail for San Blas on October 14 and arrived there on December 5. López de Haro had already reported the Russian plan to take over Nootka Sound in 1789. Joined by Narváez and the other *pilotos*, he had also lodged a strong complaint about Martínez's careless, irresponsible leadership.[22]

Prior to the publication of my translation of Narváez's journal of 1788, one of the few historians who consistently defended Martínez's conduct during this voyage was University of Calgary history professor Christon I. Archer. He blamed the "López de Haro faction" and its leader for undermining the voyage's results by provoking a near mutiny. "López de Haro prejudiced any case he might have had by neglecting his vice-regal orders to examine Prince William Sound, Nootka Sound, and to navigate as close to the coast as was feasible on the return voyage," argued Archer after reading Viceroy Flórez's letter of November 26, 1788, to Minister of Navy Antonio Valdés.[23] "Then he broke his orders from Martínez, when he decided to return to San Blas to report, rather than awaiting the *Princesa* in Monterey."

Archer also claimed that a visit to Nootka Sound could have alerted the viceroy to England's activities on the Pacific Northwest Coast, thereby giving Spain time to formulate a strategy to avoid the explosive confrontation that followed in 1790.[24]

Archer's first allegation is disproved by Narváez's penetration of Prince William Sound to a point above 60° north latitude on June 10, 1788, at López de Haro's orders. If Martínez had not disputed the almost unanimous advice of his subordinates, the expedition would have sailed into Prince William Sound through its eastern entrance three weeks earlier and probably reached Valdéz Arm at 61° N, which remained unexplored. All of López de Haro's subsequent decisions — supported by Narváez and other *pilotos* — were coloured first by Martínez's mishandling of this initial controversy and then by his outrageous conduct at Unalaska.

Although Archer's second criticism has some theoretical merit, both Martínez and López de Haro had agreed that reporting the perceived immediacy of the Russian threat necessitated an immediate return to San Blas via Monterey. After losing contact with Martínez, López de Haro made a responsible decision to sail directly to the expedition's home base so its important intelligence could be reported as soon as possible. Part of that report included the information about Captain Douglas' fur-trading activities on behalf of British interests.

When Martínez finally returned to San Blas in December of 1788, he acted as if he had been in full control of the expedition throughout the voyage. Disregarding the grievances against him that had been submitted and López de Haro's summary report, Martínez immediately wrote to Viceroy Flórez in Veracruz, warning of the Russian menace on the Pacific Northwest Coast. Eager to compete with Russian and British expansion, he greatly exaggerated the number of Russian fur traders involved (Narváez estimated there were about three hundred men at Unalaska and another sixty at Kodiak) and reported that the Russian Navy was coming. He advised that the Aboriginal settlement in Nootka Sound — called Yuquot ("wind come from all directions") by the

Mowachaht peoples who had occupied the site for thousands of years, known as Cala de Los Amigos among the Spaniards, and named Friendly Cove by English mariners — should be occupied by a garrison early in the next year to establish Spanish possession of the coast from Nootka Sound to San Francisco. Convinced of the Northwest Coast's strategic and trading importance, Martínez offered to lead the project.

Martínez envisioned a new Spanish empire in the North Pacific Ocean, in which Aboriginal peoples would be exploited in various ways. His ambitious scheme included a chain of Spanish missions operated by a private joint stock company, a shipbuilding industry employing Indigenous workers from Nootka Sound to California, Spanish domination of the fur trade with China, and the conquest of the Hawaiian Islands.[25]

As an unpredictable patriotic visionary and scheming rogue, Martínez was not the level-headed diplomat Spain needed to negotiate

Aerial view of present-day Yuquot, also known as
Cala de Los Amigos or Friendly Cove.

relations with either European nations or Indigenous peoples on the Northwest Coast of North America. His wild swings of mood, temper tantrums, drinking bouts, and abusive manners were notorious. Nevertheless, Viceroy Flórez, who may have been Martínez's uncle, gave him the benefit of the doubt in the rift with his subordinates. Flórez dismissed López de Haro's report of the incident as being improbable, and he suggested José Camacho, acting commandant of San Blas, investigate the allegations that Martínez had inflicted unwarranted punishment on crew members. By the end of 1788, the viceroy was much more interested in sending Martínez north to Nootka Sound to address the apparent Russian threat.

For the Spaniards, the message was becoming increasingly clear — both the Russians and the English aimed to exploit the lucrative maritime fur trade along the upper Pacific Northwest Coast, establish political control of the huge area with outposts at Nootka Sound and elsewhere, and continue the quest for the elusive Northwest Passage. Although Spain's assessment of the bi-national mercantile threat was correct, political developments in Europe were already forcing Russia to abandon its imperial ambitions in the Pacific Northwest.

In the late summer of 1787, Turkey and Sweden went to war with Russia. This meant Captain Grigorii Mulovskii's naval ships, which had been sent out from the Baltic to protect and extend Russian interests in the Pacific Northwest, would be needed closer to home. Consequently, Empress Catherine II cancelled the expedition, and thereby ended the Russian bid to win control of North America's Northwest Coast.[26]

If any dispute over possession rights at Nootka Sound should arise in the future, the Spaniards knew they held the whip hand with Russia. If the Russians ever moved in, Spain could simply withdraw privileges Russia enjoyed in Mediterranean ports. However, Madrid remained acutely afraid of England's imperial ambitions. To counter this threat, the viceroy gave Martínez a much weaker, almost absurd argument to use with the English. Flórez instructed his impetuous captain to point out that Spanish discoveries at Nootka Sound obviously preceded Cook's because the latter had purchased from the natives two silver tablespoons, which Martínez alleged had been stolen from him by

Aboriginal people at Nootka Sound on his first expedition to the Pacific Northwest Coast as a *piloto* for Captain Juan Pérez in 1774.[27]

In fact, the Pérez expedition had only anchored briefly about twenty-five kilometres *south* of Nootka Sound in June 1774, where the Spaniards bartered with a few Hesquiaht fishermen who paddled their canoes alongside the sailing vessels. The voyagers threw things over the side to the Hesquiaht, who never came aboard. So it is unlikely that any spoons could have been stolen there. The Spaniards did not come ashore at Hesquiaht at this time, nor did they enter Nootka Sound or take possession of the land at either location.[28] Later, Alejandro Malaspina, one of the most important Spanish explorers, would claim that the spoons were stolen or lost when Aboriginal warriors attacked one of Pérez' vessels on the Washington coast and killed seven crew members.

To fend off challenges to Madrid's claims along the coast, Flórez instructed Martínez to build "a large hut" at Cala de Los Amigos and "pretend that you are engaged in settling yourself in a formal establishment." He also told Martínez to have López de Haro use the *San Carlos* to chart the coast between Nootka Sound and Alaska and take official possession of that part of the country. The *Princesa* and the *San Carlos* set sail from San Blas on February 17, 1789, commanded respectively by Martínez and López de Haro. As usual, Narváez assisted the latter as first mate. Martínez's junior officers included *pilotín* Juan Carrasco, a talented cartographer, who would work closely with Narváez between 1789 and 1803. He had been educated at the Naval Academy of San Telmo in Seville for four and one-half years between 1775 and 1780. He served in the Philippines under the highly skilled navigator Francisco Antonio Mourelle and came with him to San Blas in 1784.

Four Franciscan missionaries also accompanied the Martínez expedition. It was destined to ignite the most explosive diplomatic conflict that has ever been seen in Pacific Northwest Coast history.

CHAPTER 3

Conflict at Nootka Sound, 1789–1790

BY 1789, INCREASING economic competition and geopolitical developments at Nootka Sound were generating international tensions that
were bound to snap one way or another. All that was needed to cause
the rupture was a few controversial incidents. Based on the way Lieutenant Commander Martínez had conducted himself during the 1788
expedition, it was not surprising that he would be the person who took
provocative action. Although Narváez did not play a central role in the
ensuing conflict, its reverberations would keep him occupied for the
next six years in several important secondary functions, surveys of two
large Northwest Coast sounds, and one major task: to explore Juan de
Fuca Strait, one of its major archipelagos, and the largest of its two interior arms.

During 1788 and 1789, England and Spain competed actively for sovereignty at Nootka Sound. English merchant mariners contended for control of the lucrative fur trade with an increasingly influential breed of American entrepreneurs. European and Indigenous lifestyles clashed repeatedly. And the quest for the long-sought Northwest Passage continued to inspire the search for a large strait that was believed to exist about 200 kilometres southeast of Nootka Sound. Whenever and wherever naval captains, merchant vessel skippers, or non-commissioned officers such as Narváez gathered, their ears perked up to catch the latest gossip, rumour, or theory about the elusive cross-continental water route.

By this time, the maritime fur trade was attracting six to eight vessels a year to the Pacific Northwest Coast, but initially their merchant captains were less interested in exploring inland waterways than they were in finding plentiful sources of easily obtained sea otter pelts along the outer coast. One of these was the English trader, Captain Charles William Barkley. In July 1787, he and his adventurous wife, Frances, were the first Europeans to see the entrance of Juan de Fuca Strait, but Barkley did not enter the passage.[1]

In mid-July of 1788, Robert Duffin — first mate to fur trader John Meares whose orders he was carrying out — entered the mouth of Juan de Fuca Strait in a longboat and explored the entrance to an uncertain distance before being attacked by Aboriginal warriors and forced to retreat. Thus Duffin became the first European to enter the waterway.[2]

About one month later, the British sea otter trader Captain Charles Duncan sailed into the mouth of Juan de Fuca Strait in the 61-ton sloop *Princess Royal* and spent two days making observations, obtaining information from the Makah people who occupied the south shore of the wide channel, and drawing the first reliable chart of the entrance along with a detailed sketch.[3] It was published in early 1790 with a note stating that the Makah called the waterway a "great sea."

In late March and early April of 1789, the American fur trader Captain Robert Gray, in command of the *Lady Washington*, spent several days around the mouth of Juan de Fuca Strait trading with the Makah and with Chief "Tatooch [Tetakü]," whose main village was located on an island off the north shore of the entrance.[4] Gray reported that "a large sea" opened to the east.

Makah Chief Tetakü by José Cardero, 1792.
(MUSEO NAVAL, MADRID)

Prior to 1789, Spain's only independent information about Juan de Fuca Strait was the unsubstantiated, vague, confused description attributed to the sixteenth-century Greek *piloto* Apóstolos Valerianos, which is summarized in the Introduction. However, Martínez and other Spanish mariners had heard about some of the recent British and American observations. Martínez claimed that, returning from his voyage to the north in 1788, he had sighted a "broad entrance" at 48°20' north latitude. More likely, the conniving captain had picked up the information while he was cooling his heels in Monterey waiting for López de Haro to rendezvous with him, assuming they would sail back to San Blas together following their contentious expedition.

While these developments had been taking place on the Northwest Coast in 1788 and early 1789, the urgent Martínez–López de Haro expedition, which had left San Blas on February 17, 1789, was sailing north to Nootka Sound, where it arrived on May 5. As noted previously, Martínez commanded the *Princesa*, aided by second mate Carrasco, while López de Haro skippered the *San Carlos*, assisted by first mate Narváez. In confirmation of the viceroy's concerns, Martínez found three fur trading vessels anchored in Cala de Los Amigos — two were American and one was British. Subsequently, three other English merchant vessels would arrive, and a major international dispute would erupt.

The first of these vessels, the *Northwest America* — a 40-ton schooner commanded by Robert Funter — cruised into Cala de Los Amigos on June 8. The small trading and coastal-exploration vessel had been built there the previous summer by about fifty Chinese carpenters under the command of the English merchant captain John Meares. Constructed around frames brought from Macao aboard the Portuguese vessel *Feliz Aventureira* (a 230-ton snow-brig owned by Meares), the fir-beamed, cedar-planked coastal schooner was the first vessel of European design built on the Pacific Northwest Coast. As part of Martínez's effort to assert Spain's sovereignty in the remote port, the impulsive, bellicose

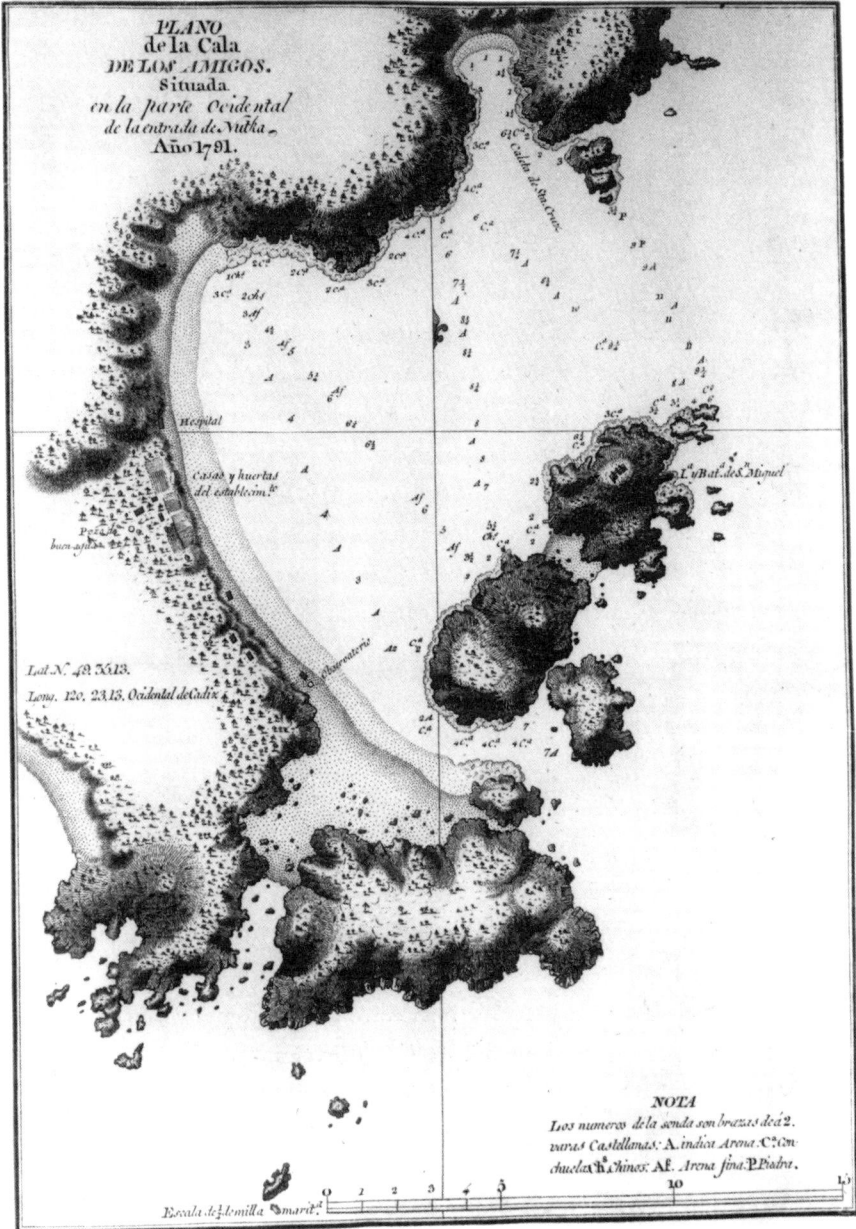

Spanish chart of Cala de Los Amigos, 1791. Along the cove's shore
is the hospital, officers' houses, observatory, gardens, and freshwater well.
The battery atop St. Michael Island guards the cove. Engraving by
José Cardero from drawing by Morata. (JOHN KENDRICK)

captain seized the *Northwest America* and subsequently claimed Funter had abandoned it. (Two years later, Narváez would use the rebuilt, and by then twice-rechristened schooner to make his major exploring expeditions on the northwest coast.)[5]

After repairing the "abandoned" vessel, Martínez rechristened it *Santa Gertrudis la Magna* — in honour of either the patroness of navigators or his wife Doña Gertrudis González, perhaps both — and placed Narváez in command. Instead of sending the *San Carlos* on an expedition northward, as the viceroy had ordered, Martínez dispatched Narváez and Carrasco aboard the *Santa Gertrudis la Magna* on June 21 to investigate three major waterways to the south of Nootka Sound: Clayoquot Sound (subsequently called Puerto Narváez by the Spaniards for a few years), which English and American fur traders had already frequented; Barkley Sound (called Entrada de Nitinat by Spanish mariners),[6] which had not attracted much fur trading; and — most important — the recently sighted and investigated entrance of Juan de Fuca Strait. The relatively short voyage would constitute Spain's first reconnaissance along the lower west coast of what is now Vancouver Island. It would also give Narváez and Carrasco their first opportunity to coordinate their skills as explorers.

On June 24, Martínez performed an elaborate ceremony of imperial possession at Cala de Los Amigos. Watched by a crowd composed of Mowachaht people and numerous English and American merchant officers and sailors, the self-important Spanish officer set up the customary cross, held a Mass, fired salutes, and gave an ostentatious speech claiming all territories as far north as Alaska for King Carlos III.

After visiting this harbour (which the Mowachaht called Yuquot) for several years, the English fur traders had decided to establish a settlement and supply base there (and dubbed it Friendly Cove). To that end, Captain James Colnett was the next British mariner to sail into Nootka Sound. After a drunken brawl with the assertive, insolent Englishman, the equally churlish Martínez commandeered Colnett's vessel, the *Argonaut*, and a 13-metre sloop under his command called the *Princess Royal*, which had arrived a few days earlier. Then Martínez arrested both crews, including twenty-nine Chinese carpenters, and placed Colnett in

Launching of *Northwest America* at Yuquot, September 20, 1788.
Drawing by C. Metz. (ALLAN E. BAX COLLECTION OF
MARITIME HISTORY, UNIVERSITY OF SYDNEY)

chains. The Spaniard's impulsive, belligerent act set off a clash between the rival nations that would take almost eighteen months to settle, and then only temporarily. The fallout from what became known as the "Nootka Crisis" would remain unresolved for several years.

Forcing the captured Chinese to work, Martínez built a small battery on an islet that commanded the entrance to Cala de Los Amigos, erected a few sheds, and started constructing a larger building on the main beach. He dubbed the outpost Santa Cruz de Nutka. Although Martínez kept Colnett confined, he allowed the other British "prisoners" to move about freely. On July 4, however, when the two American captains in port invited all officers in Cala de Los Amigos (Friendly Cove, to Colnett) to join them in honouring the United States, Colnett was released for the celebration. Subsequently taken to San Blas and jailed, he would eventually suffer a mental breakdown and attempt suicide.

Meanwhile, Narváez and Carrasco had been exploring the three large waterways to the south. We do not know exactly what they found in either Puerto Narváez (Clayoquot Sound) or Entrada de Nitinat (Barkley Sound) because both of the mariners' journals are missing. Nevertheless, we do have Martínez's record of what Narváez reported. Based on that, Narváez penetrated Juan de Fuca Strait for more than 139 kilometres (to approximately today's Port Townsend and the mouth of Puget Sound). Then he returned to Cala de Los Amigos on July 5 with Spain's first precise verbal descriptions of the large channel on which Martínez placed great importance. Although, as noted earlier, other mariners previously had found and probed the strait's mouth, Narváez became the first European to explore the interior of its long throat. He has also been credited with naming Punta de Bonilla and Punta de Martínez at the entrance to Juan de Fuca Strait, as well as other possible places.[7] Today, the international boundary between Canada and the United States follows the centre line of this wide and important strait. Narváez told Martínez: "From side to side it measured [34 kilometres], continued on inland for almost the same width as far as one could see, no horizon being visible in the east-southeast, and [is] the strait which they call Juan de Fuca. Inside [the entrance] is a habour named San Juan [Port Renfrew] which is a good place to anchor in, to take on water and wood, and to provide oneself with timber for planks and masts. It is at the farthest north and west point."[8]

Martínez was convinced the strait led to the fabled Northwest Passage, sought by maritime explorers for decades. He believed it might connect to either the Mississippi River or the legendary Strait of Fonte in the area of Hudson Bay. Furthermore, he was confident that confirmation of its exact location would startle everyone in Europe. He viewed Spanish control of Juan de Fuca Strait and similar waterways to the north as essential parts of a grand politico-economic scheme to dominate the entire Pacific Northwest Coast. In his opinion, this vital passage had to be explored further as soon as possible.

First, Martínez had to deal with another English fur trader who sailed into Nootka Sound aboard the sloop *Princess Royal*. Captain Thomas Hudson, seeking Colnett, tried to contact Martínez through the Mowachaht people living around the entrance of Nootka Sound. However, the wily Spaniard lured Hudson into Cala de Los Amigos, captured his vessel, and took the commander and crew prisoners. Martínez was on board the seized vessel on July 13, when Chief Callicum — Chief Maquinna's son-in-law, and one of the most respected warriors among the Mowachaht — came alongside in a canoe, shouting accusations about Martínez being a thief. Infuriated by the insults, Martínez grabbed a musket, drew a bead on the incensed chief, and pulled the trigger. Martínez would later claim his gun misfired and a Spanish sailor fired another gun, killing Callicum on the spot. It remained unclear whether the chief was accusing Martínez of stealing the English vessels, misappropriating lumber from the Mowachaht, or interrupting the lucrative trade the Aboriginal people had cultivated with the British merchants. In any event, the Mowachaht people would remember the incident with bitterness for years.

On July 27, 1789, Martínez placed López de Haro and Narváez in command of the *San Carlos* and the captured *Princess Royal* respectively, and sent them to San Blas with the news about discovering what he thought was the entrance to the alleged Northwest Passage. Apparently, Martínez believed that Viceroy Flórez would promptly dispatch a properly supplied expedition to carry out further investigations. López de Haro and Narváez reached their home port by the end of August. However, Viceroy Flórez — alarmed by reports about Martínez's impulsive behaviour — already had sent a vessel to Nootka Sound with orders for him to end the "pretended" settlement before winter set in. To house his captive mariners at Cala de Los Amigos, Martínez had been building a jail aboard another captured vessel. In accordance with his new orders, the acting commandant completely evacuated the Spanish outpost on October 31 and set sail for San Blas with his prisoners and captured vessels. (The latter included the former *Northwest America*, reconditioned and renamed *Santa Gertrudis la Magna*.) Although it had been ordered by the viceroy, Martínez's dramatic departure left Spain's claim to the surrounding territory in serious jeopardy.

Maquinna, hereditary chief at Nootka Sound in 1791.
Drawing by Tomás de Suría, ca. 1788. (MUSEO NAVAL, MADRID)

Maquinna welcomes his younger brother Comekela on his return
from China, May 16, 1788. T. Stothard engraving of sketch by unknown
artist in 1788–1789. (VANCOUVER MARITIME MUSEUM)

Flórez knew that Martínez's fight with Colnett would stir up trouble
with England, but the viceroy had already resigned, so he simply filed a
full report with Madrid and waited for his successor to take over. Although Flórez's dispatch recommended reoccupation of Cala de Los
Amigos, it failed to mention his latest order to Martínez , recalling him
to San Blas. The diplomatic firestorm set off by Martínez's reckless

conduct at Nootka Sound would be dumped in the lap of a new administration — one that was even more determined to secure Spain's position on the Pacific Northwest Coast.

～

In mid-August of 1789, Viceroy Juan Vicente de Güemes Pacheco de Padilla Horcasitas y Aguayo, Segundo Conde de Revillagigedo, landed in Veracruz with seven top-flight naval officers and four surgeons assigned to the Pacific Northwest Coast. The assignments demonstrated Madrid's commitment to reoccupying Nootka Sound as Flórez had recommended. The senior naval officer was Juan Francisco Bodega, who would serve as commandant at San Blas until his death in 1794. His genial, diplomatic style made him the ideal man to take charge of the contentious developments taking place at Cala de Los Amigos. The calm, conciliatory commander spearheaded Spain's intensive exploration of the Northwest Coast, which picked up steam in 1790. This initiative would give Narváez many opportunities to use his navigation and cartographic skills.

Revillagigedo would emerge as one of the greatest viceroys to govern New Spain. When he took over from Flórez on October 17, 1789, he faced two major questions: What to do about the captured Englishmen and their vessels in San Blas? How to hang on to Nootka Sound? Giving the second challenge priority, he wrote Bodega in early December, instructing him to "relieve Martínez" and replace him with an officer "who might be more worthy of confidence" to occupy and fortify Nootka [Sound] and explore more thoroughly *within* Juan de Fuca Strait. In his opinion, however, Martínez's notion of a "northwest passage" belonged to "the same sphere of dreams" as other mythological voyages.

To Bodega's consternation, Martínez arrived in San Blas on December 6, only a few days after the viceroy's letter was delivered. With good reason, Bodega decided to make Martínez the scapegoat for evacuating Nootka Sound. Two days before Christmas, the commandant answered Revillagigedo saying: "The total state of abandonment in which Martínez left Nootka [Sound] and the necessity of keeping possession of it are today the principal objects of my attention." Bodega gathered all the artillery he could find and loaded it aboard the frigate *Concepción*, the *San Carlos*, and the English sloop which had been renamed *Princesa Real*. Unfortunately, Bodega had no senior officers available at San Blas to take on his challenging orders to reoccupy Nootka Sound without repeating Martínez's over-aggressive methods. Therefore, Bodega appointed another fellow Basque, Lieutenant Francisco Eliza (1759–1825), to become commandant of the outpost. He also ordered Ensign Salvador Fidalgo and Ensign Manuel Quimper to accompany Eliza. Reluctantly, he agreed to send Martínez along as an unranked special officer, with no responsibility.

LEFT: Viceroy of New Spain, Count Revillagigedo;
RIGHT: Juan Francisco de la Bodega y Quadra.

The first item in Bodega's secret instructions to Eliza stated that the expedition's primary objective was to fortify Cala de Los Amigos before some other power took over. In addition, Bodega said, "The King requires that you do not molest the English . . . nor prevent them by force from establishing themselves in the neighbourhood." Next, he was to explore the entire coast, including the full extent of Juan de Fuca Strait. As soon as Eliza returned to Nootka Sound from this exploratory expedition, he was supposed to send a vessel straight to San Blas with charts and detailed results, including careful records of the 6,000 pounds of large copper sheets, measuring 66 centimetres by 56 centimetres and "thick as a real," which he carried to trade for furs. The introduction of processed sheet copper by European traders and explorers in the 1790s would make the shiny, pliable metal a highly prized item among all the coastal peoples from Alaska to Juan de Fuca Strait. Among many Indigenous chiefs on the lower Pacific Northwest Coast, the acquisition of stylized "coppers" soon became a complex way of demonstrating excess wealth, conspicuous consumption, cultural nourishment, spiritual power, generosity, and prestige.

Commanding the frigate *Concepción*, Eliza sailed from San Blas on February 3, 1790, in charge of the largest Spanish force sent northward to that time. He was accompanied by two vessels: the packetboat *San Carlos* under Ramón Saavedra's command with Juan Pantoja y Arriaga aboard as first mate, which carried vital supplies for the distant outpost; and the sloop *Princesa Real*, skippered by Quimper. On board the flagship were all the construction materials of the *Santa Gertrudis la Magna*, which Bodega had ordered dismantled at San Blas so Eliza could return it to Cala de Los Amigos, knowing a small schooner would be needed for coastal exploration.[9]

Fortunately, when Eliza arrived at Nootka Sound on March 26,[10] the outpost at Cala de Los Amigos was unoccupied by either English or Russian fur traders. For the time being, the Spanish had the hotly contested site to themselves, and Eliza intended to maintain a strong presence there. Even the Mowachaht had left the sheltered bay adjacent to Cala de Los Amigos, where they had long maintained a favoured summer settlement. They had pulled up stakes and moved because they had been alienated by Martínez's killing of Chief Callicum. At the same time, they clearly wanted to recover their village site. For the next two years of Spanish occupation, the Indigenous people plagued the intruders with questions about when they expected to leave.

Veteran first mate Juan Pantoja recorded some superficial observations about Mowachaht customs. He described the Mowachaht as "docile and cowardly" compared with the more warlike Aboriginal people farther south. He said they lived in board-roofed post-and-beam longhouses. The men wore "pine-bark" capes over calf-length undergarments. The women wrapped themselves in a breechcloth. Pantoja also reported that the Mowachaht enslaved enemies taken in war and that the chiefs occasionally ate some of the youngest captives.[11]

This perceived, but largely misunderstood aspect of the Indigenous culture conveyed, to some extent, the gap in understanding that existed between the two cultures. It also became a primary element of the Spaniards' justification for purchasing Indigenous youngsters.

"Fifteen Indians of both sexes from four to ten years of age have been obtained in exchange for copper and [abalone] shells," said Pantoja. "The principal land and sea officers undertook to raise and educate them."[12] In fact, the record would reveal that it was priests, sailors, and ordinary soldiers — not officers — who bought most of the Aboriginal children.

Having engaged in trade with mariners from various nations for some time, the Mowachaht had become adept at bartering whatever they could to obtain items that they either needed or, as in Maquinna's case, wanted to enhance their status. Once it became obvious that the Europeans were interested in obtaining children, for whatever reasons, the Mowachaht were quick to offer orphans and the offspring of slaves captured in war, both of whom they considered expendable as trade bait. Unfortunately, the Spaniards' participation in such trade was clouded by suspicion, ignorance, and misunderstanding. This kept them from grasping the cultural values of the people with whom they were trading, and it caused them to formulate a questionable rationalization for such trade. Consequently, these commercial transactions would become increasingly awkward and embarrassing for the authorities in New Spain.

As the Spaniards tried to settle in at Cala de Los Amigos in April 1790, they found it extremely difficult to adapt to their drastically different environment. Pantoja stated that poor diets and the long, wet northwest winters left the Spaniards suffering from colds, colic, rheumatism, scurvy, and diarrhea or bloody dysentery. "The last two are very common and almost incurable in this climate," he said.

In May 1790, Eliza ordered reconstruction of the disassembled *Santa Gertrudis la Magna*, and Captain Pedro Alberni supervised the installation of the keel for a new schooner, which would soon play a key role in several expeditions under Narváez's command.[13] It would take four months to complete the transformation.

At the end of May, Eliza sent out two expeditions. Fidalgo and first mate Esteban Mondofia sailed aboard the *San Carlos* to explore the Alaska coast in more detail. Quimper left on the *Princesa Real* with first mate López de Haro and second mate Juan Carrasco to chart both interior coasts of Juan de Fuca Strait as far as the San Juan Islands.

During the Quimper expedition into Juan de Fuca Strait, Carrasco entered a narrow waterway to the north that he named Canal de López de Haro (Haro Strait), but he made no attempt to navigate it very far. On June 30, Quimper wrote in his diary: "The longboat came back with the second piloto [Carrasco] who told me that he had been in the channel and that it . . . extended a long distance."[14] It would become the first place in Juan de Fuca Strait that Narváez and his colleagues would re-investigate in 1791.

While Quimper charted the broad outlines of the large strait using a rough chart drawn by Narváez in 1789, Carrasco made several short probes in the longboat. On one of these voyages, he located two other places near the eastern end of Juan de Fuca Strait, which he and Narváez would revisit in 1791: Puerto de Quadra (today's Port Discovery) and Isla de Carrasco (Protection Island) — a small island at the entrance of this large harbour. More important, he sighted what appeared to be a channel leading northward, which invited further investigation. In the summer of 1791, it would lead Narváez and Carrasco toward one of the most significant explorations in early Pacific Northwest Coast history.

After several months of exploration, Quimper completed his careful investigation and, as planned, he headed back to Nootka Sound. However, unfavourable winds, foggy weather, and westerly currents forced him to sail south instead, and he arrived in San Blas on November 13, 1790. Fidalgo also returned to Mexico. With the assistance of López de Haro and Carrasco, Quimper produced the first detailed chart of the interior of Juan de Fuca Strait. Although some Indigenous people in the area led Quimper to believe there might be two large channels at the strait's eastern end, one tending northwest and one south, he concluded that it was a dead end.[15] European discovery of the waterway that is now considered the Salish Sea's northern arm would have to wait another seven months.

Despite the long delay, the small, shallow-draft schooner that would prove indispensable during this next voyage of discovery was launched at Cala de Los Amigos on September 26, 1790.[16] On November 1, Eliza christened the sleek, functional vessel *Santa Saturnina*, alias *La Orcasitas*.[17] Eliza named the schooner after his wife Saturnina Norberta Caamaño,[18] who remained in Cadiz during her husband's fourteen-year-long assignment in New Spain. The vessel's alias paid tribute to Viceroy Revillagigedo by using one part of his long official title.[19]

Left at Cala de Los Amigos, Eliza would not find out what Quimper had learned from his exploration of Juan de Fuca Strait until the spring of 1791. Meanwhile, Frigate Lieutenant Jacinto Caamaño, Eliza's brother-in-law, had arrived at Cala de Los Amigos in command of the *Aránzazu* in late June 1790, with Narváez on board. (Bodega had recruited both Caamaño and Eliza in 1789.) Eliza had already started

Scale drawing of *Santa Saturnina*. (STEVE MAYO)

constructing several buildings on shore. He immediately transferred Narváez to the depot-guard ship *Concepción*. For the next two years, Narváez would remain under Eliza's command as the Spanish commander made cautious, sporadic, and largely ineffectual efforts to impede English trading ships from taking *de facto* possession of this important outpost.[20] As the only non-Indigenous establishment between San Francisco and Prince William Sound, it had become a diplomatic bone of contention at the highest levels of government in Spain and England.

Martínez's seizures of English vessels had enraged the British public, sparking the famous Nootka Sound controversy. British negotiators sought to secure undisputed fur-trading rights to the north Pacific. Spain clung to its time-worn theory that it possessed complete sovereignty in the South Sea, given to her by Pope Alexander VI in 1493 when he divided the New World between Spain and Portugal. Spain feared that settlements established on the Pacific Northwest Coast by heavily armed British fur-trading vessels would endanger its possessions in Alta California. When Britain threatened to declare war over the controversy, Spain decided to sign the first Nootka Sound Convention on October 28, 1790, effectively abandoning its claim of exclusive sovereignty. The convention left ownership of the region unsettled, however, and gave Britain and Spain equal trading rights.

Meanwhile, explorers of all the nations that had economic, political, and military interests on the Pacific Northwest Coast continued to search for a Northwest Passage — that elusive link between the Atlantic and Pacific Oceans. One of these navigators and cartographers would be Narváez.

PART II

The Key
Expedition

CHAPTER 4

In Quest of the
Northwest Passage, 1791

EXPLORING UNCHARTED territory is an undertaking of the imagination, the mind, and the will. However, Narváez's fascination with searching for the fabled Northwest Passage was also fueled by his own practical, first-hand initial investigations in the North Pacific, two large archipelagos along the Pacific Northwest Coast that became known as Clayoquot Sound and Barkley Sound, and especially the tantalizing Juan de Fuca Strait. Like other mariners of his day, he was also aware of fanciful stories and theories about a large transcontinental river. Some of these tales would lead directly to Narváez's most significant assignment: exploration of what was then an unknown huge inland sea that constituted the northern extension of Juan de Fuca Strait.

The legendary tale of Apóstolos Valerianos about his alleged voyage through what became known as the Strait of Juan de Fuca in 1592 was not the only fable that had inspired Spanish imaginations to envision a northern route from the Atlantic to the Pacific Ocean. In 1609, Captain Lorenzo Ferrer de Maldonado, a respected navigator from Madrid, had presented a long report to the King describing a remarkable voyage he pretended to have made in 1588. Ferrer claimed he had sailed from east to west through the Strait of Anian, crossing the North American continent at about 60° north latitude. His proposed scheme for securing control of the imaginary passage came to naught. But the illusion persisted.

Two Frenchmen — cartographer Nicolas Delisle and geographer Philippe Buache — were dazzled by the novelty and importance of this tall tale when they came across a remarkable letter that had been published in 1708. The writer was Bartolomeo de Fonte, a Spanish admiral who claimed he had explored the Strait of Anian for the viceroy in 1640. Although it was another fake, Delisle and Bauche became convinced of its authenticity and presented it as a true document to the Académie des Sciences in Paris in 1750. Bauche said this was indeed the long-sought route between the Pacific and Atlantic oceans. Two years later, the Frenchmen published an imaginary map, which retained its credibility for more than 40 years.[1]

On November 13, 1790, cartographer Jean-Nicholas Buache de la Neuville, nephew of Phillippe Buache, reignited the controversy when he read a paper before the Académie des Sciences, defending the existence of the imaginary passage and endorsing the credibility of the recently revived manuscript describing Ferrer's trip through the "Strait of Anian."[2]

To test Buache de la Neuville's opinions, Spain would order the corvettes *Descubierta* and *Atrevida* — commissioned for a major politico-scientific voyage around the world and harboured in Acapulco — to survey Juan de Fuca Strait along the way. With Alejandro Malaspina in command, the two ships would eventually sail north from Acapulco on May 1, 1791. On June 23 Malaspina would verify earlier surveys by Captain Cook, but he would not enter the strait.[3]

Meanwhile, Bodega had organized another probe of the waterways that were suspected to exist beyond the interior of Juan de Fuca Strait.

In February 1791, Ensign Ramón Saavedra left San Blas in command of the supply vessel *San Carlos* and sailed for Nootka Sound, with first mate Juan Pantoja aboard. Saavedra carried indispensable supplies and Viceroy Revillagigedo's new instructions for Eliza, which were prompted by Quimper's discoveries during the previous summer. The viceroy specifically requested Bodega to include second *piloto* Narváez and the experienced *pilotín* Juan Carrasco in the new exploratory expedition.[4] When the *San Carlos* arrived at Nootka Sound on March 26, Eliza learned that he was expected to undertake the challenging task of extending exploration of Juan de Fuca Strait into the uncharted waters of what is now known as the Salish Sea's northern arm (Georgia Strait).

Despite growing skepticism, many explorers, merchant mariners, military leaders, and geographers from several powerful countries were convinced that Juan de Fuca Strait represented the throat of the fabled Straits of Anian, which allegedly led from the Pacific Ocean back to the Atlantic. Geopolitically, it had become clear that whoever pushed through this waterway first would secure considerable power, authority, and prestige for their king. Spain was determined to win the race.

On April 3, 1791, two Mowachaht men approached Eliza's headquarters at Cala de Los Amigos in a canoe and seemed to report that they had seen five large sailing vessels outside the Bahía de Buena Esperanza (the open ocean north of today's Maquinna Point), and that four of the vessels had two masts and one was a three-master. Alarmed by the possible arrival of what sounded as if it might be a significant English naval force, Eliza prepared for the worst. He ordered all of the *Concepción*'s artillery — thirty cannon of twelve and eight pounds each — to be mounted. He also had eight cannon placed in battery on the *San Carlos*. Then the commander sent *pilotín* José Verdía in a longboat about seven kilometres south to Punta del Bajo (Escalante Point), where all the sea to the northwest could be surveyed easily on a clear day. Verdía returned at six o'clock in the evening to report that he had seen nothing.

Nevertheless, Eliza was determined to prepare as strong a defence as possible to avoid being taken by surprise during the dark, rainy night. He doubled the sentinels, ordered them to make their rounds both on land and water, and required them to maintain close communication. To prevent a beach landing behind the fort, which was located on a small hill at the entrance to the port, Eliza had two eight-pound cannons mounted there. Finally, he ordered the fort to be garrisoned with enough troops to man all the cannons: two twenty-four pounders, eight twelve-pounders, and one six-pounder.

On April 4, the expedition was reinforced by two more frigates: the *Princesa*, carrying Narváez as first mate under the command of Lieutenant Jacinto Caamaño, and the *Aránzazu*, commanded by Juan Bautista Matute. The following day, Eliza had the ketch-rigged *Santa Saturnina* fully armed and manned with fifteen seamen and four soldiers. Placing second *piloto* Narváez in command, Eliza ordered him to sail inland through two narrow channels that ran north and then west behind the large Isla de Mazarredo (Nootka Island) to the Bahía de Buena Esperanza (Esperanza Inlet). The objective was to verify Verdía's earlier report without being seen from any vessels that might be offshore. If Narváez saw no foreign vessels in the immediate area, he was supposed to continue farther north to obtain any information he could from Indigenous people living along the outer coast. This assignment indicates that, by this time, the Spaniards were aware of this interior waterway, which the Aboriginal people used extensively, yet held little interest for fur traders. It also showed that Eliza knew the route encircled a large island that extended northwest from Cala de Los Amigos.

This sixty-to-seventy-kilometre-long inside route could be managed efficiently in an Aboriginal canoe or a European longboat. It was not easily undertaken in a sailing vessel, however, and it could not have been accomplished in anything larger than Narváez's small schooner, which had to be rowed much of the way using up to eight long, two-man oars. After heading north about thirty kilometres in the relatively narrow Tahsis Inlet, Narváez had to glide west through an extremely tight passage into Hecate Channel, which runs northwest ten kilometres until it reaches the head of Esperanza Inlet. From there it is an easy twenty-kilometre downstream run to this waterway's large mouth. In

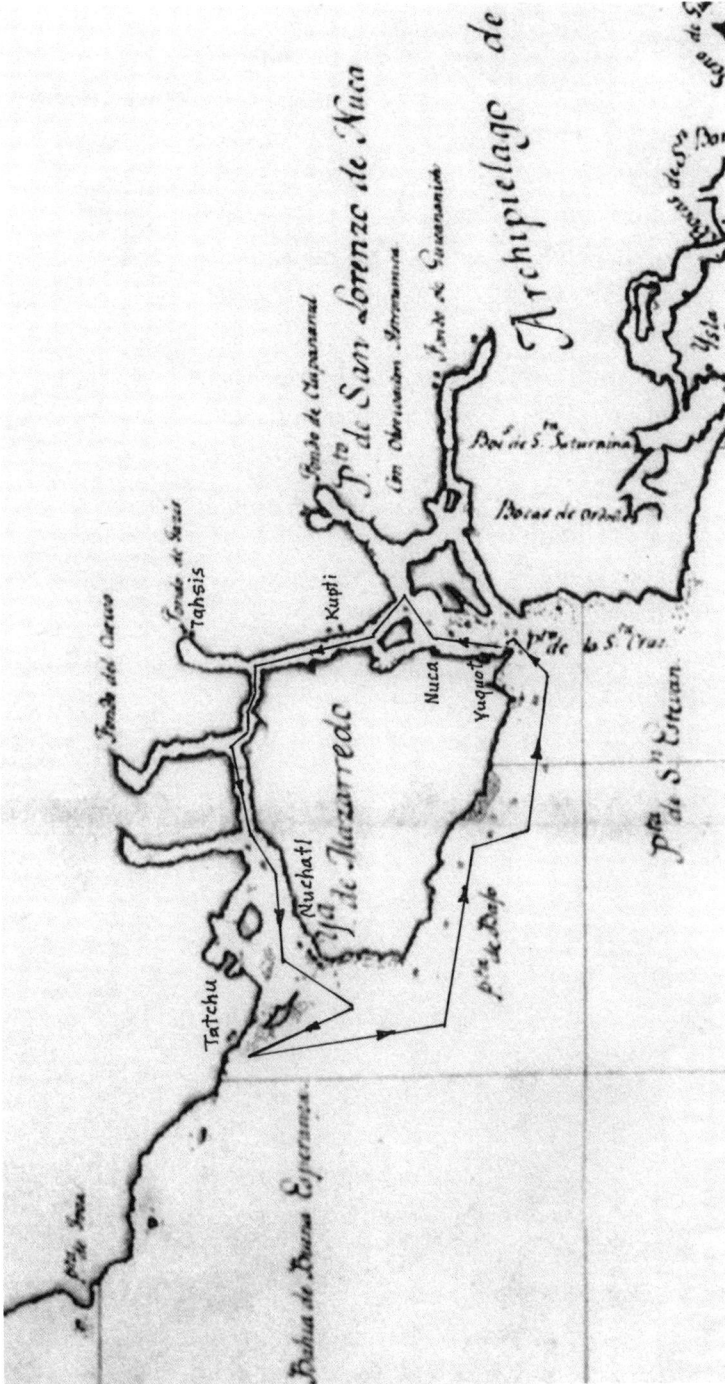

Author's adaptation of Carrasco's *Carta que comprehende* ... showing Narváez's reconnaissance at Nootka Sound, April 1791. (WAGNER)

view of the fact that Narváez did not return for five days, he must have visited Mowachaht villages along the first inlet and might well have made contact with Nuchatlaht and Ehattesaht people who had settlements around the entrance to Esperanza Inlet, about forty-five kilometres northwest of Nootka Sound along the oceanfront. When the *Santa Saturnina* returned to Cala de Los Amigos (probably by the more direct seaward route), Narváez reported that he was uncertain what the Aboriginal people had tried to communicate about the presence of several large sailing vessels.

Meanwhile, Eliza's interpreter, Corporal Gabriel del Castillo, learned from Mowachahts living along the shore of Bahía de Buena Esperanza that, four months earlier, four English vessels had sailed from Cala de Los Amigos (Friendly Cove) under Captain Mier, one of which had twenty guns. Furthermore, two days earlier a large schooner had sailed for Clayoquot Sound. Apparently, these were the vessels that the first two Mowachaht men had mentioned.[5]

Although this incident proved to be a false alarm, it showed the leadership Eliza was capable of exercising within the base. It also demonstrated his confidence in Narváez's expertise as a responsible mariner.

Eliza's orders were modified in late April, when the frigate *Aránzazu* arrived from San Blas with a supplementary letter from Bodega related to the recently completed Nootka Sound Convention. Eliza was given the additional weighty task of thoroughly exploring the entire coast between Bucareli Bay (now in Alaska) and Puerto de la Trinidad (about forty kilometres north of today's Eureka, California).[6] Bodega also enclosed a general plan of the Pacific coast, which summarized Spanish exploration between Acapulco and the Aleutian Islands up to 1791. Eliza was expected to confirm everything that previous expeditions had charted and fill in any gaps. Bodega had finished this *Carta General* in San Blas in March and sent the original to Madrid. The chart showed Juan de Fuca Strait as a wide, deep indentation in the coast, but the *absence* of two soon-to-be discovered geographical features stand out: a

López de Haro's chart for Quimper of Juan de Fuca Strait, 1790. (NATIONAL ARCHIVES UK) large island directly north of the strait, and an inland sea east of that island. One of Bodega's notes on the chart stated: "El Estrecho de Fuca, it is said, was discovered in 1592; and although surveyed and taken possession of in 1789 and 1790 by Don José María Narváez and Don Manuel Quimper [respectively], yet one [interior] mouth has not yet been inspected, but it is purposed to do so this year." (This referenced the Canal de López de Haro.) During the next year, Bodega would update this map three times to show corrections and recent observations, but none of them would show a large offshore island or details of a supposed large inland waterway running north from the interior of Juan de Fuca Strait.

The special expedition that Eliza was instructed to command would lead to Narváez exploring two previously uncharted archipelagos on the southwest coast of today's Vancouver Island, another unknown archipelago beyond the Canal de López de Haro, and then mapping the inland sea that would become his major discovery on the Pacific Northwest Coast. As commander of the overall mission, Eliza would eventually receive most of the credit for this key expedition, but he actually left all the exploration and cartography to Narváez and three other experienced *pilotos* on the voyage. Their findings would precipitate major changes in the cartography of this part of the Pacific Northwest Coast.

CHAPTER 5

Surveying "Puerto Narváez," May 1791

ON MAY 3, Lieutenant Eliza's expeditionary force placed the statue of the mariners' patron saint, Señora del Rosario la Marinera (the Seafarers' Lady of Rosary),[1] in the carpenter shop at Cala de Los Amigos, decorated it with flags and flowers, and held a special Mass. Firing rifles and shouting "*Viva la Virgen*," the crew members boarded their vessels. Eliza placed Saavedra in charge of guarding Nootka Sound with about eighty-five sailors and thirty-one soldiers under Captain Pedro Alberni. Most of the rank and file troops were Mexican.[2]

The following day, Eliza warped[3] out of the harbour in command of the *San Carlos*. His officers were first mate Juan Pantoja and second mate José Verdía. The latter, who had only reached the rank of brevet (apprentice) second *piloto*, had served as a *pilotín* (apprentice *piloto*) under Narváez on Martínez's expeditions to Alaska in 1788 and to

Nootka Sound in 1789. The 196-ton packetboat — basically a frigate with heavy armaments replaced by stowage space — was 22 metres long (at the keel), making the hull about 26 metres long. It had a 6.7 metre beam, a 4.6 metre draft, and it carried sixteen four-pound cannons. José Joaquín Villaverde, an army captain, and Father Juan Ferrón, a surgeon, were also on board. The lead vessel carried an 8.5 metre long-boat, which had thirteen oars but little space for storing provisions.

The larger vessel was accompanied by the 32-ton schooner *Santa Saturnina*, which had a 10-metre-long keel that would have given her a total hull length of about 12.8 metres.[4] It was commanded by first mate Narváez, with the veteran *pilotín* Juan Carrasco serving as second mate. This much smaller vessel had a shallow 1.5 metre draft. It was outfitted with eight two-man oars and armed with four three-pound cannons on deck. She carried a twenty-day supply of food for both her crew and the longboat's small expeditionary force. Between them, the two vessels carried ten soldiers.

Narváez must have experienced a sense of exhilaration and anticipation as Eliza led the two vessels north from Nootka Sound. He not only had his own vessel to command, he knew he would have key roles to play in several important aspects of the expedition's demanding assignment. Furthermore, he was looking forward to working closely with his fellow *piloto* Juan Carrasco, who was an experienced navigator and competent cartographer. Both men, however, knew that the expedition could take several months, and that foul weather would arrive in early fall, as it always did. This left them wondering if Eliza would have time to complete the large number of investigations, explorations, and charting tasks that Bodega had assigned.

After fighting stiff headwinds for three days, Eliza was forced to recognize two realities: first, his orders to explore the entire coast between what is now Alaska and San Francisco in three to four months were completely unrealistic; second, the *Santa Saturnina*, which was essential for probing inlets, could not make sufficient headway against the strong, contrary northwest winds that the expedition was encountering.[5] Reversing his course, the cautious captain wisely decided to concentrate on exploring two uncharted large archipelagos along the coast southeast of Nootka Sound and, most importantly, what appeared to be the openings (*bocas* or "mouths") of two channels in the interior of Juan de Fuca Strait — one on the northern shore and another at the eastern end. At that time, it was still thought that any of these three large waterways might have interior reaches that led to an undiscovered passage eastward across the continent. The *Santa Saturnina* and the longboat would be required for all three tasks, and Narváez would take the lead role, assisted primarily by Carrasco, and secondarily by Juan Pantoja and José Verdía.

On May 7, 1791, both vessels entered what the Spanish mariners for three years had been calling Puerto Narváez (Clayoquot Sound) — the first major archipelago south of Nootka Sound on Vancouver Island's west coast. Narváez had briefly visited some part of this large waterway in 1789, but it had not been charted by Spanish seafarers. Although English and American fur traders had become more familiar with the area than the Spaniards, they tended to be more intent on engaging in commerce than making accurate maps and hydrographic charts. This aspect of the expedition also held important diplomatic significance for the Spanish. While British and American traders had established effective relations with the most important Aboriginal chief in the region, mariners from New Spain had yet to meet him in person. Narváez would be among the first to have that opportunity.

As the Spanish vessels anchored inside Puerto Narváez near what is now Tofino at about six o'clock in the evening, they were immediately visited by Tla-o-qui-aht people in numerous canoes, which carried four to twelve persons each. According to Eliza, by sunset fifty-eight canoes of all sizes had pulled alongside the *San Carlos* and the nearby *Santa Saturnina*. One of the Indigenous vessels carried the exceptionally wealthy and powerful Chief Wickaninnish and his three sons.

Since 1787 — two years after the maritime fur trade started — commerce along Vancouver Island's west coast had been controlled by three large trading blocks that were dominated by a trio of powerful chiefs.[6] Although each governed a separate territory, all three, along with their closest subordinates, were related by marriage. In the south was Chief Tetakü, whose main village was located on an island at the entrance to

Juan de Fuca Strait. In the north was the Mowachaht Chief Maquinna, who lived in Nootka Sound. In between, Chief Wickaninnish's oligarchy ruled the central coast from his villages in Clayoquot Sound. The biggest Tla-o-qui-aht village, which was also the largest Indigenous settlement on the entire Pacific Northwest Coast, was located at Opitsaht on the southern point of what became known as Meares Island.

Wickaninnish's three sons went aboard the *San Carlos*, while the chief inexplicably remained in his large canoe. Pantoja described him as being "fifty to fifty-five years of age, fat, robust, of pleasing appearance and at the same time very grave in his gestures, signs and conversations."[7] Eliza gave the trio a copper sheet and a dozen abalone shells. When Eliza asked how long it had been since any sailing ships had entered the sound, he learned that twenty days had passed since a frigate apparently commanded by Captain Robert Gray and a packetboat probably skippered by William Douglas had left carrying "many sea-otter skins" which had been exchanged for "large copper sheets."[8] At nightfall, Eliza ordered a cannon fired to inform the Tla-o-qui-aht that trading was finished for the day and it was time to retire.

At six o'clock the next morning, more than five hundred Tla-o-qui-aht people of all ages came back out to the vessels in about eighty canoes, eager to trade. Early in the afternoon Wickaninnish's sons visited the *San Carlos* again. To show respect, Eliza gave them two sheets of copper, and the chief's sons reciprocated with two sea otter skins.[9] By evening Eliza had moved his vessels across the sound to within a kilometre of the main village at Opitsaht, where he managed to moor them at the most protected anchorage in the area.

On May 9, Eliza ordered Narváez and Pantoja to prepare their respective vessels — the *Santa Saturnina* and the longboat — for exploring several inlets, the mouths of which were located to the northwest and southeast. However, these plans were interrupted when Wickaninnish invited Eliza and his officers to attend a welcoming ceremony at his longhouse the next morning.

Honoured by the invitation, Eliza, Narváez and the other three *pilotos*, the first chaplain, and the surgeon went ashore the following day to formally present their compliments to Wickaninnish. It would prove to be a memorable experience for all the Spaniards. Carrying a present of abalone shells and a bundle of ship's biscuits, the Spanish contingent strode along a narrow alley for about twenty paces until they came to a "very large figure" carved out of one of the huge posts that supported large timbers which held up the building's roof. The mouth of the figure constituted the door to the longhouse. One at a time, the mariners entered the "huge gallery" and saw Wickaninnish standing at the other end. The chief welcomed the Spaniards "imperiously" and invited them to sit down, along with a large number of his followers. Then Wickaninnish called for a song of welcome. "An old man [probably a shaman], taking in his hands a string of shells, began the chant which they all continued with such noise and cries that at the end . . . they gave (in musical time) a roar so loud and terrible that . . . it seemed to make those three huge [roof] timbers tremble," wrote Pantoja. He estimated the longhouse could lodge nine hundred to one thousand individuals. According to Pantoja, Eliza was informed by Wickaninnish that he had not boarded the *San Carlos* with his sons the previous day because his brother had once fallen in the water and drowned while he was descending a ship's ladder.[10]

Eliza felt he had managed to establish a strong relationship with the powerful chief. "In a dance of young men which Guicananich gave me

LEFT: Clayoquot woman shaman; RIGHT: Clayoquot girl. (CURTIS)

in his house, more than six hundred took part," wrote Eliza. He said the Clayoquot had five large settlements, each of which was occupied by about fifteen hundred people. According to Eliza, the largest community was "Guicananich" (Wickaninnish) with 2,500 inhabitants.[11] The Spanish mariners left the celebration at noon that day in their longboat, accompanied by Wickaninnish's sons and his father, and they all ate together on board the *San Carlos*.

The following morning, Wickaninnish's sons and some other Tla-o-qui-aht chiefs came out to the *San Carlos* to announce that a feast celebrating the birth of a son by one of Wickaninnish's several wives was being held, and to invite the mariners to participate. Because Eliza had no trinkets to distribute to a large number of people, he gave the chiefs a few more abalone shells and excused himself from attending. According to Pantoja, "none of the principal officers went ashore [because] the natives . . . never cease asking for something."[12]

At 1:30 that afternoon, Eliza sent Narváez and Carrasco off on the *Santa Saturnina* to explore interior inlets southeast of his anchorage. (The following day, Eliza would dispatch Pantoja to take the armed longboat and investigate waterways that were northwest.) With Narváez in command of the *Santa Saturnina*, the two *pilotos* sailed about fifteen kilometres southeast past what is now Indian Island to the head of a channel which they named Canal y Seno de Poco Fondo ("Canal and Bay of Little Depth"), which is now Grice Bay. Narváez would report finding the surrounding land "flat," compared with the mountains that rise to the north. Furthermore, from the head of this heavily silted bay, it is only a one-kilometre walk to the open ocean.

Turning northward, Narváez proceeded to penetrate a twenty-kilometre-long channel which he named, Canal y Seno de Gervete ("Canal and Bay of Gervete"), in honour of his mother, Úrsula Gervete. (One year later, Captain Dionisio Alcalá-Galiano would rename the channel Tofino Inlet, to recognize Admiral Vicente Tofiño, who had taught Alcalá-Galiano cartography at the naval academy in Cadiz that Narváez had attended.) Along the way he saw four rivers which entered the channel, the largest of which he named Río Caudaloso ("Abundant River")[13] — shown on Carrasco's chart at the location of today's Kennedy River, the outlet of the expansive Kennedy Lake into Clayoquot

Carrasco's chart *Plano del Archipiélago de Clayocuat . . .*, 1791, showing exploration routes taken in "Puerto Narváez" (Clayoquot Sound) by Narváez (continuous line) and Juan Pantoja (broken line) May 10–20, 1791. (WAGNER)

Sound. Nothing indicates that the *pilotos* saw the large lake that fed this important waterway.

After reversing direction to sail out of this long channel, Narváez found an arm that reached northwest. Continuing inland about five kilometres the *pilotos* reached the end of this inlet, which they named Brazo y Seno de San Juan de Dios ("Arm and Bay of San Juan of God"), now Tranquil Inlet. Narváez would inform Eliza that there was a river (today's Tranquil Creek) at the end and that the surrounding land was extremely mountainous.[14]

From Carrasco's chart it is clear that when Narváez sailed southeast in the newly named Canal y Seno de Gervete, a decision was made not to explore the channel (today's Fortune Channel) that heads due north above Indian Island. Although no explanation is given in any of the mariners' journals for this decision, there are at least two plausible reasons: first, heavy fog commonly rolls in at this time of year and it may have obscured the entrance; second, the passage into this channel can be extremely risky for a relatively shallow wooden boat that needed to be kept sound for the extensive explorations that lay ahead.[15]

On May 14, Narváez and Carrasco returned to where the *San Carlos* was anchored, and the two *pilotos* began collaborating on drafting a chart of what they called Puerto Clayucuat, which would incorporate Narváez's findings with those of Pantoja.[16] (A small portion of it would appear later as an inset on Carrasco's chart of the entire voyage.)

Meanwhile, from May 11 to 19, Pantoja — in command of the eight-and-one-half metre longboat and fourteen armed sailors — investigated the sound's network of inlets and channels northwest of Opitsaht. Covering a remarkably extensive area, enduring uncomfortable living conditions, and encountering hostile Aboriginal resistance, Pantoja would return with an impressive amount of information that was new to the Spanish. During the eight-day exploration of this complex archipelago, he identified at least eighteen locations, which would be added to Carrasco's chart.

Rowing northwest in the channel on the east side of Isla de Feran (Vargas Island), Pantoja crossed the sound inside Bocas de Saavedra (Russell and Brabant Channels), and entered a long northwest-trending waterway (Millar Channel) on the east side of the very large Isla de Flórez (Flores Island), the first part of which he named Seno de San Juan Bautista. (Unknowingly, he passed the large Ahousaht settlement at Marktosis, which was located near the entrance to this channel.) In the middle of this widening channel he rounded a small island, which he named Isla de San José (McKay Island). To the east Pantoja saw two openings which he named Bocas de San Bonifacio, because they seemed to lead to another inlet. (If Pantoja had had more time, he would have found the northeast trending waterway now known as Herbert Inlet.)[17]

Staying in the main channel, Pantoja headed the longboat northwestward into what he called Canal de San Antonio (the northern section of Millar Channel). Reaching the head of the canal on what appears to be May 15, the expedition made its way around the north side of Isla de San Pedro (Obstruction Island), entering at Puerto de San Isidro in the east and emerging in the west at Puerto de Rivera. Heading west in Canal de San Antonio (now Shelter Inlet), Pantoja's explorers entered Canal de San Francisco (Sydney Inlet). (Its large entrance had been seen earlier by passing Spanish vessels and named Puerto de San Rafael. Pantoja would later inform Eliza that it had a "well sheltered port inside" where "many vessels could winter.")[18]

Turning south and heading downstream toward the open ocean, Pantoja sighted two Aboriginal settlements, one on each shore, and directly opposite each other. These would have been Ahousaht summer villages of Sumaxqwuis on the west shore and Mañu7is (later the Openit Reserve) on the east shore. The tribe's winter village of Atm7a was located near the head of Canal de San Francisco.[19] As the Spanish boat appeared, warriors from both villages came out in large war canoes and fired arrows at the intruders. When Pantoja's crew waged a "prompt defence" with musket fire, at least one Ahousaht was hit. Deciding it was prudent to catch the onshore wind and retreat upstream, Pantoja ordered one cannon shot to be fired at the shore. The barrage of arrows subsided, and the longboat headed northwest into Canal de San Francisco, followed by several canoes full of Ahousaht warriors.

Nevertheless, Pantoja had probed deep enough into the long canal to realize it led to at least two smaller channels, and he named the location

Bocas de Órdenes. Reversing direction, Pantoja sighted what appeared to be the mouths of two inlets to the northwest, which he named Bocas de Santa Saturnina (today's Holmes Inlet to the west and Young Bay to the east). Seeing another Aboriginal settlement — the aforementioned Ahousaht winter village — at the second location, he decided to camp for the night on a small island opposite the long canal's confluence with Canal de San Antonio. Continuous shouting by the Ahousaht warriors during the foggy night gave the exhausted mariners little sleep. With only a few days left to complete his assignment, Pantoja decided it was time to turn back and investigate a large waterway he had seen north of Opitsaht.[20]

At sunrise on May 16, Pantoja began the return journey around the east side of Isla de Flórez. The morning was uneventful until the long-boat reached the narrows at the southeastern tip of the island, where a canoe full of Ahousaht warriors from the village of Ma-qtusus (Mark-tosis) challenged the intruders. Ignoring the hostile encounter, Pantoja continued southeast before turning east and then northeast through a passage that he named Canal de San Juan Nepomuceno, as it was the feast day of this fourteenth-century saint. (Carrasco subsequently re-named the inlet Canal dt. Norueste ["canal trending northeast"] on his chart.) From there, Pantoja explored two other inlets: Puerto y Seno de Güemes (Bedwell Sound), which ran north a considerable distance, and Puerto de Guiraldes (Warn Bay), which reached northeast a lesser distance. Although Pantoja took the longboat about halfway downstream in the canal (Fortune Channel) that ran southeast from Puerto de Guiraldes, he inexplicably reversed course and returned to Opitsaht via the route he had just taken. If he had continued, the longboat could have easily made it through the narrow mouth of this waterway where it joins the long canal that Narváez had explored earlier. Then the two explorers would have realized they had encircled a large island (later named Meares Island).[21]

On May 19, Pantoja returned to the *San Carlos*, which was still an-chored at Opitsaht. He was eager to report his findings and add them to the chart that Narváez and Carrasco had been drafting for five days. However, the three *pilotos* would have less than a day to collaborate, because Eliza was about to issue new orders. Consequently, Pantoja shared the various field surveys that he had made, showed his fellow *pilotos* how they fit together, and left this material with them to complete the chart which he and Eliza could review later. As New Spain's first comprehensive, detailed map of this extremely important waterway it confirmed that this large archipelago did *not* have an arm that extended eastward beyond the mountains.

One might have expected that Eliza, as commander, would lead the way on the *San Carlos* during the expedition's next phase, which was aimed at exploring what the Spanish had been calling Entrada de Nitinat (today's Barkley Sound) to see if it might have an internal channel that penetrated the mountains. But Narváez had given Eliza two reasons for investigating this second uncharted sound differently. First, Narváez had convinced Eliza that he already was familiar with the area because "he was the only one who had been there in ... 1789" during Narváez's brief, and fairly superficial investigations for Martínez of the same three large bodies of water that were now being explored more thoroughly. Secondly, Narváez had advised that "the packetboat could not enter [the waterway] as there was absolutely no shelter for a large vessel."[22]

Eliza readily agreed, and, on May 21, he instructed Narváez, as captain of the *Santa Saturnina*, to sail southeast about forty kilometres, with Carrasco as his first mate, and explore the Entrada de Nitinat. Eliza also informed Narváez that, as soon as possible, he would be leaving Clayoquot Sound and sailing south to Puerto de Córdova in Juan de Fuca Strait to prepare for the most critical part of the expedition. To this end, he ordered Narváez to join him at Córdova after he had finished charting Entrada de Nitinat.

CHAPTER 6

Charting "Entrada de Nitinat," June 1791

NARVÁEZ AND CARRASCO sailed the *Santa Saturnina* out of Clayoquot Sound on May 21, 1791. They headed southeast on the open ocean for fifty kilometres, and entered the southern channel of Entrada de Nitinat (Barkley Sound) on the same day. The two mariners would be involved in charting this archipelago for the next twenty days.[1] Their primary objective, however, was once again to verify whether or not this large sound had an interior arm that might extend eastward deep into the continent. Together they would produce the earliest detailed information about the geography, hydrography, and ethnology of Vancouver Island's largest sound. This particular part of the overall expedition in which Narváez was engaged is interesting because it reveals more clearly how effectively he collaborated with Carrasco, and the exploratory methods that they developed, which would serve them well when they undertook the biggest challenge that still lay ahead of them.

Unfortunately, Narváez's journal of this expedition does not exist, Carrasco makes one brief comment about it in his *Excerpt of the Voyage . . . , 1791*, and Eliza simply summarizes what Narváez reported to him three weeks later. Consequently, the only other primary documents are three charts, each of which displays the same configuration of geographic features, which corresponds with present-day maps except for the duplication of a four-island chain on the south side of the sound.

The first chart, *Plano del Archipiélago de Carrasco situado . . . reconocido en los años de '89 y '91 por Don José Narbáez*, was probably drafted by Narváez as an initial, rough working chart of his observations in 1789 and 1791. There are no place names, route markers, or Indigenous settlements, and only a few sounding numbers. (This *plano* is not shown herein, but it is cited as a source.)

The second chart, *Plano del Archipiélago de Nitinat ó Carrasco situada . . . descubiertos sus interiores por el Theniente de Navío de la Real Armada Don Francisco de Eliza en este prescrito año de 1791*, is commonly attributed to Narváez, and the title is in his handwriting. This appears to be a more refined working chart. Although there are no place names, and nothing to indicate the exploratory route that was taken, there are small squares marking five major Indigenous settlements, and some sounding numbers. Despite the limited information contained on this chart, it is the one that has consistently been published to illustrate Narváez's discoveries in this large waterway.

The third chart, which is published here for the first time, is much more informative. Although it has also been attributed to Narváez, it appears to have been drafted by Carrasco, because the handwriting is his and the inscription contains another clue. Titled *Plano del Archipiélago de Nictinac ó de Carrasco en la Isla de Quadra y Vancuber en la costa No. de América*, it was apparently a final chart that summarized the expedition's findings. It contains numbers for soundings, a few place names, letters presented alphabetically to indicate the order in which geographic sites were visited, anchors to show what were probably one-to-four night stops, and squares for Aboriginal villages. The fact that the huge island referenced on this chart — La Isla de Quadra y Vancuber

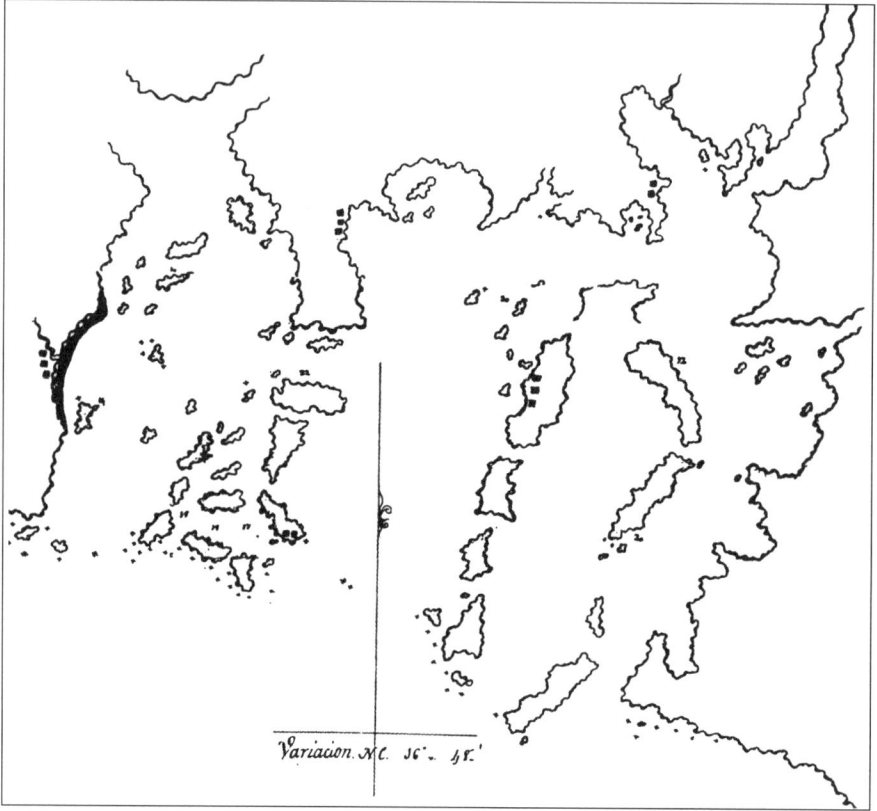

Narváez's chart *Plano del Archipielago de Nitinat ó Carrasco ...* , 1791,
detailing Boca Carrasco, now Barkley Sound. (MUSEO NAVAL, MADRID)

(Vancouver Island) — did not acquire that dual name until 1792, would
suggest that this hydrographic map was drafted by Carrasco sometime
during the year *after* Eliza's larger expedition finished its work.

By combining information shown on this chart with current post-
contact ethnographic and cartographic data,[2] the author was able to
recreate a fairly clear picture of how Narváez surveyed these uncharted
waters and what he found. Because there was nothing that specified the
expedition's timeline, the author allowed for about three days of recon-
noitring from each of the seven anchorages shown on Carrasco's chart.
(Although the author has drawn lines to show the explorers' probable

route, there was not enough space to insert the current place names that are mentioned in the text. Therefore, some readers may want to have a contemporary map of the area for reference.)

A notation on Carrasco's chart due west of Punta de Alegría (Cape Beale) reads "Entrada de *Santa Saturnina* en Mayo de 21," which indicates where and when the explorers entered the sound on their schooner. Carrasco's dotted line shows the route that they initially travelled. Coasting northeast through what appears to be Hammond Pass in the Deer Group chain of islands, they sailed between Folger Island (to port) and King Edward Island (to starboard). Passing Diana Island (to starboard), they swung into their first anchorage (marked with the letter "A") at the south end of Fleming Island.

From this location, Narváez and Carrasco would have been able to look south across Trevor Channel into a long bay behind Cape Beale where the Huu-ay-aht (formerly Ohiaht) people had a large settlement at Kixin (later, Keeshan Reserve).[3] Carrasco's chart indicates that they next sailed northeast in Trevor Channel along the east shore of Fleming Island, and then tacked northwest along the east shore of Tzartus Island, the largest in the Deer Group chain. While making this fifteen-kilometre survey, Carrasco drew the east shore of Trevor Channel with sufficient accuracy to show the large bay where the Huu-ay-aht had another village at Numaqamis (later, Numukamis Reserve). Apparently the explorers did not encounter any Huu-ay-aht, because neither of the two villages, nor another one a short distance inland at Sarita, are marked on the chart. That night, the expedition anchored in twelve fathoms of water in a small bay near the northeast end of Tzartus Island (B).

Looking eastward from there, the two hydrographers sighted a large bay, which appeared to have a river entering into it from the northeast. This was likely today's Ritherdon Creek. Carrasco named the bay Ensenada Alegre ("Cheerful Bay"). Narváez sailed the *Santa Saturnina* northwest across the channel to survey Seddal Island. (Part of the route here is represented by a dotted line across an incomplete land form, which the explorers misconstrued, but did not erase.) Then the expedition investigated Rainy Bay and may have gone ashore, because the

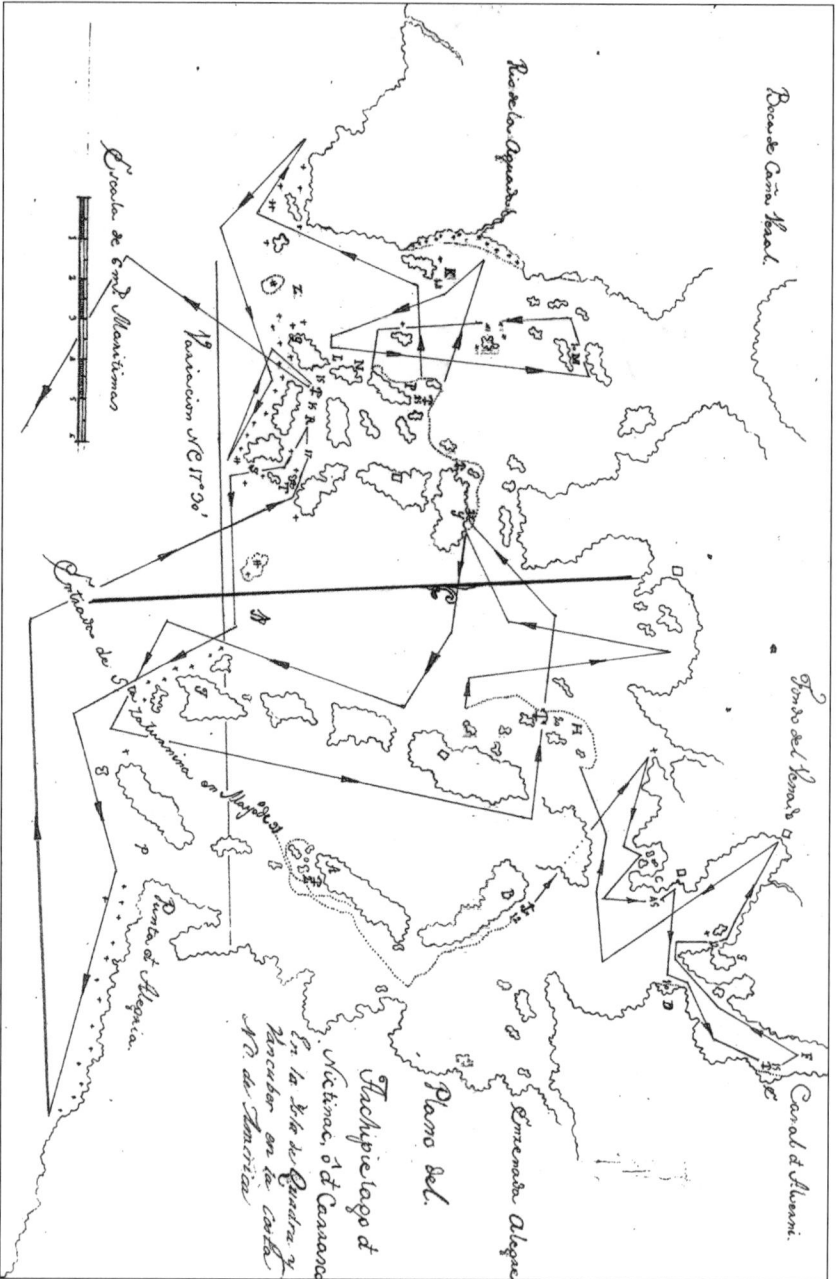

Carrasco's chart *Plano del Archipielago de Nictinac ó de Carrasco en la Isla de Quadra y Vancuber en la costa No. de America*, c. 1792, showing exploration route taken in Boca Carrasco (Barkley Sound) by Narváez from May 21 to June 10, 1791 in command of *Santa Saturnina*. (UBC SPECIAL COLLECTIONS)

letter "C" is marked on the chart there. Rounding Chup Point, the explorers headed northeast in forty-five fathoms of water and passed the large Tseshaht tribal village of Quwasut (later, Cowishil Reserve), which Carrasco marked with a square.

Having sighted two large inlets that needed investigation — one that ran northwest (Uchucklesit Inlet) and another that reached northeast — Narváez decided to probe the latter channel first. Heading due east across the mouths of these inlets, the explorers reached the east shore, where they paused in a bay (D), which was at least ten fathoms deep. From there, the expedition sailed northeast in the lengthy channel, which Carrasco named Canal de Alberni (Port Alberni Inlet). They passed Nahmint Bay on the west shore, and anchored in fifteen fathoms of water on the east shore below what is now Stamp Narrows (E).

After probing the swift-flowing narrows a short distance, Narváez decided to turn back (F) and explore the other inlet they had seen reaching northwest. Taking the *Santa Saturnina* downstream, Narváez rounded the headland at the mouth of today's Uchucklesit Inlet, and then tacked northward to reach a small bay in twelve fathoms of water (g).

Bearing northwest, Narváez took the schooner deep into the interior of what is now Uchucklesit Inlet, where the explorers saw, and probably visited, the large Uchucklesaht tribal settlement at Huchuqtlis (Elhlatesse Reserve). It is also marked with a square on Carrasco's chart. He named the site Fondo del Venado ("locale of the deer"). This relatively remote village might have been the place where Narváez gained the impression, which he reported later to Eliza, that the Indigenous people "were surprised to see the schooner and, according to their explanations, had never seen [such] a vessel inside" the sound.[4]

Reversing direction and sailing southeast in the long inlet, Narváez steered the *Santa Saturnina* into the large archipelago's southernmost channel. As Narváez swung west at the north end of Tzartus Island, it would appear that he may well have become disoriented, possibly by fog. Carrasco sketched the crown of this large isle immediately west of where he first drew the entire island, but he left the remainder of Tzartus undetermined. Although the explorers must have recognized that this was the same island they had observed earlier, at this point they may have realized it was actually at a slightly different location. A dotted line a short distance from this approximate location indicates Narváez headed slowly west and then slightly south around the northwest side of Tzartus Island searching for a safe place to anchor. Fortunately, he found an anchorage in twenty feet of water between Weld Island and Diplock Island (H), which are located a short distance west of Tzartus Island, near the northeast end of Imperial Eagle Channel, the sound's central and largest waterway.

On May 25, the same dotted line indicates that the explorers continued south from this anchorage for a short distance along the west coast of Tzartus Island before they were forced to change course. It may have been too foggy to safely reconnoitre the islands they were trying to locate more accurately, or this may have been one of the points at which they were threatened by Indigenous warriors. (When they subsequently recharted Tzartus Island, Carrasco placed a small square on the lower west side of this large island to mark a Huu-ay-aht village. The Huu-ay-ahts controlled territory along the sound's eastern shore and the off-shore islands on that side of the waterway.)

Whatever caused Narváez to change his route, he reversed direction and sailed north toward the head of the sound until the *Santa Saturnina* reached Vernon Bay where the explorers sighted what would seem to be a Toquaht tribal village at Tlutsp'it-is. It is marked on Carrasco's chart with a square on the east shore of this large bay. Because the expedition's next anchorage was not a great distance away, it would appear that the explorers spent some time visiting this settlement. If that is correct, then this is another place where Narváez might have acquired the impression that the *Santa Saturnina* was the first sailing vessel to penetrate the sound. From Vernon Bay, Narváez sailed southwest about ten kilometres, completely missing the entrance to Effingham Inlet, which reached inland to the north about twelve kilometres. Tacking west, he passed through Seachart Channel and anchored in about twenty-two fathoms of water at a small bay on the west side of Nettle Island (I), the most eastern of the Broken Islands. (The explorers evidently did not see the Toquaht tribal village of Tlhuwa, which was located here and later became Cleho Reserve.)

If the weather cleared on May 26, the two explorers would have been able to reorient themselves and recognize the need to rechart the entire Deer Group of islands that ran southwest from Tzartus Island to the open ocean. To this end, Narváez headed southeast across Imperial Eagle Channel — maintaining a safe distance from the Huu-ay-aht village they had seen earlier — and then sailed south along the west side of two other islands to King Edward Island (J). From this location, Narváez probably sailed north along the east side of the same islands, so the correct alignment could be determined and drawn on the chart. Assuming the weather was relatively clear, the explorers might have realized at this stage of their investigations that the sound consisted of two distinct archipelagos that were separated by at least one large channel. This would explain why Carrasco proceeded to redraw the same series of islands that he had drafted earlier, except that this time they were each slightly larger and they were located somewhat farther west of the sound's eastern shore.[5] Then the *Santa Saturnina* returned to the anchorage at (I).

From this anchorage, a dotted line indicates the route Narváez followed next. Considering the locations of the capital letters Carrasco placed on the chart, it seems that Narváez took parts of this course at two different times. This would have involved considerable navigation in the unfamiliar, complex waterway that could be subject to highly variable weather conditions. Sailing southwest through current-day Peacock Channel, Narváez passed the Brabant Islands (to starboard), swung west around Doud Island, and then headed farther west across the open waters of Loudoun Channel to explore the sound's northwestern shore, which was about twelve kilometres away. The expedition reached Forbes Island (K), where the *Santa Saturnina* probably stood offshore while sailors rowed in to the beach to obtain fresh water from the nearby Toquart River, which Carrasco named Río de la Aguada. His chart shows that a Toquaht settlement, which was either the main winter village of Macoah or the fishing camp of Hiikwis (later, Equis Reserve), was located nearby. The Toquahts controlled the sound's western shore and the centrally located Broken Islands.

From there, Narváez headed southeast and recrossed Loudoun

Channel with the intent of investigating the interior of the Broken Islands. However, when the *Santa Saturnina* reached the passage (L) between Trickett and Turret Islands to the southwest and Willis Island to the northeast, Narváez abruptly changed direction and sailed due north a long distance. It is reasonable to assume that this was one of the two occasions Narváez would report having been attacked by two hundred "warlike and daring" Indigenous warriors, whom he managed to hold "in check by means of some cannon shot."[6] These were undoubtedly Toquaht warriors who had come over to protect this western entrance into the heart of their territory, which was controlled from their large settlement of Humuwa (later, Omoah Reserve) on Effingham Island, located at the head of a bay near the eastern side of the Broken Islands. It is one of the seven Indigenous villages shown on Carrasco's chart.

After a brief encounter, Narváez prudently reversed course and sailed north hoping to explore a large bay that he had seen earlier, which seemed to have two channels that extended farther inland. Carrasco named the western channel Boca de Caña Veral ("bay of veined reeds"). Pressing northward in foul weather, the expedition managed to reach a temporary refuge in twenty fathoms of water between the two Stopper Islands (M) at the mouth of Torquart Bay. Forced to turn back here, Narváez would inform Eliza: "In the interior there were two arms which [I] could not finish exploring on account of contrary winds and continual rain."[7] Heading due south in Loudoun Channel with the wind at his back, Narváez took the *Santa Saturnina* downstream to the northwest point of Willis Island (N) in the Broken Islands, before coming about and beating his way northward close to shore until he could slip in behind Doud Island and anchor the *Santa Saturnina* in fifteen fathoms of water (P). Presumably, the letter "O" was not used on the chart because it would be mistaken for a non-existent island.

Despite the previous violent encounter with the Toquaht, Narváez again sailed southeast in Loudoun Channel to what should have been the mouth of Ucluelet Harbour. However, Carrasco did not show either the geographical features of the area, two more large Toquaht settlements (Ch'uumat'a and T'ukw'aa)[8] inside the entrance on the north shore, or its important Ucluelet settlements, which were controlled by

Chief Wickaninnish. The omission may have been because the harbour was well-known to mariners, or Narváez decided it was prudent to show respect for the Clayoquot chief's authority by staying out of his territory.

Instead of charting Ucluelet Harbour, they turned south and, working from northwest to southeast, took soundings at regular intervals across the entire entrance to Loudoun Channel until they reached Wouwer Island (q) — the southwesternmost isle in the Broken Islands. At this point, Narváez appears to have continued making soundings southeastward across the western front of the Broken Islands, before doubling back to Wouwer Island (q) and entering the archipelago from the southwest through Coaster Channel between Benson Island to the northwest and Wouwer Island to the southeast. Then he anchored the schooner in fifteen fathoms of quiet water south of Cooper Island (R). This was a bold move by Narváez, because he was surrounded by Toquaht villages. The large settlement on Effingham Island was less than five kilometres away, and three other Toquaht summer villages were nearby: Cisha on Benson Island, Maktltsi on Wouwer Island, and Hucacwit on Dicebox Island. He must have been confident that he could either repel any attack or escape quickly from his position, which was not visible from Humuwa. In any case, the expedition was nearly complete, and it must have been running low on provisions.

From this anchorage, it would appear that Narváez exited through the channel (S) between Dicebox Island and Howell Island and took more soundings across the entrances to Imperial Eagle Channel and Hammond Pass, and along the shore beyond Beale Point. At some point along this oceanfront, he reversed course a second time, entered the Broken Islands through the channel (T) between Dicebox Island and Bauke Island, and anchored at the same protected location he had used previously. Although the explorers may have felt secure that night, they would soon discover that they had stretched their luck too far.

Based on Narváez's report that he had been attacked twice by a force of two hundred Indigenous warriors, it was probably the Toquaht who launched a second assault as the expedition prepared to leave on June 10.[9] Using the *Santa Saturnina*'s four three-pound cannons, the handful of soldiers on board kept the warriors at bay as the schooner sailed southeast to exit the bay. Narváez had left himself three escape routes: the two channels (S and T) which were a fair distance southeast, and nearby Coaster Channel, the strong currents of which, if the tide was favourable, could help carry the *Santa Saturnina* swiftly southwestward into the open ocean. If the second attack occurred at this time, presumably Narváez fled through Coaster Channel, firing small cannons at the Toquaht warriors, and headed out to sea.

The expedition led by Narváez with Carrasco's assistance produced Spain's first rough but fairly detailed picture of this large archipelago's geography, its navigable waters, and the people who had lived there for thousands of years. Both Narváez's *Plano del Archipiélago de Nitinat ó Carrasco situada* . . . and Carrasco's *Plano del Nictinac ó Carrasco en la Isla de Quadra y Vancuber* . . . revealed an island-strewn waterway that Narváez said was about twenty-two kilometres from north to south and twenty-seven kilometres from east to west. He showed that at least two inlets reached farther inland from the sound's interior, but did not appear to penetrate the mountain range beyond. Narváez also advised that large vessels should avoid entering what the Spanish began calling Carrasco Sound, because "there was no anchorage except close to the islands," and the waterway "was very much exposed" to inclement weather. Notations on Carrasco's chart indicated the quality of each of the sound's three entrances. The letter Z at the northwestern entrance (Loudoun Channel) cautioned against entering this opening which was filled with reefs. What appears to be the image of a "floating body" placed at the central entrance (Imperial Eagle Channel) marked a deep but hazardous route which contained at least one major underwater reef. The letter "P" at the southwestern entrance (Trevor Channel) pointed to a safer passage.[10]

Although Carrasco had charted seven Indigenous villages, Narváez reported seeing "five large settlements" which he thought "contained more Indians than Nuca [Nootka] and Clayocuat." (Spanish chroniclers would estimate the population of Carrasco Sound at more than 8,500 people compared with 4,000 at Nootka Sound.)[11] Narváez said "the customs of the natives, their clothing, and their method of living are in every respect similar to those at Nuca, except the language, of which a few words vary." (Although Narváez had not demonstrated great linguistic facility, he had attempted rudimentary communication with Indigenous people on many occasions. Evidently, this enabled him to recognize variations in words for certain common, frequently referenced terms.) According to Narváez, "the country promised no fertility for crops as it is all mountainous" and mostly rocky.[12] Unfortunately, the inclusion of the words *Nitinat* and *Nictinac* in the titles of the two hydrographic charts was somewhat misleading, because the archipelago was not located in Ditidaht (formerly Nitinaht) territory, which was farther southeast and included two large settlements: one on the coast at Cloose and one inland at Nitinat.

For a short time while the Spaniards pressed their claim of discovery with the English regarding the archipelago of Barkley Sound, they referred to it as Puerto de Boca ó Carrasco, using the charts produced by Narváez and his first mate as evidence. Of equal importance was the fact that Eliza's most experienced *pilotos* had proved that both of the large archipelagos on Vancouver Island's lower west coast were "closed" (in other words, did not lead to a river route across the continent).

Having finished this challenging assignment, Narváez began the 150-kilometre voyage southeast toward his rendezvous with Eliza at the Puerto de Córdova, which was about 105 kilometres inside the entrance to Juan de Fuca Strait. Depending on weather conditions, the journey could often take three to seven days. Because Narváez and Carrasco would need only one day for the voyage, they both must have been keen to engage finally in the primary, far more extensive exploration which Eliza's expedition had been instructed to undertake.

CHAPTER 7

Reconnaissance of an Unknown Archipelago, May–June 1791

WHILE NARVÁEZ AND CARRASCO were charting Puerto de Boca ó Carrasco (Barkley Sound), Lieutenant Eliza had left Clayoquot Sound on May 21 and sailed the *San Carlos*, with its longboat on board, southeast well beyond the large waterway the two *pilotos* were surveying up the coast. After stormy weather prevented Eliza from entering Juan de Fuca Strait for several days, he finally made his approach on May 26, and, sailing gradually inland, anchored at the entrance to Puerto de Córdova (Esquimalt) on the 29th.[1] Although the sheltered harbour had been thoroughly surveyed by Quimper and Carrasco in 1790, and occupied by Lekwungen peoples for about four thousand years, Eliza made no mention of contacting the Lekwungen-Esquimalt band upon his arrival. This Central Coast Salish group, which spoke a Northern Straits language, were the ancestors of today's Esquimalt and Songhees First Nations.

Two days later, Eliza sent José Verdía — the least experienced of the expedition's four *pilotos* and still apprenticing as a second *piloto* — to explore the Canal de López de Haro, the *entrance* of which Carrasco had been the first European to find and navigate during Quimper's expedition the previous year, but he had not investigated the interior.[2] Therefore, this canal had become another waterway that the Spanish speculated might reach eastward a great distance and penetrate the continent.

Verdía commanded the supply vessel's longboat, which could carry about a dozen sailors and a few armed soldiers. Leaving the anchorage at Puerto de Córdova, Verdía instructed his thirteen sailors to row west along the shore toward Punta de San Gonzalo[3] (Gonzales Point). (On this section of the chart which Carrasco eventually would draw of the entire expedition, one can see that what is now Victoria Harbour was not observed.) Rounding Trail Island, which is shown on the chart but not named, and Punta de San Gonzalo (Gonzales Point), Verdía continued north into the entrance of Canal de López de Haro (Haro Strait), staying close to the west shore. After sailing about fourteen kilometres from Puerto de Córdova, the longboat reached what appears to be today's Gordon Point, located at the southern end of what is now Cordova Bay, where the chart shows four Lekwungen-Songhees villages were located — two at the point and two more near mid-bay.

To Verdía's surprise, his boat was suddenly approached by six large Lekwungen-Songhees war canoes that were paddled out from shore. According to Verdía, each vessel carried sixteen to twenty men armed with "long [bone-tipped harpoon-like] spears," and each warrior carried "his own bow and arrow[s]." Verdía said, "They began to menace our longboat, even overtook it, so it [became] necessary to open fire on them to get away." To further justify his use of arms, which Bodega had strictly prohibited except in desperate situations, Verdía reported that he heard a drum beating and saw many more warriors running along the beach, launching additional canoes, and paddling furiously toward the longboat as they yelled and shot arrows. Although the Spaniards' firepower killed several Lekwungen-Songhees men and sank one canoe, Verdía still feared being overwhelmed by the growing mass of attackers. Consequently, he beat a hasty retreat and headed back to Puerto de Córdova.[4]

Portion of Narváez's chart *Carta esferica que comprehende* . . . , of Gran Canal. Arrows show Verdía's skirmish at Gordon Head, May 31, 1791.

According to Pantoja, Verdía returned "in great haste" at 10:30 that evening to report that he had been forced to turn back by a large number of Indigenous warriors "on whom he had found it necessary to fire to avoid the loss of his longboat and men."[5] Although Eliza must have questioned the *piloto* thoroughly, his journal does not provide much insight into how he evaluated the incident which, if Verdía's report was accurate, almost cost the loss of an extremely useful boat, a *piloto*, a few soldiers, and several sailors. Was Eliza's decision to dispatch the unaccompanied probe naïve, careless, and premature? Did Verdía misread the situation, fail to follow established procedures, or overreact? What did Eliza think motivated the Lekwungen-Songhees to launch their show of force?

The imaginative, enthusiastic local historian John Crosse, who was fascinated by the Narváez expedition for many years, used to call this encounter "The Battle of Gordon Head," as if it were equivalent to a major naval encounter. Realistically, the brief skirmish was the predictable result of a first contact between strangers who had markedly different agendas: on one hand, a small number of uninformed, inadequately prepared, armed intruders rowing a single small boat into territory they knew almost nothing about; on the other, a large settlement of Indigenous people who exercised their ancient responsibility to protect and defend their traditional territory. In describing the "battle," Crosse correctly dubbed the episode a "foray" (in other words, a raid), but he neglected to point out that it was the Spanish intrusion that provoked a violent defensive reaction by the Lekwungen-Songhees. This incident, in addition to what Narváez would soon report about his experiences in "Entrada de Nitinat" (Barkley Sound), would convince Eliza that Aboriginal people in the area were hostile, violent, and dangerous, but no match for Spanish weaponry. This direct encounter with European firepower undoubtedly spurred the Lekwungen-Songhees to begin thinking about trading pelts for guns, instead of settling for beads, trinkets, and brass sheets.

Whatever else Eliza learned from the incident, he prudently "decided to wait for [Narváez and] the schooner [to arrive] before he went on with his examination [of the canal]."[6] This aborted probe would be the only active exploration that Eliza supervised directly between May 31 and July 26 — the most critical period of the entire three-month-long voyage — yet he would garner most of the credit, not Narváez and the other *pilotos* who would actually perform the explorations. As another informed historian has noted, Eliza "was not the most resolute of the Spanish mariners [to be stationed] on the Northwest Coast."[7] Robin

Inglis, a widely recognized expert on the Spanish presence on the Northwest Coast, evaluated the situation even more thoroughly. "Although [Eliza] was a less than energetic or curious explorer," said Inglis, "the activities of his subordinates — Narváez, Pantoja, Carrasco, and Verdía — ensured that the expedition was a success."[8]

After sailing the *Santa Saturnina* southeast from "Entrada de Nitinat" (Barkley Sound), Narváez rendezvoused with Eliza at Puerto de Córdova on June 11. Receiving Narváez's report of his exploration (of which we only have Eliza's brief summary), the commander seemed to be particularly impressed by Narváez's observation that some of the Indigenous people in the extensive archipelago "were surprised to see the schooner and, according to their explanations, had never seen a vessel inside."[9] Based on the number of fur traders who had worked the large sound for several years, Eliza's interpretation seems to be an exaggeration, possibly intended to impress his superiors. It is also contradicted by the fact that Narváez had also sailed into some part of the sound in 1789.

With all four of his *pilotos* now on hand at Puerto de Córdova, Eliza launched the first part of the expedition's primary objective — exploration of any and all waterways to the north of Juan de Fuca Strait's interior that might lead to a transcontinental river route. From the onset, however, Eliza seemed to create some ambiguity about lines of authority and accountability among his four *pilotos*. When he dispatched the mariners on June 14, it was not altogether clear which *piloto* was actually appointed commander of the investigation. "Having provided the *schooner* with water, wood and food, I issued an order [to Narváez, who was still in command of the *Santa Saturnina*] to explore the Canal de López de Haro," wrote Eliza. "And that the task might be completed as quickly as possible, I dispatched the armed longboat in *her* company under the command of second *piloto* Don Juan Pantoja"[10] (emphasis added). At the same time, Eliza placed Pantoja in command of the entire expedition, which he anticipated would be a short, concentrated reconnaissance of whatever lay beyond the entrance of the previously unexplored canal now known as Haro Strait. Although Eliza had not bothered to observe the mouth of this nearby waterway himself, he made two assumptions: first, compared with Juan de Fuca Strait, a relatively narrow canal had to be investigated; second, if he sent two vessels to survey opposite sides of the channel, the task should take only four days. "Everything, however, came out exactly contrary," wrote Pantoja after the first day of exploring. The assignment would actually take ten days.[11]

To avoid a repetition of Verdía's recent misadventure, Eliza made sure that the longboat was "fully armed and the schooner was supplied with twenty-five shots for the six cannon and swivel guns she carried," wrote Pantoja. Noting that Eliza had ordered him to "punish the Indians in case they came back or tried to attack us [again]," Pantoja said Eliza "manned [the vessels] with thirty sailors and eight able-bodied and spirited soldiers of the Volunteers of Catalonia."[12]

The Volunteers of Catalonia

After years of routine garrison duty in Guadalajara and San Blas, the First Company of Volunteers of Catalonia had been assigned to duty on the Pacific Northwest Coast in response to the Nootka Crisis ignited by Martínez. Arriving at Nootka Sound in April 1790, they rebuilt the abandoned Spanish fort and became the first regular European military unit posted in present-day British Columbia. Their mission was to secure Spain's claims to the vast region — potentially an essential role on the Eliza expedition, but one that had to be employed with restraint.

Leaving Eliza to watch after the *San Carlos*, protected by some soldiers, all four *pilotos* left Puerto de Córdova on their two vessels on June 14 at nine o'clock in the morning. In the longboat, Pantoja and Verdía took the same route west in Juan de Fuca Strait that the latter had taken fifteen days earlier. Farther offshore, Narváez sailed the *Santa Saturnina* in the same direction, with Carrasco pointing the way toward the channel he had discovered the previous year. One-and-a-half hours later, Pantoja led both vessels north into the Canal de López de Haro. Pantoja noted that his vessel battled "a strong current, which made such large whirlpools that we seemed to be sailing along a very copious river."[13]

Santa Saturnina, San Carlos, and longboat off Puerto Cordova (Esquimalt Harbour), June 14, 1791.
(WATERCOLOUR BY GORDON MILLER)

Nevertheless, the explorers managed to pass the headland and bay where Verdía had been attacked. They not only met no resistance from the Lekwungen-Songhees, they also saw no Indigenous people at all there. The tribe probably withdrew into the forest or may have moved out temporarily to avoid an anticipated violent retaliation for their attempt to halt or at least discourage the previous intrusion by uninvited foreigners.

By eleven o'clock in the morning, the mariners were well into Haro Strait and trying to stay on opposite sides of the canal. Following present-day Cordova Channel, they had begun passing a series of reefs and small islands (D'Arcy, James, and Sidney Islands) that appeared to form a long chain, which Carrasco would name Islas de San Antonio[14] on his comprehensive chart (see Chapter 9). The passage is not named on the charts of Narváez and Pantoja.

About noon, they crossed today's Sidney Channel, where the wind became so strong from the southwest that Pantoja could not keep up with the *Santa Saturnina*, which was running the "baseline" between two "stations" from which bearings were taken for triangulating various survey points. Coordinated surveying became impossible. Consequently, Pantoja furled the longboat's sails, took down its two masts, and had his men row through seas that were so choppy he was "taking plenty of water over the gunwale." When Narváez saw that the longboat was unable to make headway, he lay to and waited for Pantoja to catch up. More than an hour later, the longboat pulled alongside the schooner, and Pantoja asked Narváez to unfurl his sails and tow the smaller vessel for the rest of the day.[15]

Riding in tow behind the *Santa Saturnina* for the next six hours must have been a relief to Pantoja, who could now devote all of his attention to survey work as the two vessels moved north through today's Moresby Pass, passed between present-day Portland Island to port and Moresby Island to starboard, and headed toward the south end of Prevost Island. (Today, BC Ferries vessels running from Swartz Bay to Tsawwassen trace this same route north past the eastern tip of Salt Spring Island and then off the east shore of Prevost Island as the ships head toward Active Pass.)[16]

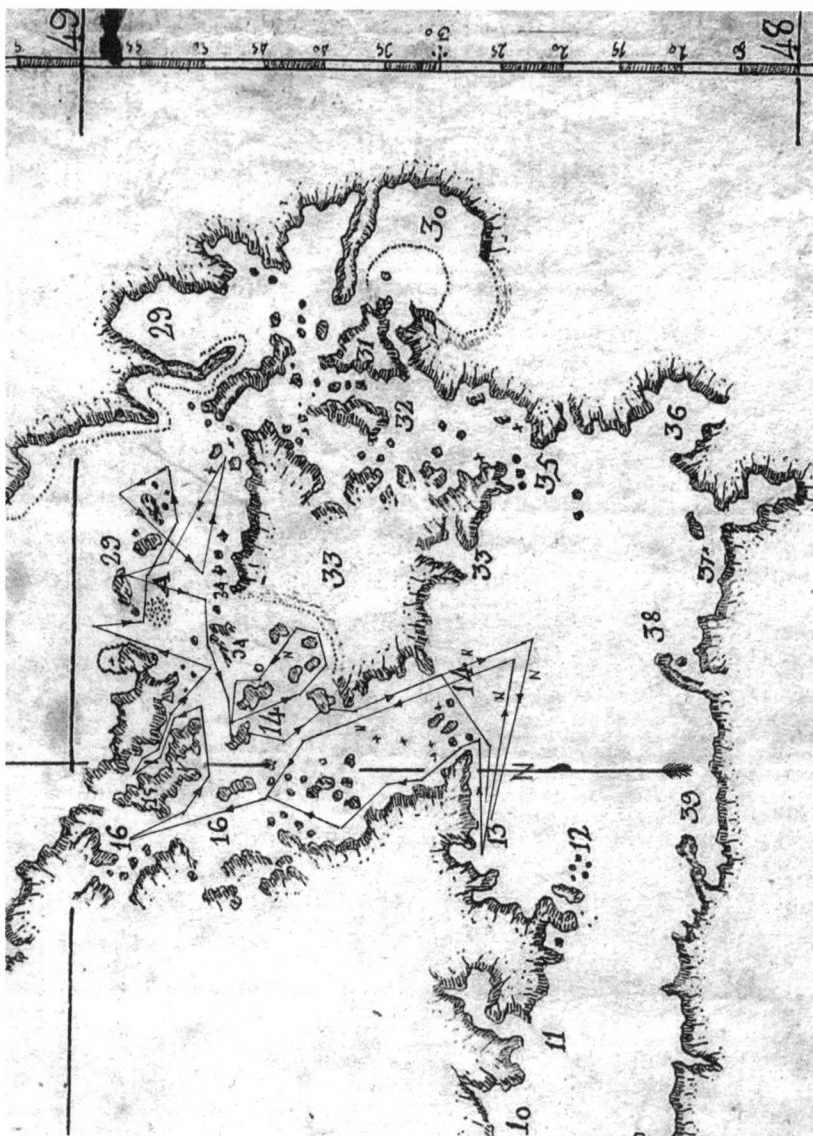

Author's adaptation of Narváez's chart *Carta esferica* . . . , to show approximate route taken by Narváez et al. during first European reconnaissance of Southern Gulf Islands, June 14–24, 1791. (N) indicates Narváez's route when two vessels sailed separately. Location numbers in order of encounter: (13) Puerto de Cordoba; (14) Boca Canal de Lopez; (15) Islas de Sallas [Zayas]; (16) Bocas de Bazan; (A) powerful whirlpool; (29) Seno de Gaston; (33) Archipielagos de San Juan y Bocas de Orcasitas; (34) Punta Sa Gil e Isla de Lemus; (37) Puerto de Quadra. Complete chart on page 171.

"During the afternoon, we [passed] on the west side various small inlets and arms, apparently formed by numerous islands, which [gave] promise of some extension," wrote Pantoja. "We did not follow these [because we realized] that to do so would require many days and we had very few allotted to us."[17] Subsequently, three of the four *pilotos* engaged in the reconnaissance — Carrasco, Narváez, and Pantoja — would produce charts of this part of the overall expedition, and they all named these openings, which appeared to be channels reaching northwest, Bocas de Bazán, after the Spanish minister of marine, Antonio Valdés y Bazán. (The southernmost of these *bocas* would have taken the explorers past the location of today's BC Ferries terminal at Swartz Bay.) During this leg of the survey, the *pilotos* also sighted an arm that reached eastward (today's Swanson Channel), which was much wider and even more promising than the ones they had seen to the west.

At eight o'clock in the evening, Pantoja realized that, with the sun setting and almost no wind, both vessels could not "reach a front of land we had marked where it seemed to us that this arm . . . ended." Consequently, he and his crew "took to the [longboat's] oars in quest of it." The "front of land" must have been the westernmost point of today's Mayne Island which — approached from the southwest — can seem to be connected in the northwest to what is now Galiano Island, until the view into Active Pass opens up. Pantoja did not see this opening because, once he "discovered that there were two entrances" to the large channel (today's Trincomali Channel) he had entered — "one towards the first quarter and the other towards the third" — he returned in the dark at 10:30 to the *Santa Saturnina* where "she was anchored [most likely in Prevost Island's Ellen Bay] close to land in thirty-seven metres of water, mud bottom."[18]

By the time Pantoja reached this anchorage, he had recognized that the assignment entailed much more than surveying a single canal. "We found ourselves in an indescribable archipelago of islands, keys, rocks, and big and little inlets," he wrote. "Therefore, we decided not to separate, not only because we might not find each other [on certain] days but because the longboat, which was very small, was not appropriate for such a task in bodies of water so wide, and [it lacked] sufficient room for the supplies necessary for such an undertaking. We therefore decided that the longboat should be towed by the schooner, aiding her with her sails when there was wind, and passing in front of the schooner to tow her when it was calm. This having been arranged, I went on board the schooner to help my companions in putting down the many marks, bearings, and elevations which had to be made." After putting in a fifteen- or sixteen-hour day, the explorers passed their first night near Prevost Island, without, as Pantoja put it, "having seen during the whole day [no] more than one Indian."[19]

Perspective drawing of *Santa Saturnina*. (G. MILLER)

During a day of surveying, the *pilotos* would work as a team. While one or more of them took charge of sailing a vessel, the other two would take bearings to establish prominent points and draw numerous field sketches. Later, these field surveys would be put together, realigned, and redrawn on a *carta pequeña* (small chart). Only two *cartas pequeñas* of the 1791 expedition have survived — one by Narváez and the other by Pantoja. The latter, however, was copied from the former. Consequently, for this ten-day reconnaissance, Narváez's *Carta esférica que comprehende . . .* is the most reliable and informative (See Chapter 9 for Narváez's comprehensive chart). Therefore, the author has adapted a portion of it to show the approximate routes that the two vessels took on this part of the overall expedition.

"The fifteenth dawned clear with a light wind from the east," wrote Pantoja. "At three in the morning we weighed anchor and went on towards the [east] with the longboat towing" Narváez's schooner, which had its eight long oars out. Their first objective was to sail southeast to investigate the large arm they had sighted the previous afternoon (today's Swanson Channel), which ran eastward between present-day North Pender Island and Moresby Island. Three hours later, after sighting "large islands," a strong wind from the east forced Narváez to anchor the *Santa Saturnina* "close to a point (today's Wallace Point on North Pender Island) where there seemed to be a small entrance."[20]

From there, Pantoja took the longboat inside the entrance and found a "small port" that was 2.4 kilometres long and 1.6 kilometres wide, sheltered "from all winds," between four and twenty-four metres deep with a sandy bottom. He named it Punta [Puerto] San Antonio (today's Bedwell Harbour, at the northern head of which is a narrow channel that separates the two Pender Islands).[21] At the time, all four *pilotos* assumed they had anchored along the southern shore of a single large island, which Pantoja recorded as Isla de Zayas, whereas Narváez used Isla de Sallas, which is an alternative spelling. The name recognized Juan Martínez de Zayas, who had accompanied Narváez to San Blas in 1787, as the first two *pilotos* on New Spain's west coast. Zayas had also served with Narváez on the 1788 expedition to the Gulf of Alaska and the Aleutian Islands. Inexplicably, Carrasco subsequently changed the name to Isla San Eusebio on his comprehensive chart, probably in recognition of Saint Eusebius, a fourth-century martyred bishop.

Shortly after nine that morning, the wind died down and Pantoja headed the longboat out to join the *Santa Saturnina*. About ten o'clock, Narváez ordered the crew to weigh anchor on the schooner, and the expedition headed eastward again with the longboat's sailors plying their oars to tow the larger vessel, which also had its eight sweeps out. (This laborious warping method, commonly employed by eighteenth-century mariners, would be used on many different occasions during the reconnaissance. On the schooner, the long oars were deployed through four oar ports in the bulwark or between up to eight pairs of removable thole pins on the rail cap, and they were pulled by pairs of sailors standing on deck who used the ports or thole pins as fulcrums.) The vessels continued in this way until noon, when they "crossed the mouth of a deep bay." The explorers would soon discover this was the southern entrance into the large channel between the Pender Islands and Saturna Island that opens into today's Plumper Sound. It remained unnamed on all three of the *pilotos'* charts.[22]

"We anchored [here] in 33 metres of water, fine pebbles, and I at once went with the longboat to explore [the channel]," wrote Pantoja. "It is 11 kilometres long from northwest to southeast and at the [northern] end are two entrances, one in the first and the other in the fourth quarter — the one in the fourth being the one which I had explored the previous afternoon." He estimated it was about four kilometres wide. Based on his cursory survey of this large waterway, it is understandable that Pantoja did not notice that a narrow passage (now called Robson Channel) in what he called the "entrance" in the "first quarter" actually led past the south side of Mayne Island into a huge inland sea. Consequently, at this stage of the 1791 expedition, it remained undiscovered.[23]

About three o'clock that afternoon, Narváez weighed anchor on the *Santa Saturnina* in a dead calm, which required the longboat to return to towing the schooner southeastward. According to Pantoja there was a large island to port and an extensive channel (today's Boundary Pass) to starboard, the currents of which were "much more rapid and violent than those of [the previous day]." He noted that the mariners saw "many gulls, seals, tunny [probably large Chinook salmon], and whales of great size."[24] The pass was a major route for both resident humpback whales and orcas that travelled throughout the sound.

The *pilotos* aimed for "a salient point which bore in the first quarter"

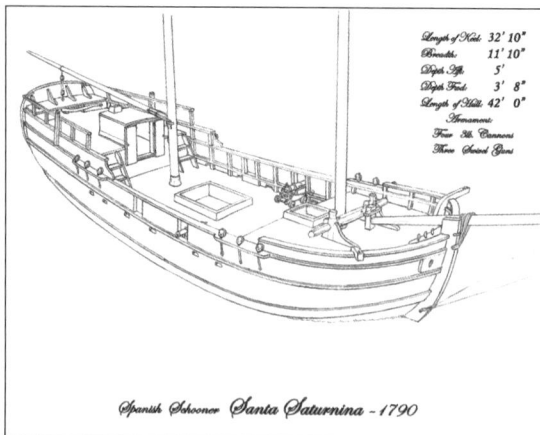

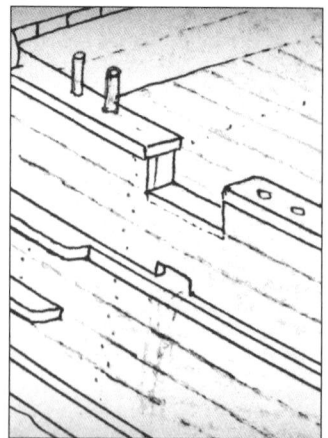

LEFT: *Santa Saturnina*'s deck; RIGHT: Both the cannon notches in the bulwark and the removable thole pins on the top rail accommodated oars. (S. MAYO)

approximately fifteen kilometres away. At seven in the evening, the exhausted crews rowed both vessels a short distance beyond this point. "No sooner had we passed it than we saw in the fourth quarter a grand and extended canal," wrote Pantoja. "As the horizon was clear, it was possible to see a long distance, and in the middle of it could be made out, at the farthest point of vision, a small hill like a sugar loaf. It may be noted that the end of land, or the points which form this canal, are very high mountains covered with snow. This [canal we] named 'El Gran Canal de Nuestra Señora del Rosario la Marinera' [The Grand Canal of Our Lady of Rosary the Seafarer] in honour of our patroness, as it was the most important place we had discovered up to the present."[25] Pantoja, Narváez, Carrasco, and Verdía believed they had found the long-sought inland sea that would lead to a passage eastward across the continent to either Hudson Bay or the Mississippi River. As seasoned mariners from a strong Catholic background, paying tribute to the patron saint of Spanish seafarers for their discovery was a natural practice. It also added a spiritually rich (although quite long) dimension to the name of this particular body of water, a designation that would soon be erased by a seafarer from another culture. The same symbolic figure who was so important throughout Latin America was also the patroness of both the *San Carlos* and the small chapel far to the south in San Blas where this expedition originated.

One can sense the feelings of amazement, excitement, and relief the Spanish officers and crew must have experienced after two long days of wending their way, mostly by rowing hour-after-hour, through a previously unexplored archipelago — littered with islands, islets, reefs, shoals, straits, channels, canals, passages, tidal currents, rapids, and whirlpools — to suddenly emerge into this grand expanse of open water. These forty-two men — four *pilotos*, thirty sailors, and eight soldiers — thereby became, on June 15, 1791, the first Europeans to cast their eyes across this part of what we now call the Salish Sea. What were the actual landmarks that they sighted?

Gazing northwest as far as they could see, the mariners said they spotted a "small hill" in the middle of the "canal" that looked like a "sugar loaf." If the explorers were far enough out in the gulf to be at least five and a half kilometres northeast of today's Tumbo Island, they could have established a direct line of sight with a telescope from the *Santa Saturnina*'s quarterdeck, or even by climbing up to the crosstrees to see the island Narváez would later name Islas de San Feliz (today's Texada Island).[26] It is about 110 kilometres away in that direction. It could not have been its nearby, considerably smaller, companion, which Carrasco later named Isla de Lasquety (today's Lasqueti Island), because this island sits too low on the horizon to be seen at water level from the explorers' position. Furthermore, the latter is not shaped like a sugar-loaf, whereas a string of four moderately high mountains on the former island definitely creates a conical shape when it is viewed from the southeast. Just as the distinguishing characteristic of Sugarloaf Moun-tain, in Rio de Janeiro, Brazil, is its shape — not its colour — that is what caught the mariners' eyes in this instance.

Looking eastward across the water as the evening sun fell behind them, the mariners were struck by the wall of "high mountains," many of which were "covered with snow." They stretched from north to south across the horizon. At the centre of this scene was the snow-capped peak that became known as Mount Baker, which can be spectacular during a mid-June sunset. To the south of this volcanic mountain the North Cascade mountain range extended into the darkening distance.

In recognition of the vital role that their schooner *Santa Saturnina* had played during this reconnaissance and others recently carried out by Narváez, they named the "salient point" that they had struggled so hard to reach, Punta y Bajo de Santa Saturnina. (Although this designa-tion would not appear on Carrasco's working chart, he did insert it on his final map which he drafted later.)[27] Eventually, the entire island would derive its name from a contraction of the headland's designation (see Chapter 9 regarding "The Naming of Saturna").

After savouring their achievement, Pantoja said the *pilotos* made "a wholly satisfactory observation for variation" in time at sunset, which occurred a few minutes after eight o'clock. Then both vessels caught a freshening wind from the northwest and sailed southeastward toward a small island, which Carrasco would later designate as Isla de Patos. (Pantoja's chart, most of which was copied later from those of Narváez

Santa Saturnina and longboat entering the Gran Canal off Saturna Island with Mount Baker in background, June 15, 1791.
(WATERCOLOUR BY G. MILLER)

and Carrasco, listed a string of three islands — Islas de Patos, Sucia, and Mal Abrigo — without indicating where they were located. Narváez simply identified these three islands and a large bay that he would survey three weeks later as Seno de Gaston ("Bay of Gaston"). Nevertheless, Narváez's *Carta esférica* has an unnamed island where Patos should be located in the eastern entrance to Boundary Pass, and his chart is the only one that shows two other interesting features: first, a large letter "A" near the place where the two vessels anchored at about nine o'clock on this memorable night (Carrasco placed a tiny anchor here);[28] second, a dense circle of tiny dots which marked a powerful whirlpool that Pantoja described as "a small vortex." The A is related to the note below the lower right-hand corner of the legend on Narváez's comprehensive chart, which reads: A. Boltise ó manestron ("Get around or get lassooed") — a cryptic warning to mariners of the need to avoid the nearby giant whirlpool that is caused by the huge volume of water which surges through this narrow channel. (To this day it remains a well-known hazard for boaters.)

On June 16, Narváez weighed anchor on the *Santa Saturnina*. Both vessels still had to be rowed, however, because there was no wind. According to Pantoja, the explorers went "in quest of the channel [to] the east, which from the first day we had intended to follow." This would seem to refer to one of the Eliza expedition's primary objectives, which was established before it left Nootka Sound: to investigate the channel at the east end of Juan de Fuca — the entrance to which was discovered by Carrasco the previous year during Quimper's exploration. Although Quimper had concluded it was only a closed inlet into the mainland, Carrasco had wanted to determine if it continued northwest into a larger waterway, as some Indigenous people had intimated. Now that the *pilotos* realized they were actually in that very inland sea, they undoubtedly thought they might be able to find the northern entrance to what Carrasco would later name Canal de Fidalgo (today's Rosario Strait).

According to Pantoja, the *Santa Saturnina* and the longboat moved "among different islands" during the next "two days," sometimes "under oars" and "at other times under sail," until the *pilotos* found themselves "in another great archipelago of [large] and small islands."[29] In the absence of Narváez's journal, and with Pantoja's sparse comments made about this part of their reconnaissance, it is difficult to determine exactly where they were anchored or which islands they had seen. Nevertheless, it is highly probable that the two vessels continued to maintain close contact for two reasons: first, the *pilotos* had established regular daily sailing procedures that were collaborative, cooperative, and interdependent; second, as the expedition's deadline approached, it would have become increasingly important to have the *Santa Saturnina*'s limited food supplies close at hand. Based on the charts of Narváez and Pantoja, on June 16 and 17 the explorers probably surveyed in order (from northwest to southeast): Isla Sucia ("dirty island"), Isla Mal Abrigo ("bad shelter island," which is now Matia Island), and then what Carrasco would indicate as Islas de Aguayo (one more part of the viceroy's name), which are today's Barnes and Clark Islands. The anchor inserted here later by Carrasco on his chart seems to confirm this route.

Although this chain of islands is only about twenty kilometres long, it runs along the northeast side of the second largest island in the "great archipelago" that the *pilotos* were just beginning to explore. As they moved southeast, they charted the large island's northeastern shore in detail for another ten kilometres. This probably brought them as far as the mouth of a channel that they hoped to find in this area. However, they would have observed two geographical features: a long front of land (today's Lummi Island, which was later named Isla de Pacheco on Carrasco's chart) blocked their way to the east, and there was a dense archipelago inside the channel to the southeast. "This we could not explore and see to what point the arms of the sea extended [inland] on account of a heavy rainstorm, which struck us from the southeast," wrote Pantoja.[30] There is no documentary evidence that indicates the reconnaissance ventured any farther

Lummi woman. (CURTIS)

east or southeast. (The explorers had actually reached the northern entrance of the waterway that they would enter two weeks later from the southwest, discover it connected Juan de Fuca Strait to the Gran Canal, and name it Rosario Strait.)

Seeking a protected anchorage, Narváez and Pantoja probably retraced their course back to Isla Sucia, which Carrasco might have named for the "dirty" weather they had to endure for two more days. Today, Sucia State Park is one of the world's most popular destinations for boaters. It is composed of an extremely small archipelago of ten islands including Sucia, Little Sucia, Ewing, Justice, Harnden, the North and South Finger Islands, and the Cluster Islands. Because Pantoja cites "a heavy rainstorm" but makes no mention of strong winds at this time, Sucia might well have offered a logical place where the *Santa Saturnina* could anchor, as long as it avoided hazardous reefs and shoals. If the wind was blowing from the southwest, the large Echo Bay on the east side, which has an average depth of about eight metres, would have been a convenient place to wait out the seemingly endless rain. It is doubtful that the schooner found shelter in the much smaller Shallow Bay on the west side. Although it averages about four metres in depth, it has an extremely narrow entrance.

Alternatively, the two vessels might not have sailed northwest to seek an anchorage. Instead, they could have remained in the southeastern part of the inland sea and taken refuge in the cove toward the northeast end of Lummi Island near today's Village Point. This route, however, probably would have brought them in contact with Indigenous people, and Pantoja made no mention of such an encounter.

"The abundant rain lasted until June 20," wrote Pantoja. "Seeing that two days more than [the four allotted for the reconnaissance] by the commander had elapsed and that we had little food, I resolved to turn back" [the next day] to "comply with my order" and "to give an account of the great amount of work that had to be done with what had been discovered."[31] It is worth noting that Pantoja used the first person singular here, when most of his account references the first person plural "we," when it came to making decisions. Does this grammatical change indicate that Pantoja had departed from the *Santa Saturnina* at this, or some earlier, point? If the two vessels separated, why did it happen? Had the three senior *pilotos* disagreed about survey priorities? Certainly Carrasco would have advocated pressing on to search for the all-important channel to the sea that he had reason to believe existed somewhere at the southeast end of the Gran Canal. Narváez, on the other hand, probably would have stressed the need to keep the vessels together. Given the absence of Narváez's journal and Carrasco's sparse comments, these questions remain intriguing, but unanswerable. Based on the mariners' charts, however, it does not appear that a separation occurred here.

Pantoja did not describe the route that the two vessels followed in returning to Puerto de Córdova. Nevertheless, his chart and that of Narváez indicate that, upon leaving the Gran Canal (probably from Isla Sucia) on June 21, they headed southwest about eight kilometres toward a passage (today's President Channel) that ran between the northwestern point of what they had been assuming was a large island and a small offshore island. Both *pilotos* named the two places Punta de San Gil and Islas de Lemus (the former for what is now Doughty Point and the latter for today's Waldron Island). In fact, one man's full name — Francisco Gil y Lemos, then Viceroy of Peru, was split to cover the two geographical features.[32] As Narváez and Pantoja passed around the outside of Islas de Lemus through the swift-moving currents of Boundary Pass, they came to two realizations: they were passing a large island to port (today's Orcas Island), and it appeared to be part of another archipelago of islands, mouths, channels, and bays. Consequently, they named it Archipiélagos de San Juan y Bocas de Orcasitas ("archipelago of San Juan and mouths of Horcasitas"— the last word, with the initial letter "H" being an English variant of one of the eight elements in Viceroy Revillagigedo's long name, and the *Santa Saturnina*'s nickname).

The two vessels may have continued southwest another twenty kilometres to present-day Stuart Island, which is located at the confluence of Boundary Pass and Haro Strait. Depending on the wind's direction, they could have found a protected anchorage for the night on either the northeast or southwest side of this sizeable island.

From this point on, Narváez's chart shows more detail than Pantoja's, which would suggest that the two vessels did not work together on the 22nd and 23rd of June. On these two days, Narváez and Carrasco may have taken some of the schooner's crew in the longboat to survey several other nearby islands. This would have given the longboat's crew time to rest and recover their strength aboard the schooner, and it would have allowed Pantoja to prepare his report for Eliza.

On the 22nd, Narváez and Carrasco may have made a twenty-to-thirty-kilometre circular survey of the other islands in the chain which ran southeast from Stuart Island toward the San Juan Archipelago. During this reconnaissance, Narváez also may have sighted present-day Henry Island and probed the excellent harbour on its northeast side.

The entire expedition might have moved to the protected anchorage at today's Roche Harbour on the 23rd, where Pantoja could have finished his paperwork and prepared to depart the next morning. (Carrasco inserted a tiny anchor near this location.) This would have given Narváez and Carrasco an opportunity to make a cursory reconnaissance of the big island's northern shorefront. Narváez's chart makes it clear that he did not try to penetrate the northwest side of the archipelago, because it is shown as a curved dotted line southeast of five smaller islands that seem to have been fairly accurately surveyed. If the *pilotos* had gone beyond these islands and entered the largest channel, they would have made two more discoveries: the waterway (today's San Juan Channel) divided the archipelago into two or more segments, and it led directly southeast to Juan de Fuca Strait.

On June 24, Narváez finished his chart, assisted by Carrasco, and prepared his report of the expedition's findings. Meanwhile, Pantoja guided his tired, hungry longboat crew, some of whom may have been sick, back towards Puerto de Córdova. Rowing about thirty kilometres south in Haro Strait against the wind, the exhausted crew reached Juan de Fuca Strait, rounded Punta de Gonzalo, and rowed to a point where they could see the *San Carlos* about eleven kilometres away. They dropped their anchor in relief about four o'clock in the afternoon. (Carrasco would insert a tiny anchor here on his chart.) Pantoja said his crew needed a rest "from their fatigue caused by the great amount of rowing done during the day." Furthermore, the wind was blowing so hard against them that they could not reach the packetboat under sail.[33]

At seven o'clock in the evening, a boat from the *San Carlos* carrying a fresh crew came alongside Pantoja's longboat to deliver an order from Lieutenant Eliza. It instructed the *piloto* to board the visiting boat, come immediately to the packetboat, and report what had been found. Pantoja boarded the *San Carlos* ninety minutes later. The deliberations that occurred that night and the following four days between Eliza and his three most experienced *pilotos* were summarized by Eliza and Pantoja in their separate journals.

After informing Eliza that he had not encountered any "Indians" during his ten-day reconnaissance of what are now the Southern Gulf Islands, Pantoja produced his working chart. According to Eliza, he took some time to study Pantoja's document and then decided on his own about how to proceed — without waiting to consult with all three of his most experienced *pilotos* the following day.

"Having informed myself [from Pantoja's report] about what they had done and of the great amount still to be explored and discovered in detail in the great Canal de Nuestra Señora del Rosario, I resolved that, as soon as they had [all] rested a few days, the schooner and the longboat should depart a second time for the purpose of carrying forward the discoveries as far as possible, up to consuming all the favourable summer season left to us," wrote Eliza. "That this should be carried out with the greatest activity, with more comfort and a quick means of support to the crews, I resolved to also enter with the packetboat into the farthest possible interior point . . . and to explore to my own satisfaction whatever could be reached with the packetboat."[34]

In short, after studying Pantoja's report, and before he had heard from Narváez and Carrasco, Eliza had made up his mind to have *pilotos* use the *Santa Saturnina* and its longboat to explore the Gran Canal, and to take the *San Carlos* himself into the unexplored waterway as far as possible to support the expedition. (Pantoja's journal echoed most of this entry almost word for word.)

According to Pantoja, Narváez returned June 25 on the *Santa Saturnina*, anchored near the *San Carlos*, and came on board the packet-boat with Carrasco to meet with Eliza and Pantoja. (Verdía was not present.) Pantoja's description of the meeting's purpose highlights a curious detail about the course Eliza assumed the expedition would take next. "The commander called us to a meeting to consider entering the Canal de López de Aro [today's Haro Strait]," wrote Pantoja.[35] Inexplicably, this was the channel the *pilotos* had just left, not the passage that Narváez and Carrasco had been planning to investigate next, which — for at least a year — Commander Bodega had considered the most likely entrance into what might be the Northwest Passage. By assuming that the expedition would return to the Gran Canal through Haro Strait, Eliza demonstrated that he had forgotten Bodega's explicit orders to find an entrance that was thought to be located at the extreme *interior* of the Strait of Juan de Fuca's throat, not one that was less than halfway inside this waterway. It also appeared that Pantoja had not informed Eliza of the decision his fellow pilots had already made about the course that had to be investigated next. In either case, Eliza's decision at this point indicated he was not sufficiently aware of how the next phase of exploration needed to be carried out.

Eliza's description of his consultation with the three *pilotos* on the 25th duplicated Pantoja's account except for the following significant passage about his initial decision to use the *San Carlos* to explore the Gran Canal. "The three *pilotos*, in compliance with their obligations, represented to me that this resolution was not feasible, nor was it convenient to the best service of the expedition for the packetboat to enter [the inland sea]. They foresaw that she would be in evident danger of shipwreck for the following reasons: the numerous islands; the few ruling winds favourable to making headway against the [strong] currents which run through each arm and through channels between the islands of this great archipelago; ... [the] great whirlpools; ... and finally the necessity of anchoring every night among so many reefs ... [and inadequate anchorages]. ... I therefore abandoned this resolution [to use the packetboat] and decided to effect this [expedition] with the schooner."[36] (Pantoja's journal left the false impression that he gave the identical cautionary advice to Eliza during their first meeting on the 24th.)[37]

As of June 25, Eliza clearly had reached two new decisions: first, *not* to use the *San Carlos* for exploring the Gran Canal; second, to lead the expedition in command of the *Santa Saturnina*. (As will be seen in the following chapter, four days later, Eliza would change his mind even about the latter resolve.) Before he could act on this determination, however, he had to move his vessels southeast across Juan de Fuca Strait, because Narváez and Carrasco had apparently reminded him about which channel had to be investigated next.

"On the 28th, having decided that the schooner and the longboat should set out again," wrote Eliza, "I weighed [the *San Carlos*] and went to anchor at Puerto de Quadra [Port Discovery on the south shore of Juan de Fuca Strait], as this was closer to the point of beginning [the principal expedition]."[38] According to Pantoja, the *San Carlos* anchored at Puerto de Quadra the same day.[39] This was the exact location that Narváez and Carrasco had confirmed years before as the best starting place for exploring a promising channel at the northeast end of Juan de Fuca Strait (not Haro Strait as Pantoja and Eliza had previously discussed).

At the conclusion of the *pilotos'* eleven-day reconnaissance of the archipelago now known as the Southern Gulf Islands, two critical factors remained in play that would affect the organization and performance of the great expedition that was about to unfold. First, there was Eliza's confused decision-making process, and second, there was an unclear operational dynamic among his subordinates. What stands out was the lieutenant's inability to provide informed, confident, clear directions without becoming overly dependent on the advice of his capable pilots, who were responsible for doing the work. Eliza demonstrated this lack of command and vision shortly after the expedition left Cala de Los Amigos in late May. It clouded his initial orders regarding the recent reconnaissance, hindered his deliberations after it ended, and it would weaken his management of the upcoming phase of exploration.

An objective assessment of the recent voyage raises two other questions. The first one is: Who had actually been in command of the task at the outset eleven days earlier: Pantoja or Narváez? As often happened during the overall expedition, the initial orders issued by Eliza had been somewhat ambiguous. Although Pantoja was nominally in charge during the reconnaissance, Narváez and Carrasco seemed to exercise as much, if not more day-to-day influence. Although Eliza was not present during this phase of exploration, and all of the *pilotos* acknowledged his role as commander of the expedition, it is not clear that any of them particularly respected his competence, commitment, and enthusiasm for the task that was undertaken.

The second question that surfaces is: How well had the four *pilotos* worked together? During most of the voyage, they seemed to perform as a functional team until Pantoja departed early, returned on his own, and submitted his report independently to Eliza. Unfortunately, all of our information about the *pilotos'* interactions is based on Pantoja's account, portions of which seemed to place his self-interest above cooperative efforts to complete a challenging task.

These questions highlight issues that directly related to understanding the developments that were about to occur at Puerto de Quadra, many of which would involve the organization, direction, supervision, and documentation of the most significant aspect of the entire Eliza Expedition — exploration of the Gran Canal. As the *San Carlos* and the *Santa Saturnina* made their separate ways toward another safe anchorage, all the mariners understood which vessels would be used for the challenging exploration, but their actual assignments remained completely unclear.

CHAPTER 8

Exploration of the Gran Canal's East Shore, July 1791

ALL THREE VESSELS INVOLVED in the overall Eliza Expedition — the large packetboat *San Carlos*, the much smaller but more versatile schooner *Santa Saturnina*, and the latter's sturdy longboat — were anchored at Puerto de Quadra (today's Port Discovery) by June 29, 1791, and the mariners were preparing for the next phase of exploration: their long-anticipated reconnaissance of the inland sea, which they had been the first Europeans to see thirteen days earlier. Unfortunately, essential organizational details of the voyage remained unclear.

Although Lieutenant Eliza had decided only four days earlier to lead the expedition as captain of the schooner, at the last moment he changed his mind, claiming he had fallen sick.[1] Nevertheless, Eliza's *Extract of the voyage...*, which he eventually sent to the viceroy, made it explicit that the entire expedition was "being commanded by the lieutenant of the royal fleet . . . Don Francisco de Eliza." His journal, however left three important factors unclear: How did he manage to command this second, most important phase of the undertaking when he did not intend to participate in the voyage? Which *piloto* did he actually place in command in his place? Why was that assignment made?

Instead of clarifying these issues, Eliza's report contains only a single, ambiguous, incorrect phrase: "I dispatched the schooner and the armed long-boat under the command of second *piloto* Don José Verdía." In fact, Verdía had not yet achieved the full rank of second *piloto*, and Eliza certainly would not have placed his least experienced *piloto* in charge of both vessels. Did Eliza simply make a grammatical error and neglect to note that Narváez commanded the schooner? Was Eliza so "sick" that he confused the surnames of two *pilotos*, both of which began with José? If Eliza was not that ill, what does the omission of Narváez's role and the mistaken identities suggest about his respect for the mariner he actually designated commander? The answers cannot be found in the journals of Eliza and Pantoja, neither of which reveals which of these two men actually issued the final orders. Based on second *piloto* Pantoja's account, he might have done so on Eliza's behalf.

Fortunately, Pantoja's journal clarifies who truly commanded the second phase of the expedition, although he has it beginning on the wrong date. "On the 30th [sic], the schooner and the longboat departed on their task under the command of the captain of the schooner, the second *piloto* Don José María Narváez," wrote Pantoja. "In the longboat went the [apprentice] second *piloto* Don José Verdía, in order to obtain the merit which he is securing in this discovery. As there was no other officer of war [on board] the packetboat than the commander, and only two [other fully qualified] *pilotos* [himself and Juan Carrasco], I remained behind to assist the commander in anything that might come up."[2] (Neither Eliza nor Pantoja mentioned Carrasco's actual role in the expedition in their journals, despite the fact that he was the oldest, most experienced *piloto* in the group.)

As a non-commissioned officer, Pantoja would not have been considered a *marinero de guerra* ("mariner of war" or warfare officer), and there were army officers present who could exercise such authority. Therefore, Eliza must have had some other reason to keep Pantoja

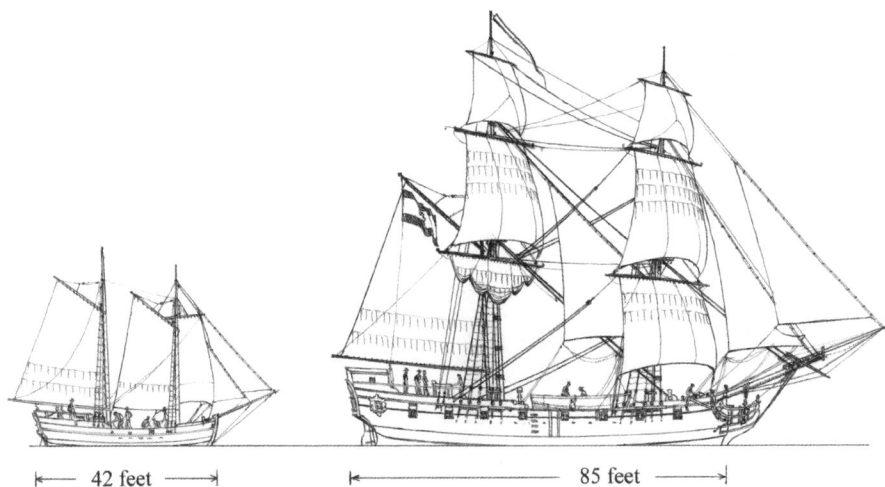

Comparison of Narváez's *Santa Saturnina* and Eliza's *San Carlos*. (S. MAYO)

rather than Verdía at Puerto de Quadra. Did Eliza need Pantoja to undertake important exploration assignments while his colleagues investigated the Gran Canal? Based on the journals of Eliza and Pantoja, the answer to the latter question is clearly negative, because not much would transpire there for about three weeks. Pantoja might have used some of the time to complete his journal of the recent reconnaissance, but he had little, if any, chart work to finish. His *Pequeña Carta* . . . was simply copied from those of Narváez and Carrasco, and it did not illuminate what occurred during the major expedition because he was not present. Perhaps Eliza was simply interested in exploiting Pantoja's self-proclaimed political connections among government officials in Peru to shield himself from criticism by his superiors for his lax performance as an effective commander.

Despite all the organizational ambiguity that clouded the expedition's departure, one thing was certain: the central figure of this narrative — the relatively young twenty-three-year-old Narváez, a *piloto* who had acquired a wealth of experience navigating sailing vessels and making hydrological surveys — was about to set off on what would prove to be his most significant voyage of exploration.

On July 1, 1791, Narváez warped the *Santa Saturnina* out of Puerto de Quadra in charge of the overall expedition's fourth and most important phase. The twenty-three-year-old mariner commanded the same two exploration vessels recently used in the reconnaissance of the Southern Gulf Islands, and presumably the crafts were manned with a similar sized crew: thirty sailors and eight soldiers.[3] With veteran *piloto* Juan Carrasco serving as his first mate on the schooner and the aspiring second mate Verdía aboard the longboat, the three mariners made a solid team of enthusiastic, diligent explorers. Narváez and Carrasco had collaborated effectively before, most recently in charting Clayoquot Sound, Barkley Sound, and the Southern Gulf Islands. By combining the younger man's proven navigational ability with the older *piloto*'s cartographic skills, they had learned how to divide the labour, share responsibility, and achieve reliable results. Having sailed to Alaska in 1788 as Narváez's assistant, Verdía was eager to take on a more independent, challenging role. Now that they knew a huge inland sea existed not too far to the north, all three men were excited about the prospect of exploring its entry and exit points, determining its actual size, and meeting the peoples who lived there.

Once the expedition was underway, Narváez began sailing northeast along the northern shore of what is today's Quimper Peninsula. Looking west from there, they could see Isla de Carrasco[4] nearby in Juan de Fuca Strait. By now, they must have realized that the large but broken front of land to the north was the south side of the Archipiélago de San Juan, which they had viewed earlier from three other directions. The two vessels continued northeast — across the wide mouth of Ensenada y Boca de Caamaño (Admiral Channel) which seemed to run southeast a considerable distance — and headed toward a point of land (today's Point Partridge) on what appeared to be the mainland (actually present-day Whidbey Island). During the Manuel Quimper expedition in 1790, Carrasco had discovered what he thought was a bay at this location, and he named it Ensenada y Boca de Caamaño. On his *Carta esférica* .. ,

Narváez left the southern end of this "isthmus" open because he planned to reconnoitre it when he returned.

Because the journal of this voyage which Narváez must have written has vanished, and because Carrasco's brief written observations relate only to the end of the expedition and its aftermath, we must rely largely on the charts drafted by these two men to illuminate the route that they followed. Narváez's *Carta esférica* ... is clearly drawn, carefully numbered and indexed, and less cluttered. Narváez used dotted lines in various locations to show sandbars, shoals, tide lines, mudflats, and areas that were left unsurveyed. Carrasco's *Carta que comprehende* ...[5] is, however, more detailed. It uses shading to mark sandbars and tidal features, has strings of numbers in several places which indicate where the longboat took soundings, and it has tiny anchors to show anchorages, some of which represent overnight stays and others that were brief stops. Fortunately, both charts contain considerable information, and they are similar enough to facilitate identification of various places by placing them side by side with detailed current nautical charts of the area.

To show the route Narváez travelled during the remainder of the expedition, the author has adapted portions of Carrasco's *Carta que comprehende* ... , each of which will introduce a different part of the exploration. The first portion covers the eastern end of Juan de Fuca Strait, its northern arm which reaches into the Gran Canal, and the archipelago east of today's San Juan Islands.

Carrasco undoubtedly pointed the way during this initial phase of the voyage, because of his experience as *piloto* under Manuel Quimper on his exploration of Juan de Fuca Strait in 1790. As noted earlier, Carrasco had made a one-day excursion northeast from Boca de Quimper (present-day New Dungeness), where Quimper had anchored, and discovered the wide entrance to what he assumed was only an inlet in the mainland. Consequently, he did not sail inside at that time. If he had proceeded, he might have discovered the inland sea to which it was linked, a year before he and Narváez saw it for the first time on June 15, 1791. During the 1790 investigation, Carrasco also discovered today's Admiral Inlet, but he named it Ensenada y Boca ("cove and mouth") de

Adaptation of Carrasco's chart *Carta que comprehende* . . . , to show the first
phase of Narváez's exploration of Gran Canal, July 1–5, 1791.

Caamaño because it, too, appeared to be a closed waterway.[6] (See Haro and Quimper's chart of Juan de Fuca Strait, 1790, in Chapter 6.)

Having sailed about thirty kilometres, Narváez and Carrasco continued north toward a point of land (the present Watmough Head) which appeared to be on a flat-topped island (López Island) that was about another twenty kilometres distant. On the way, they anchored briefly at a tiny island near mid channel that Carrasco named Isla de Bonilla (today's nearly non-existent Smith Island). This route was taking them toward the seven-kilometre-wide mouth of the waterway Carrasco had discovered one year earlier, but did not enter. To the northwest of Isla de Bonilla they saw an opening in the Isla y Archipiélago de San Juan which was not shown on the chart Quimper had made the previous year. Consequently, the two *pilotos* decided to at least investigate the entrance when they reached the southern shore of what still appeared to be a single huge island. To the east they sighted the narrow mouth of an entrance that Carrasco had discovered in 1790, named Boca de Flon (today's Deception Pass), and assumed it was another closed inlet. Narváez decided not to investigate it, and both mariners left it open on their charts.

At the entrance to the main channel that ran north, there were two islets and three reefs, which Narváez named Islas de Fidalgo on his chart. (Later, Carrasco would name the entire waterway Canal de Fidalgo on his *Carta que comprehende* . . . .) Based on the tiny anchor Carrasco placed on his map just west of these islands, it would appear that the explorers dropped anchor in today's McArdle Harbour, a short distance west of Watmough Head, to stay clear of the heavy current flowing out of the canal. From there, they could take their bearings, locate reefs that had to be avoided at the entrance, and possibly wait for the tide to change. The detailed drawing of shoals along the northwest and northeast shores of this headland on Carrasco's chart indicates that the longboat was used to make these observations. In the process, the mariners reached the opening in the Isla y Archipiélago de San Juan which they had seen earlier, but they did not enter. Nevertheless, they could see that it appeared to have two mouths inside. On their charts, Narváez and Carrasco named the opening they had discovered Bocas de Orcasitas and Boca de Horcasitas, respectively, in recognition of the viceroy, and they left the possible inlet (today's Griffin Bay and the southern entrance to the San Juan Channel) open-ended.

Returning to where the *Santa Saturnina* was anchored, the longboat was rowed northeast into the channel that Narváez was most interested in exploring, in search of a safe anchorage inside that would be out of the main current. About five kilometres north of the entrance along the west side of the channel the scouting party evidently found what became known as Shoal Bight, and today's Lopez Pass. At this location a vessel can stand to westward facing into the bay in eleven metres of water and anchor in a mud bottom less than one kilometre from shore.[7]

After the longboat returned to the schooner — where both vessels may have waited for a rising tide — the smaller vessel was used to tow the *Santa Saturnina* through the entrance to this anchorage, using all the oars on both vessels. Two sighting marks on Narváez's chart on each side of the canal inside the entrance indicate that he took these bearings en route. Anchoring overnight at Shoal Bight, which had a relatively low island behind it and an even larger landform farther west, the explorers must have begun to realize that this was another side of the Isla y Archipiélago de San Juan, which they had now viewed from every direction of the compass. That, however, raised several questions in their minds: How long is the canal that they were in? Would they be able to buck its powerful current, even on a strong incoming tide which appeared to run three to seven knots (1.5 to 3.6 metres per second) in the narrows? Were there side channels that might offer easier routes northward into the Gran Canal?

Early on July 2, the mariners headed northeast across the four-kilometre-wide canal, being careful to avoid being pushed by the current against either of the two dangerous islands (Bird Rocks and Belle Rocks) that stand in the centre of the channel about 6.5 kilometres inside the southern entrance. Rounding a headland on the east side of the channel, Narváez guided the vessels about two kilometres farther and anchored in what is now Ship Harbour (where today's Washington State Ferries dock at Anacortes before wending their way westward through the San Juan Islands to Sidney on Vancouver Island's Saanich Peninsula). A tiny anchor marks the location on Carrasco's chart.

Working from this anchorage, with little or no onshore wind, the explorers probably rowed both the longboat and the schooner — as far as tidal changes allowed the latter to proceed — to survey the surrounding waters. Directly north of them was a moderately large island which they named Isla de Güemes. In the middle of the main canal there was a slightly smaller island which they named Isla de San Vincente (today's Cypress Island). Because both of these are drawn fairly accurately on Carrasco's chart, it would indicate that the explorers penetrated the channel between them (today's Bellingham Channel). It is also probable that the longboat was used to round the northern end of Isla de San Vincente, cross Fidalgo Canal to the east shore of today's Orcas Island, and probe a large opening (now known as Obstruction Pass), which seemed to lead in two directions to a larger waterway (today's López and East Sounds). Inside this pass, the explorers sighted the Central Coast Salish village of Whuht'k-aw-ch'lh, which was occupied by the Swehluhkh people, a Lummi group that spoke the Northern Straits language. The settlement is shown on Carrasco's chart near what became known as Buck Bay.[8] From this location, the longboat would have been able to ride the current downstream, cut across the canal, and return to the anchorage in Güemes Channel.

The shaded area around the headland and shore due south of this anchorage indicates this area was also thoroughly surveyed, possibly in the afternoon while both vessels moved east through today's Güemes Channel, with regular soundings being made aboard the *Santa Saturnina*. After sailing eastward about seven kilometres, the expedition entered a large bay, which Narváez and Carrasco named Seno de Padilla. (The names of this bay and the two large islands to the west all paid tribute to Viceroy Revillagigedo, by using parts of his long name.) Narváez anchored the *Santa Saturnina* for the night southeast of today's Hat Island at about 48°31' north latitude, while the longboat continued to survey the breadth of the closed bay to the south, which the receding tide revealed was filled with mudflats.

On the north side of this bay the explorers observed a long, narrow point of land (today's Samish Island), which Carrasco named Punta de Solano ("Point of Sunshine"). It reached northwest and created one side of another bay that stretched farther north. Carrasco's chart shows the large village of Eh-tseh-kun, a Central Coast Salish group of Samish people who spoke a Northern Straits dialect, located toward the southeast end of Punta de Solano. According to Pantoja, who was not present on this voyage, Narváez reported seeing "many Indians after shellfish" in the wide mudflats at this time.[9]

Having observed several tidal changes in the last two days, the Narváez expedition left Seno de Padilla on Sunday, July 3, rowed northwest and then northeast around Punta de Solano into present-day Samish Bay. Continuing northeast under sail across this waterway, Narváez entered the mouth of today's Bellingham Bay and anchored the *Santa Saturnina* in deep water on the east side of the entrance, off what is now Post Point just north of today's Chuckanut Bay. Then he placed a landing party aboard the longboat and sent it inside to investigate the cove at the north end of the long bay. Carrasco placed tiny anchors at both locations, and named the place Puerto del Socorro ("port of relief"), probably because the crew obtained fresh water from Chuckanut Creek. Given that Sunday was a day of rest, the crew enjoyed easy access to drinking water and opportunities to hunt for shellfish and wild game. The surroundings were so pleasantly beautiful, the expedition probably stayed here two nights. (In passing, it is worth noting that a tiny island across the bay from the south end of Chuckanut Bay was subsequently named Eliza Island, in recognition of the lieutenant who would receive most of the credit for this entire expedition even though he did not participate directly in any of it.)

From the soundings shown on Carrasco's chart, it appears that on July 5, the expedition proceeded across the broad entrance of Bellingham Bay, which Narváez named Seno de Gastón. Although it reached another ten kilometres north, they could see that it was closed. Consequently, the explorers decided it was unnecessary to survey inside. It was more important to keep pressing northward into the long inland sea that they knew could not be too far distant. Rounding today's Portage Island at the southern tip of the current Lummi Indian Reserve Lands, the *Santa Saturnina* would have turned northwest and headed into today's Hale Passage, which runs between the mainland and present-day Lummi Island, which Carrasco named Isla de Pacheco. If the

Santa Saturnina and longboat crossing Seno de Gastón (Bellingham Bay), July 5, 1791. (WATERCOLOUR BY S. MAYO)

wind was favourable, the schooner could have sailed through the channel. Otherwise the two vessels would have employed their usual warping method. When they emerged from this waterway, the explorers had their first opportunity to view the Gran Canal from its southeastern end. They could also look across to the southwestern end which they had surveyed a few weeks earlier before they stopped short of entering. They now knew it was the Canal de Fidalgo, which is about forty kilometres long. From this vantage point they would have realized that Isla de Pacheco was the long stretch of land that had blocked their way in June, and caused them to miss surveying the swift-flowing Canal de Fidalgo that flowed past its southwestern side and eventually ran into Juan de Fuca Strait. In 1790, Carrasco had sensed the existence of this primary connection between an inland waterway and the Pacific Ocean. Now, he and Narváez had found it.

The forty-one-member expedition proceeded to anchor for the night on the mainland side of the Gran Canal in the shallow Lummi Bay. Carrasco's chart shows that it was sheltered to the northwest by what he named Punta de Loera (now Sandy Point), in recognition of Nicolás de Luera of San Blas, chaplain of the frigate *Concepción*, which was stationed at Cala de Los Amigos.

Father Nicolás de Luera's Purchase of Aboriginal Children

The extent to which Father Luera deserved such acknowledgement depends to a great extent on how one views the purchase of Indigenous children at the Spanish outpost, a practice that had been underway for some time. According to Alejandro Malaspina, who arrived in Nootka Sound in August 1791, Father Luera "distinguished himself particularly for his disinterested zeal in this kind of acquisition. Afterward he kept watch over their good habits and their social and Christian instruction. Ultimately he entrusted them for their dress, food, and subsequent instruction to those individuals of the crews who could take care of them and realize some benefit within their families from adopting these children."[10] Fearing the practice could easily lead to what he diplomatically called "indelible mastery over these unfortunates," Malaspina thought it should be curtailed. Nevertheless, this mariner who in many ways epitomized the enlightened scientist, accepted six boys from Luera, who had paid for them with guns.[11]

Lummi Bay lies at about the same latitude as Patos Island, where the expedition had anchored on June 15 after sighting the inland sea for the first time. Now that Narváez had succeeded in taking the explorers through the tortuous, complex southeastern waterways of the San Juan Archipelago and reached open water to the north, his skills as a leader and navigator would be thoroughly tested by the challenges that lay ahead. Having used up four of the twenty-one days allotted to survey the entire area of what was clearly a huge body of unfamiliar waters, he would have to maintain a fairly tight schedule, plan ahead, and manage his time carefully. Ensuring the safety and condition of both vessels — one of which was their home at sea and the other was their lifeline to the outside world — was essential. Narváez would also have to maintain his crew's health, morale, and discipline. Given cramped quarters on the *Santa Saturnina* and the limited supply of rations on board, making certain that all forty-one men — especially those who were required to pull the oars of both vessels hour-after-hour for long periods of time — would prove to be a major task. In addition to these responsibilities, Narváez had to plan daily surveys, delegate authority to Carrasco and Verdía as required, draft daily field sketches, and maintain a journal.

Heading north from Punta de Loera into the Gran Canal on July 6, Narváez continued charting those parts of the eastern shore that he could see. Now that they were in open water, the three mariners could follow their customary procedure of having two *pilotos* on the *Santa Saturnina* run the baseline offshore, while a third *piloto* in the longboat took soundings and surveyed the land from point to point close to shore. Probably Narváez and Carrasco were usually on board the schooner — one navigating and the other taking bearings, noting relevant geographic features, and sketching contours — while Verdía was largely in charge of the longboat. Narváez was in command, but each man respected the other's skills, and they worked as an effective team, exchanging places when the need arose. Every evening, Narváez and

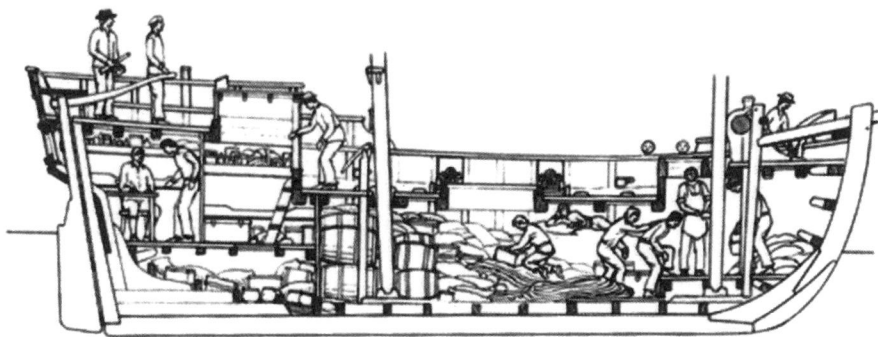

Scale drawing of *Santa Saturnina*'s interior showing crew's cramped quarters. (S. MAYO)

Carrasco would record the day's observations on their charts. The next portion of Carrasco's *Carta que comprehende* ..., which the author has adapted, covers the southern end of the Gran Canal where the expedition was working.

After travelling about six kilometres, the expedition anchored just south of today's Cherry Point, where a landing party apparently trekked inland about one kilometre, following a river that led to a lake. Carrasco named the location Punta y Laguna del Garzón. The "Laguna" was obviously present-day Lake Terrell. However, the "Punta" Carrasco had in mind is today's Point Whitehorn, which is northwest of Cherry Point.

With a new supply of fresh water on board and possibly some fresh meat obtained by hunters, Narváez sailed about fourteen kilometres more, travelling north around Point Whitehorn, northeast across an

Adaptation of Carrasco's chart *Carta que comprehende* ..., to show the second phase of Narváez's exploration of Gran Canal, July 6–8, 1791.

unnamed bay (today's Birch Bay), and then northwest and north around a headland that Carrasco named Punta de San José (present-day Birch Point). A short distance beyond this point, the *Santa Saturnina* dropped anchor in today's Semiahmoo Bay, close to the mainland shore and just north of the entrance to what became Drayton Harbour. Looking west, Narváez would have seen the southern end of what appeared to be a large island that Carrasco would name Isla de Zepeda (now known as Point Roberts) in honour of Félix de Cepeda, adjutant to Bodega. On the eastern shore of the bay in which they were anchored, members of the expedition sighted two Aboriginal villages, which are marked on Carrasco's chart with small squares (near present-day White Rock). Narváez had entered the territory of the Semiahmoo people, a large Central Coast Salish group that spoke the Northern Straits language and controlled the bay and its surrounding shores.[12]

Using Verdía's longboat the next morning to survey the east shore of Semiahmoo Bay, the explorers reached a prominent point of land that Carrasco named Punta de San Rafael. The Semiahmoo people used this site for spiritual renewal and named it Kwomais ("place of vision"), because of its high bluffs and unobstructed views of the surrounding waters and islands. They undoubtedly used it as a lookout point. Today Kwomais Point appears on nautical charts, and Kwomais Park occupies the location.

If Narváez's survey team climbed this bluff to scan what lay ahead of them — *and the weather was clear* — they would have had a panoramic north-to-southwest view: to the north, a mountain range and forests in the distance, forested hills in the near distance that descended to lowlands, which came down to the mudflats of the waterway (Boundary Bay) below them; to the northwest across the bay, lowlands that seemed to have nothing behind them except water and mountains on the horizon; to the west, the previously sighted Isla de Zepeda, which they should have been able to see was connected to the mainland by a low isthmus, thereby making today's Boundary Bay closed. If the explorers had seen these features, their charts would have reflected this sort of detail, because they consistently drew what they saw. Carrasco and Narváez both left places they did not investigate blank or open-ended.

Sometimes Narváez used dotted lines to show he passed the area but did not penetrate it.

If the weather was *not clear*, however, and the area to the north was obscured by fog and rain, the explorers might have been unable to determine whether Boundary Bay was open or closed and how far north it extended. This is what seems to have been the case, because Carrasco's chart left the northern part of this waterway open and its eastern seashore undefined and vague, even though he showed shoals that were supposedly surveyed along this shore for a considerable distance beyond Punta de San Rafael. (If a longboat survey of this length had been conducted, the explorers would have encountered — within a few kilometres — mudflats and marshlands which circled west toward Isla de Zepeda.) On Narváez's chart, the eastern shore is more detailed but entirely hypothetical, and no shoals are shown as being surveyed.

In either case, instead of penetrating the waterway (Boundary Bay), and surveying it thoroughly, the commander and his mate — after probably being socked-in by fog for two days — formed the impression that the inland sea extended, without any landward interruption, far to the northeast, possibly reaching a channel which Narváez later named Boca de Bodega on his chart. Consequently, when the Narváez expedition subsequently warped around Islas de Zepeda (today's Point Roberts), the *pilotos* continued to believe it was an island. Their assumption actually bore some prehistorical validity. For most of the past twelve thousand years, this large headland was actually one of the Gulf Islands, and geologists still call it Roberts Island. A low land bridge did not begin to link the island to the delta until about three thousand years ago.[13] It is possible that, if the surrounding area was inundated in July 1791, water from the sea could have briefly covered, or nearly concealed the relatively narrow spit. (This specific hypothesis was advanced in 1986 by historian Thomas Bartroli, who concluded that spring runoff in the Fraser River might have flooded a large part of its delta, creating the impression of a huge expanse of water.)[14]

Eleven months after Narváez left Boundary Bay, however, another Spanish expedition led by Dionisio Alcalá-Galiano would use Narváez's findings to search from this approximate location for the large *boca* (mouth) shown on Carrasco's chart. Not surprisingly, these explorers would find a huge land mass (the present-day municipalities of Delta and Surrey) blocking the way. Their reaction to this discovery, so contradictory to what their predecessors had suggested, is reflected by the name they gave to the area: Ensenada del Engaño (Bay of Deception). One way or another, Narváez and Carrasco had been deceived by the elements.

Rounding the south end of Isla de Zepeda (Point Roberts) on July 8, Narváez sailed northwest about fourteen kilometres along the shore, and then navigated through what he later reportedly told Eliza seemed to be effluent from a "very copious river, [because] for a distance of [eleven kilometres we] sailed through a line of white water [that was] more sweet than salt."[15] This would indicate that, Narváez and Carrasco

Adaptation of Carrasco's chart *Carta que comprehende . . .* , to show the third phase of Narváez's exploration of Gran Canal, July 9–11, 1791, including tiny anchors off Islas de Lángara, Rio de la Aguada, and Isla de San Ignacio.

had some awareness of a vast amount of fresh water flowing from the east into the sea as the *Santa Saturnina* and its longboat traversed the waters offshore from today's Roberts Bank and Sturgeon Bank. There is no clear indication on either *pilotos*'s chart, however, that it was actually three large mouths of the great Fraser River which they were passing, because they did not probe any of these openings, nor did they have any concept of the geography inland from the coast. Nevertheless, on his *working* chart, Carrasco inserted the following descriptive handwritten note immediately behind this broken shore: Islas bajda y aguadas ("low islands and watering places"). This revealing notation does not appear on Carrasco's final chart. Both Narváez and Carrasco drew four openings between what they assumed were three low-lying islands. From south to north the latter would have been today's Westham Island (now farmland and wildlife sanctuaries), Lulu Island (now the city of Richmond), and Sea Island (now Vancouver International Airport). Between these islands, the openings that were drawn would have been (south to north) today's Canoe Pass, and the Fraser River's south, middle, and north arms.

After sailing about five kilometres north of the northernmost opening, Narváez anchored the *Santa Saturnina* off a prominent headland, later called Point Grey. Two tiny anchors are located here on Carrasco's final chart, which suggests that the expedition stayed here at least two nights. Narváez assumed it was the northernmost of two islands in the area — marked Islas de Lángara on Carrasco's chart. (During the period when Spanish explorers were charting the Pacific Northwest Coast, they named several land formations after Don Juan Francisco de Lángara, a Basque-born naval commander and cartographer, who became head of the Spanish Navy.) The other island must have been the previously mentioned Sea Island.

If Narváez's designation for this headland had survived, the lowlands behind it, which were then Aboriginal territory that later became Canada's largest west coast metropolis, might well have been named the City of Langara. Now, that name is applied only to Langara College and an adjacent golf course in what became the City of Vancouver ninety-five years later.

At this anchorage, Carrasco inserted three squares to indicate the presence of Halkomelem-speaking Coast Salish villages (Musqueam settlements probably observed at Steselax on the Fraser River's north arm, Máləy where the Musqueam Reserve is now located, and Ee'yullmough or "good spring water" at Jericho Beach).[16] Soon after the expedition arrived, large numbers of Musqueam people paddled out from their settlement at Steselax, which was about nine kilometres to the southeast near the mouth of the last "opening" Narváez had passed.

First contact between European invaders and Indigenous people in this part of the Gran Canal occurred on July 8 or 9 when the Musqueam, paddling slim dugout canoes,[17] approached Narváez's schooner as it rode at anchor below the headland that the Squamish called Chitchula-yuk (today's Point Grey).[18] At the time, it marked the boundary between Squamish and Musqueam territories. The explorers were alarmed until they realized these people did not carry bows and arrows. Instead they brought several kinds of fish, including large freshly caught salmon, for bartering. They also traded deer and elk meat; edible wild plants, berries and fruits; fresh water; and firewood. In exchange, they received scraps of copper, pieces of iron, and barrel hoops. The Spaniards noticed that the Musqueam language (Hunquminum, which was a dialect of Halkomelem) was different from that of the Mowachaht in Nootka Sound. Using sign language, the Musqueam people made it clear that the Gran Canal continued much farther on. They also managed to explain that vessels much larger than the *Santa Saturnina* had sailed earlier somewhere in the Salish Sea (probably in Juan de Fuca Strait), and that one vessel carried brass bracelets engraved with knives.

Although the Musqueam probably had not seen these vessels themselves, the appearance of large sailing vessels certainly would have been communicated among the numerous Coast Salish and Nuu-chah-nulth settlements located around the inland sea. As mentioned, at least one of these vessels — the Spanish sloop *Princesa Real*, commanded by Manuel Quimper — had sailed deep into Juan de Fuca Strait for two months during the summer of 1790, at which time the *alférez de navío* (ship's ensign) gave presents to First Nations people in exchange for valuable geographical information. He also traded copper, iron, beads, fish hooks, and other small items for a large quantity of sea otter skins.

According to Pantoja, who transcribed the verbal reports Narváez

Musqueam leader Qeyupulenuxw whose people met Narváez at Punta de Lángara (now Point Grey), ca. July 8–9, 1791. Drawing by José Cardero, 1792. The oldest known image of an Indigenous person who lived in what is now Greater Vancouver. His name evolved into the word Capilano. (MUSEO NAVAL, MADRID)

made to Eliza after the voyage ended, the explorer's purser, José Ignacio González, bought an eleven-year-old Musqueam boy. From the youngster, the Spaniards learned that many Indigenous people came on horseback from "flat country" in the northeast to trade iron, copper, and blue beads for fish. Their visits lasted two months.[19] There is no record of the Spaniards going ashore to visit the Musqueam villages.

Another large Indigenous settlement composed of three villages is shown on Carrasco's chart at Punta de la Bodega y Quadra (a point of land at the mouth of today's Capilano River, which is also on the north side of the narrow entrance into present-day Burrard Inlet — Vancouver Harbour).[20] Therefore, we can be sure that the voyagers observed the shores of today's West Vancouver, where the Squamish people resided in a large village at Homulcheson, beside the Homulcheson River.[21] In fact, on one day "bad weather" forced Narváez to move away from the shores of today's Point Grey, and he anchored the *Santa Saturnina* about three kilometres outside the entrance of Burrard Inlet. Looking east from this vantage point (approximately due south of today's Navy Jack Park on the West Vancouver waterfront), he realized there was a "very copious river" nearby and sent the longboat to collect some "sweet water."[22] Evidently, this led Narváez to venture a short distance inside the mouth of the adjacent inlet.

Carrasco's chart shows the northern shore of a large bay where Burrard Inlet is located today and the mouth of a wide, open-ended channel trending northeast apparently indefinitely, which is named Boca de Florida Blanca, thereby invoking the surname of Spain's prime minister. Narváez named the same channel Boca de Bodega y Quadra on his chart. In both cases, it is unclear whether this was simply the most northern latitude the expedition reached in the large gaping bay (today's Boundary Bay) that the explorer's had hypothesized earlier but left unnamed, or if it represents today's Indian Arm which runs northeast from Burrard Inlet and is much closer to the 49°25' north latitude shown on Carrasco's chart. In either case, the absence of a dotted line across the Boca de Bodega y Quadra to show the south side of this hypothetical canal indicates the expedition did not penetrate these waters. Nevertheless, this channel became one of two unexplored waterways that the Narváez expedition would point to as possible routes to the tantalizing Northwest Passage.

Narváez would have had three practical reasons for not sailing farther east to investigate. First, he was already into the tenth day of an expedition for which he only had twenty-one-days'-worth of provisions. Second, he still had to reconnoitre a large portion of the Gran Canal to the northwest before returning to Puerto de Quadra. Third, because the northwesternmost end of the Gran Canal appeared to extend a long distance, it also had to be surveyed. Consequently, Narváez headed west toward present-day Point Atkinson.

What was probably the Squamish village of Skeawatsut[23] is located on Carrasco's chart at the eastern entrance to Bocas del Carmelo (one of the "mouths" of today's Howe Sound), near Point Atkinson. Although this had been the westernmost point of territory occupied by the Tsleil-waututh for at least three thousand years, by 1791 this group seems to have pulled back to the mouth of today's Seymour River where it had a large village at Chaychilwuk.[24] The Tsleilwaututh exercised control of present-day Indian Arm, the interior of what is now Burrard Inlet, and a large area of land to the north and east.

Narváez surveyed the Squamish outpost at the mouth of Howe Sound on Sunday, July 10, along with the Islas de Apodaca (present-day Bowen Island and its nearby islets). Instead of entering this large sound, Narváez sailed northwest along the coast and anchored at a watering place he named Río de la Aguada (probably Chapman Creek at today's Mission Point), about two kilometres due north of what are now called the White Islets.

We have documentary evidence, therefore, which shows these explorers went ashore at three locations near what is now Greater Vancouver: they collected fresh drinking water at Point Grey, at the mouth of the Capilano River, and then at Chapman Creek. From Narváez's next anchorage off Isla de San Ignacio (today's Thormanby Island) on July 11, he sailed between the large island he named Islas de San Félix (changed later to Isla de Texada by Carrasco) and the two mainland locations of Boca de Moñino (the entrance from Malaspina Strait into Agamemnon Channel and Pender Harbour) and Punta de Arze (Cape Cockburn on Nelson Island).

Because the feast of San Félix is held on July 12, and the Spanish mariners tended to use feast days to name various locations, we can assume that was the date on which the expedition reached Islas de San Félix. Most of the expedition's anchorages (each of which is indicated on Carrasco's chart with a tiny anchor) involved overnight rest stops. Consequently, using anchorages to work backwards from July 12, it is reasonable to estimate that the expedition had anchored in a large bay near today's Vancouver on July 8 or 9, 1791.

After reaching Islas de San Félix on July 12, Narváez continued a short distance farther north in what is now Malaspina Strait. Examination of four charts — one made by Narváez and Verdía, Pantoja's copy of that chart (about two-and-a-half months after the expedition ended), the comprehensive chart produced collectively by Carrasco and Pantoja (about five months after the exploration), and a chart made the following year by López de Haro (who did not participate in the expedition) — indicates that the explorers did not observe the large entrance to

Plaque located at Spanish Banks, Vancouver, B.C., marking Narváez's anchorage off Isla de Lángara (Point Grey) in July 1791.

Monuments about Narváez

Today, two monuments remind British Columbians of Narváez's explorations in the Vancouver area. In 1941, the Lions Club of West Vancouver, erected a large stone monument and plaque in Ambleside Park, commemorating the 150th anniversary of Narváez's arrival. Based on limited and partially incorrect information supplied by Major James S. Matthews (1878–1970) — the City of Vancouver's first archivist — the plaque commemorated Narváez's "arrival July 1st 1791" as "the first white man to visit the mainland of western Canada."[25] Although the latter racially tinged assertion is true, we now know that Narváez began his expedition at Port Discovery on July 1 and did not go ashore near what is now Vancouver for another seven or eight days. Unfortunately, the cairn fails to note that it was Narváez, not Captain Vancouver, who first sighted the entrance to Burrard Inlet, which is now synonymous with Vancouver Harbour — one of the world's finest landlocked ports.

For several years, a small, easily missed plaque also stood in the shadow of a stylized concrete anchor on Spanish Banks beach. It was placed there on July 4, 1986, by the Government of Spain as part of the City of Vancouver's centennial celebrations. The brass plate stated that it "honours the accomplishment of Spanish explorer Don José María Narváez, the first European to visit these waters on July 5, 1791." Although this date is also questionable, the statement was clear, correct, and succinct. Furthermore, the site is close to the place where Narváez anchored off Point Grey and went ashore for fresh water. Regrettably, this historic marker was removed or stolen about 2013, and it has not been replaced. A slightly larger plaque nearby, installed in April 1991 during the "bicentennial of the Spanish expeditions to the Northwest Coasts of America," recognizes two events: Narváez's arrival in July 1791, and the meeting of Galiano, Valdés, and Vancouver in 1792 that led to "the first circumnavigation of Vancouver Island by Europeans." (It would be timely for the governments of Spain, Mexico, and British Columbia to jointly install a new, separate marker that restores due recognition to Narváez for his singular accomplishment.)

Outdoor wall murals often commemorate early explorers. Unfortunately, two of these large paintings that feature Captain Vancouver's voyage do not portray Narváez's earlier arrival. One is in Dundarave Village, West Vancouver; the other is on the backside of the Vancouver Maritime Museum.

Adaptation of Carrasco's chart *Carta que comprehende* . . . , to show the fourth phase of Narváez's exploration of Gran Canal, July 12–15, 1791.

Portion of Lopéz de Haro's 1792 chart showing Bocas de Flórez. (WAGNER) what is now Jervis Inlet. This suggests that the expedition probably went no farther north than today's Point Cockburn, approximately 250 kilometres by sea from where it started in Puerto de Quadra and at about the same latitude as Nootka Sound (about 49°35' north latitude). Running low on rations, Narváez decided it was time to turn back. Reversing course on July 13, the two vessels sailed south in Malaspina Strait, and then rounded the south shore of present-day Lasqueti Island.

Narváez named it Isla de Texada. (As noted earlier, Carrasco would eventually transfer this name to the larger island which is immediately north and renamed this smaller one Isla de Lasquety.)[26] Then Narváez sailed north far enough to sight Punta de Lazo de la Bega [Vega] to the northwest on Vancouver Island.[27] Both Narváez and Carrasco placed this name on the relatively high point of land that is about five kilometres southeast of today's Little River ferry terminal at the southeast end of Kye Bay. This large, precipitous headland is now called Cape Lazo. On a clear day, it offers a commanding view of the Gran Canal about fifty kilometres to the northwest, forty kilometres to the southeast, and eighty kilometres to the Coast Mountains in the northeast.

From this approximate vantage point on the water, Narváez apparently was able to see northwest to two high hills at the head of the gulf: Campo Alange (probably on Quadra Island north of Cape Mudge, which appears to be a rounded hump) and Punta de San Luis (possibly Cortes Island, which can be seen as another curved mound above and behind Hernando Island). To Narváez, these easily observed features seemed to be separated by a canal. Although neither he nor Carrasco named it on their charts, it was named Boca de Flórez (today's Sutil Channel) on the chart that López de Haro drafted in San Blas in January 1792, seven months after Narváez's exploratory voyage ended.[28] This Boca ("mouth") — probably given the viceroy's name to advertise its importance — would become the second prospective entrance to the hypothetical Northwest Passage that this expedition would suggest needed further exploration.[29]

Narváez had no other place names on his *Carta esférica* north of this latitude, but Carrasco's chart shows two more names on the mainland side of the canal, south of Punta de San Luis, both of which could have appeared to be headlands: Punta de Romay (probably today's Savary Island) and Punta de Camino (now Harwood Island, off the north end of Texada Island). European exploration of the Salish Sea north of this location would not occur for another year.

CHAPTER 9

Exploration of the Gran Canal's West Shore, July 1791

AS WE HAVE SEEN, by about mid-July of 1791, Narváez had managed to locate what he thought were entrances to two promising wide waterways that seemed to penetrate the continental shore and might possibly lead to the long-sought Northwest Passage. The first had been east of today's Burrard Inlet, and the other was at the northern end of the Gran Canal. In both instances, however, he realized that it was impossible to investigate them further in his small vessels which had limited supplies. Earlier, Narváez had simply pressed onward in the huge inland sea. Now, he prudently reversed course.

Heading southwest opposite Punta de Lazo, he passed a long, extremely shallow bay known today as Balmoral Beach before rounding a point of land which Carrasco designated Punta de Araus,[1] and Narváez left unnamed. Today this relatively low headland forms the Willemar

Adaptation of Carrasco's chart *Carta que comprehende . . .* , to show the fifth phase of Narváez's exploration of Gran Canal, July 16–18, 1791.

Bluffs, which storm waves have attacked for about ten thousand years, creating a long-shore drift system that has transported sand and gravel southwestward. This has formed the large Goose Spit[2] at the mouth of present-day Comox Harbour at about 49°40' north latitude and a broad, largely underwater sandbar offshore now known as Sandy Island Marine Park.

Sensibly sailing well east of these shallow waters, Narváez was still able to see inside Boca de Valdés (Comox Harbour), which he charted on the east shore of Vancouver Island. Continuing southwest, the expedition sailed past the east side of the Islas de Lerena (Hornby Island and Denman Island) and then kept the same course until it reached a position on Vancouver Island which Narváez named Punta de San Leonardo (a low point of land at the north end of what is now Qualicum Beach). Carrasco's chart shows that the vessels anchored on the south side of this point. Narváez undoubtedly sent a shore party to fetch fresh water from the nearby Little Qualicum River, which empties into the Salish Sea here and forms a large estuary. The sailors may well have hunted, fished, and even encountered some Indigenous people. According to Thomas Kinkade Jr., son of the first landowner of Little Qualicum estuary, "There were deer, elk, bear, ducks, geese, brant, and grouse as tame as chickens. Trout were very plentiful ... at any time of the year." Kinkade also stated that a large 25-metre by 122-metre Aboriginal longhouse had been located nearby until the late 1880s.[3]

In 1791, the Qualicum people had several settlements in the surrounding area. A small monument located near the old Qualicum Beach E&N Station,[4] which is now used only by the heritage Alberni Pacific Railway, is titled "Qualicum Beach from the Beginning to 1913." It states that the Qualicum descended from Pentlatch people, the southernmost group of the Kwawaka'wakw First Nation, who had lived in this locale for many thousands of years. According to the plaque, the name Qualicum was derived from the Pentlatch word for chum salmon, *squal-li*. The same marker incorrectly states, however, that "the first European to visit the area was Spanish Commander Juan Quadra [sic], who mapped the east coast of Vancouver Island in the late 1700s." (The historical plaque needs correction. Bodega y Quadra was not involved in the expedition, and he never visited the area. José Narváez deserves recognition.)

Continuing southwest close to shore on July 14, Narváez sailed about ten kilometres before anchoring again just south of the mouth of a small inlet that Carrasco named Río de las Grullas ("river of the cranes"), which is present-day French Creek, where a private passenger ferry connects Qualicum Beach with Lasqueti Island. The river empties into a small estuary which is a natural habitat for migratory ducks and geese. Consequently, it might well have been a promising place for the hungry sailors to stock up on wild game.

On another low, heavily forested headland about eight kilometres southeast of Río de las Grullas, Carrasco's chart shows a cluster of three Qualicum villages. The traditional land and sea territory of this Northern Coast Salish group extended from about twenty kilometres inland on Vancouver Island in the west to the entire west shore of Texada Island in the east, and from present-day Little River in the north to Parksville in the south. This ancient domain also included a pair of small islands offshore that Narváez named Islas de Ballenas ("islands of whales") after encountering a pod of whales nearby on July 15. The sighting strengthened his conviction that the Gran Canal probably had a second connection to the ocean from the north. The pair of islands still bear that name. Although it is not indicated on Carrasco's chart, today's large Englishman River empties into a huge estuary, which the Spaniards likely sighted directly north of the headland Carrasco indicated was occupied by the Qualicum people. The estuary may have inspired the explorers to hunt more wildfowl, unless it was low tide, when the ocean can recede up to a kilometre, making access to the huge sandy beach difficult. That easily could have caused the mariners to miss sighting the river flowing into the estuary. Nevertheless, they would have observed the large Qualicum settlement from the south side of the heavily forested headland, which is known today as Brant Point in the large Rathtrevor Beach Provincial Park.

From there, Narváez sailed southeast about another thirty kilometres on the 15th, passing Entrada de Rualcava (today's Nanoose Bay) en route, until he reached the entrance to a bay that he named Boca de Hijosa (present-day Nanaimo Harbour), in recognition of Francisco Hijosa, a naval administrator in San Blas. Later, Carrasco changed the name of the spacious, protected waterway to Boca de Wenthuysen after Francisco Javier Winthuysen, head of the Naval College in Madrid. Based on

Snunéymux^W chief.
(MUSEO NAVAL, MADRID)

Carrasco's chart, it would appear that the explorers cruised around the main harbour, rounded today's Duke Point and looked into the mouth of present-day Stuart Channel, but did not investigate it further. Narváez must have assumed that it was closed at the southern end where Mudge Island occupies most of the canal. If he had continued, he would have found a narrow opening to the side and discovered the two long channels that run southeast to the Southern Gulf Islands and Haro Strait, which the expedition had explored in late June.

(These routes and the associated archipelago would remain uncharted for more than six decades.)[5] Furthermore, Narváez certainly would have made first contact with the Snunéymux^W people, a large Island-Halkomelem-speaking group whose main settlement of Tle:lwx, occupied by more than one thousand people, was located at False Narrows — one of the two passes around Mudge Island.[6] (This might well have been the location of the Snunéymux^W chief whose portrait was drawn in 1792 by José Cardero, during the expedition that followed up on Narváez's discoveries.)

Instead of pursuing this southerly route, Narváez reversed his course and sailed east around a large island (today's Gabriola Island) to starboard of the *Santa Saturnina*. Rounding its northwest end, which Carrasco named Punta de Casatilli (today's Orlebar Point), Narváez started southeast in open water. Carrasco's chart shows that the expedition anchored, probably for the night, on the east side of this island about four kilometres south of Punta de Casatilli along what is now Whalebone Beach. Carrasco also named the next headland, which is another four kilometres to the southeast, Punta de Gaviola (subsequently corrupted to Gabriola),[7] where he drew three squares to indicate a Snunéymux^W village. It was probably either a hunting-fishing camp or a lookout. With no journals by any of the three *pilotos* on the expedition to rely on, it is impossible to explain how the explorers could have avoided meeting any people from this major Central Coast Salish group, whose vast traditional territory extended across the Salish Sea from the central mountain range on Vancouver Island in the west to the mainland in the east, and from the northern end of Texada Island in the north to the Gulf Islands in the south.

When Narváez left this anchorage on July 16 and continued southeast, it appears that neither he nor Carrasco saw the narrow channel at the south end of Gabriola Island (now known as Gabriola Pass), which separates it from the next island to the south (later named Valdes Island). After sailing a total distance of about twenty-five kilometres, they sighted a larger passage, which both *pilotos* charted as mouths and Carrasco named Boca de Poliel (today's Porlier Pass at the south end of Valdes Island). Travelling another twenty kilometres southeast along the shore of what soon became known as Galiano Island, Narváez took a sighting near a headland that on his chart was located at approximately 49°10' north latitude — about the same latitude as Isla de Zepeda and Punta de San José, which he had previously located on the eastern side of the sea.

A short distance beyond this observation point, both Narváez and Carrasco must have noticed a significant opening between the land they had passed (today's Galiano Island) and what appeared to be another island (the current Mayne Island), because an open-ended mouth appears on the charts of both hydrographers. This is the present-day Active Pass, which Pantoja almost discovered a month earlier from the opposite direction. It was here that the two parts of the expedition initiated by Eliza on June 15 intersected, the results of which would soon give Euro-American explorers their first realistic comprehension of the geographic and hydrographic scope of these two sections of the Salish Sea.

From here, Narváez continued to follow a southeastern course for about eighteen kilometres along the shore of what the *pilotos* assumed was a single island. (Neither Narváez nor Carrasco realized they were passing what are now Mayne Island to the north and Saturna Island to the south.) However, by the time they reached the strong current off tiny Tumbo Island at the entrance to Boundary Pass, the explorers must have known exactly where they were. Both Narváez's chart and that of Carrasco show a dotted line around all or part of Tumbo Island and its surrounding reefs. The line that Narváez drew here is distinctive in several ways: it is more pronounced than Carrasco's, darker than similar lines Narváez used to show shallows, exaggerated in size, and a complete loop encircling a tiny cross which Narváez inserted at various places to show where he took sightings. This would suggest that, to confirm the exact location of the place where they had first seen the Gran Canal, Narváez made one final observation on Sunday, July 17.

The Naming of Saturna Island

It is worth noting here, that neither Narváez's chart nor Carrasco's *working* chart named the point of land on the large island west of Tumbo Island, and it remained unnamed on Spanish charts for another year. However, Carrasco's *final* chart, on which he had written Pta. y Bajo de Sta. Saturnina ("Point and Shoal of Santa Saturnina") clearly paid tribute to Narváez's vessel and warned mariners about the reefs around Tumbo Island. Furthermore, it evidently inspired the lead Spanish explorer who followed in Narváez's wake (carrying Carrasco's *final* chart) to give the island its present name. After reconfirming and correcting Narváez's discoveries, Captain Dionisio Alcalá-Galiano drafted two charts of the Gran Canal del Rosario in 1792, which identified Isla de Saturna for the first time by that name.

In the first instance, Alcalá-Galiano hand-drew a sketch map, titled *Carta esférica de los reconocimientos hechos en 1792 en la costa N.O. de América*, and wrote the name Iª de Saturna (Isla de Saturna) just offshore from a landform that is now two islands: Mayne and Saturna. Later in the same year, Alcalá-Galiano placed the name Saturna *on* this same landform when he drafted his *Carta esférica de la parte de la Costa N.O. de América comprehendida entre la entrada de Juan de Fuca y salidas de las goletas con algunos canales interiors.*[8]

From there, all of Narváez's attention must have shifted to returning to Puerto de Quadra as soon as possible. His crew was tired, hungry, and growing weak. Food supplies were nearly exhausted. Consequently,

Narváez undoubtedly considered which of two routes would be the most familiar and direct to take before he entered the challenging canal that ran straight south to Juan de Fuca Strait: head directly east about thirty kilometres across the Gran Canal to anchor again at Punta de Loera (Lummi Bay) on the mainland, or continue southeast about twenty kilometres via the previously visited Isla de Sucia to an anchorage made earlier at the Islas de Aguayo. The former course was considerably longer, but it offered safer options in case of unfavourable winds or inclement weather; the latter was well-known, more direct, and shorter. Presumably, on July 18, Narváez took the first route, headed for the Islas de Aguayo, and anchored his vessels there for the night on the east side of the main island (today's Clark Island). Although the west shore has a sandy beach, strong currents can dislodge anchors. Smooth pea gravel forms the bottom on the east side, which offers the most direct access to Canal de Fidalgo (Rosario Strait).

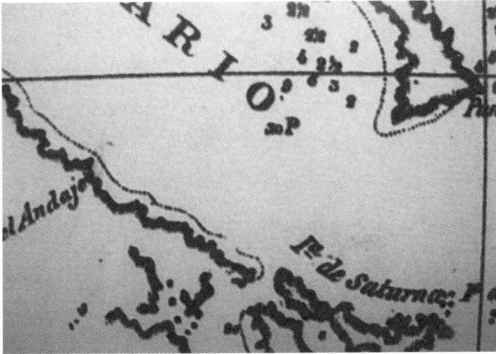

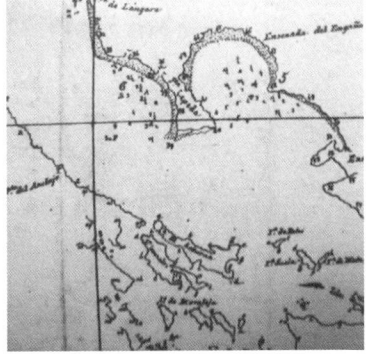

LEFT: Excerpt of Galiano's *Carta Esferica de la Reconocimientos . . .* , 1792;
RIGHT: Extension of Galiano's *Carta Esferica de la parte . . .* , 1792.

On July 19, Narváez entered the canal's powerful flow which he knew would take the expedition south about eighty kilometres to its urgent rendezvous with the supply vessel *San Carlos*. The *Santa Saturnina* sailed swiftly along the southwest side of Isla de Pacheco (Lummi Island) toward a small island which the *pilotos* had not charted earlier (today's Sinclair Island). Narváez had to make a quick decision: tack to starboard around the west side of this island and stay in the canal's

Adaptation of Carrasco's chart *Carta que comprehende . . .*, to show the sixth
phase of Narváez's exploration of Gran Canal, July 19–22, 1791.

surging current, or bear to port and cruise through quieter waters across
the entrance into Bellingham Bay. Being a prudent, cautious navigator,
Narváez probably took the latter route and coasted into the peaceful
anchorage at Punta del Socorro (Chuckanut Bay) which he had visited

earlier. Here, the hungry crew could obtain fresh drinking water, collect a plentiful amount of shellfish for a nourishing stew, and possibly shoot some wildfowl.

Staying out of the swift-flowing Canal de Fidalgo as long as possible while continuing to move southward, Narváez took his two vessels on July 20 through the quiet waters of Seno de Padilla (Padilla Bay) and then to the safe anchorage in Güemes Channel, which he had visited at the beginning of the expedition. From here, Narváez could observe the tidal changes, and plan a timely downstream departure the next day.

On July 21, Narváez roused his weary crew early to prepare for the final stretch of the expedition. The young navigator was eager to get underway because he had saved exploration of the critically important Ensenada de Caamaño (Admiralty Inlet) until the end of the voyage and he knew it would require as much time as possible. After both the *Santa Saturnina* and the longboat were rowed out of Güemes Channel into Canal de Fidalgo's main current, Narváez and Verdía steered their respective vessels due south twenty-five kilometres, avoided the two reefs at the entrance, and coasted out into the eastern end of Juan de Fuca Strait. Although the vessels were only about forty kilometres from Puerto de Quadra, the wind was so light and variable that the longboat had to be used to pull the schooner. Even though the twenty-one oarsmen maintained steady rotations and the tide was going out, it was grueling work on a mid-summer morning.

By noon, Narváez's vessels had managed to reach the tiny Isla de Bonilla (Smith Island) in the middle of the strait, where he could look into the Boca y Ensenada de Caamaño which was still about twenty kilometres away to the south. His men, however, were exhausted, famished, and discouraged. They still had some drinkable water on board, but there was no more food. With no wind to fill his sails, Narváez had only one option: give the crew a long, well-deserved rest and hope that the wind picked up. Even if it did, he realized he would not have enough time to explore the large waterway that seemed to extend southward a great distance.

In 1791, Smith Island and the much smaller Minor Island to the east were connected by a low sand spit, which ocean currents and tides pulled eastward from eroding, eighteen-metre-high cliffs on the west side of Smith Island. The low, grassy islands had a few trees that were important habitats for seabirds, and the beaches were a resting site for sea lions. (Today, both islands have been almost totally eroded by weather and rising sea levels.) Narváez knew it would be too risky to remain long in his present position, exposed to unpredictable weather. He decided to head for a safe anchorage near shore as soon as the men recovered some strength.

According to Narváez's later report to Eliza, by two o'clock in the afternoon the weather still remained unchanged. Furthermore, there had been an extremely low tide about one o'clock, so he now faced a strong incoming surge that would last several hours. Consequently, he explained the situation to the crews of both vessels, and the men reluctantly returned to the back-breaking, protracted task of towing the schooner while its eight oarsmen did their best to assist. Because momentum had to be maintained, the sailors took turns resting. By evening, they managed to reach an anchorage at a low point in the land along the north shore of Quimper Peninsula near today's Point Wilson. They had reached the west side of the Admiralty Channel's mouth and they were less than twenty-five kilometres from the supply vessel waiting in Puerto de Quadra. Knowing his men were too worn out to continue, Narváez sent the longboat to look for shellfish along the sandy shore and ordered two other parties to hunt game in the fields and forests above the bluffs. After consuming a rustic but nourishing stew, everyone on board collapsed for the night.

Fortunately, Narváez was able to catch a falling tide about five o'clock in the morning of July 22, and a few hours later the *Santa Saturnina* pulled into the anchorage inside Puerto de Quadra where Lieutenant Eliza had been waiting for twenty-one days aboard the *San Carlos*. What he and his right-hand man, Juan Pantoja, accomplished during this three-week period remains both unimpressive and murky.

⌒

On July 1, Eliza had claimed he could not lead the Gran Canal expedition because he was suffering from an unspecified illness. Since neither he nor Pantoja mentioned it again in their journals, it would appear that they were both healthy, able-bodied mariners, capable of using this opportunity to engage in exploration activities that would contribute in significant ways to the overall expedition. Surprisingly, that did not happen.

Eliza records doing only three things at Puerto de Quadra during Narváez's absence. First, he "looked over the country finding some level pieces of land for crops." Second, he became aware of "a great abundance of deer."[9] In this regard, Pantoja also reported that, on July 13, a "gunner" killed "a quadruped," which, based on the *piloto*'s long description was clearly a large elk.[10] According to Eliza it "served for food in abundance for three days for the crew ... which consisted of seventy persons, besides leaving a quarter for the wardroom."[11] ("We dined on it bountifully in the cabin for four days," wrote Pantoja, "and the crew for two.") Third, Eliza found "clay ... of a superior quality for any construction which one may wish to make," and he brought some back to "use for making an oven" on his vessel.[12] He excused his failure to describe any other wildlife than the single large quadruped (the description of which seems to have been derived from Pantoja's long account) by suggesting he had seen "all the animals" Quimper had described in 1790. Furthermore, of the three activities Eliza recounts in his single paragraph on this subject, only one of them (the elk episode) definitely occurred at Puerto de Quadra. The other two seemed to happen at Puerto de Córdova or at both places.

In any case, it is abundantly clear that, during this three-week-long interlude, Eliza neither conducted nor ordered any new explorations by sea of waterways on "the inside of Fuca" in accordance with "the plan" which accompanied his secret instructions from Commander Bodega.[13] The plan Eliza cited was the chart of Quimper's expedition in 1790, which clearly indicated three *open, discovered* but *unexplored* waterways (Canal de López de Haro, Boca de Fidalgo, and Boca de Flon) on the north side of Juan de Fuca Strait, and one large *apparently closed* bay (Ensenada de Caamaño) near the southeast end of the Strait that required further exploration. The Pantoja reconnaissance had dealt with the canal, and the Narváez expedition was addressing the two *bocas*. The Ensenada de Caamaño, however — which was only eleven kilometres east by sea of Eliza's anchorage at Puerto de Quadra — had not been investigated. If Eliza had bothered to take even a day-cruise there or ordered Pantoja to undertake a short expedition overland or by sea in a longboat, one of them certainly would have discovered what Narváez had recognized immediately during the first day of his expedition to the north: this bay definitely was *not* closed; it led to a wide, navigable canal that seemed to extend southward.

In presenting second-hand information about various occurrences during the Gran Canal exploration, in which he did not participate, Pantoja asserts at one place in his journal that the Ensenada y Boca de Caamaño "could not be explored [by Narváez] for lack of time."[14] In another section, however, he states on July 23, the day after Narváez returned, that there still appeared to be "sufficient time . . . to examine the *new* Boca de Caamaño"[15] (emphasis added). This clearly indicates that both Pantoja and Eliza had belatedly recognized the importance of exploring this waterway, which they had made no effort to investigate to even a limited extent, when they had plenty of time to do so.

Pantoja's journal makes it fairly clear how he spent his time at Puerto de Quadra during Narváez's absence. "As we were anchored in this port twenty-five days . . . we ascertained that it abounded in various kinds of fish, especially those called flounder, turbot, and dog-fish," he wrote. "The ground, although fertile, is of very little use for crops as water is lacking and it is all hilly [and] very rugged by reason of the many declivities in their sides. Among these the sailors and the troops saw bears, leopards [more likely cougars], coyotes, wolves, deer, hares, rabbits, two kinds of doves, and chickens [probably grouse]. They killed more than fifty of these birds and a few of the four-legged [animals], which served all as moderate refreshment, since we were in great need. To this is to be added the great abundance of a special thick bramble [wild blackberries] which at the end of July began to ripen." Pantoja also described seeing in the woods "some canoes closed with boards and capes, very well tied, which had inside some human skeletons, although there is no settlement in the neighbourhood of the port. Only some Indians came from outside from time to time in their canoes to trade boys."[16] These would have been Clallam people from either the village of Shkwee-uhn at the mouth of Entrada de Bertodano (Sequim Bay) or today's Diamond Point at the mouth of Puerto de Quadra (Discovery Bay).[17]

Although Eliza's instructions included an order to "examine carefully the true . . . character and number of Indians," this directive apparently did not filter down to his chief assistant at Puerto de Quadra. When Pantoja stumbled upon what was either a Clallam or Chimakum cemetery, which he neither understood nor honoured, he proceeded to label the entire bay — and thereby all the Indigenous people who lived there — a *matadero de racionales* (slaughterhouse of humans).[18] Pantoja's behaviour in this instance raises questions about his competence as an effective explorer. Instead of using his time at Puerto de Quadra to interact with the two Central Coast Salish groups whose traditional territories had overlapped on the Quimper Peninsula for several thousand years, Pantoja focused on a single incident to spread misinformation, bias, and disrespect about Indigenous people.

As commander of the expedition, Eliza clearly knew that Indigenous children had been bought by members of his expedition while it was at two locations. "During [our] stay in Clayacuat and in [Juan de Fuca Strait] seven Indian girls and thirteen Indian boys between four and twelve years of age were purchased for copper sheets," he would write on October 10, 1791, at Puerto de Santa Cruz de Nuca (the harbour at Cala de Los Amigos). "The naval officers [of which there were five], calkers (sic), carpenters, and some of the gunners have taken charge of them to educate and train them." Based on the record, it was Carrasco who transported twenty-two of these Indigenous youngsters back to San Blas (see Chapter 10). Although it is impossible to assess Narváez's involvement in this illicit trade, he had to have known what was going on.

The practical, altruistic rationale for engaging in trafficking Indigenous children advanced by Eliza had been recirculated for several years by Franciscan priests and Spanish officers. Based on the record, however, it rings hollow. Beyond the vague claims of one or two priests who hoped families in Mexico would raise young adults who might be sent back to their people as messengers of the new religion, there is no evidence that any education occurred.

A second justification that the Spaniards advanced for buying Indigenous children was the claim that they were saving the boys and girls from a worse fate at the hands of their own people. With little or no understanding of Mowachaht culture, the European intruders believed that the youngsters offered for trade — almost all of whom were either slaves or orphans — might be eaten during certain ceremonies. This alleged consumption of children was part of a long-held preconception among Europeans about cannibalism by Aboriginal peoples, which was based on ignorance, prejudice, recirculated misconceptions, rumour, and second-hand reports. The alleged practice of anthropophagy was also advertised enthusiastically by Maquinna and other trade-wise Indigenous chiefs who — knowing the European intruders better than they knew themselves — were skilled at simultaneously exploiting their property, increasing their wealth, and enhancing their charismatic power.[19]

In July of the following year, Eliza would state that, during his stint on the Pacific Northwest Coast a total of fifty-six Indigenous people had been "secured by purchase except [for] three men and a woman who voluntarily said they wished to accompany him to Spain."[20] If buying human beings, especially children, was representative of the "gentle" imperialism that some self-styled "post-colonial" writers claim the Spanish intended to practise on the Pacific Northwest Coast in order to gain the support of the people they were suppressing and colonizing, it was doomed to fail. Aboriginal resentment that smoldered for several generations after the Spanish departed, inevitably led to backlash, uprisings, and rebellion.

When the *Santa Saturnina* and her longboat finally pulled into Puerto de Quadra on July 22, Narváez and Carrasco went on board the *San Carlos* to give Eliza an overview of the expedition's results. Narváez noted that, during the first day of his departure from Puerto de Quadra, he had noticed that the Ensenada de Caamaño (today's Admiralty Inlet) was not "closed" as Quimper had thought. As Carrasco noted, it "is not an ensenada but an arm of the sea which trends to the southeast."[21] Because it was only about eleven kilometres from Puerto de Quadra, Narváez said he had planned to explore it on his return.[22] He had been unable to do this the previous day, however, because he had run out of food at the end of the voyage and his men were exhausted.

According to Pantoja, the next day Eliza "ordered the schooner to be hove down [careened] for cleaning her bottom, and to be supplied with food, water and wood [because] there [was] still sufficient time for the schooner and the longboat to examine the new Boca de Caamaño and [possibly] advance the discoveries in the [Gran] Canal." In the same ambiguous paragraph, however, Pantoja noted that Eliza had already prepared the *San Carlos* for departure and "determined to leave this port and the strait and direct his course for Noca (Nootka Sound)."[23]

Despite the fact that Narváez had been eager to explore the Boca de Caamaño and Pantoja had thought there was sufficient time to undertake that important task, all the mariners knew it was imperative to exit Juan de Fuca Strait as soon as possible. At this time of year, four factors made it difficult for sailing vessels to make headway westward: balmy days of little or no wind, inconsistent light breezes from the east, strong incoming summer tides, and the threat of unrelenting winds from the northwest. The latter were sometimes powerful enough either to force a vessel to remain inside the strait for days or drive it onshore, causing serious damage if not shipwreck. If the commander hoped to return to Nootka Sound before the heavy northwesterly storms commenced, he had to act decisively.

Although Eliza made no mention of intending to send Narváez to investigate the nearby bay that the commander had ignored for more than three weeks, he did indicate his departure plan in two ways. First, he reassigned some personnel.

"On the 24th, the captain and *piloto* of the schooner, José María Narváez, and four out of the five soldiers of the schooner were transferred, by order of the commander, to the packetboat [*San Carlos*]," wrote Carrasco.[24] If Eliza had ever intended to explore the promising "arm of the sea" that trended southeast, he had now clearly made up his mind to take another course of action. Carrasco was given command of the schooner *Santa Saturnina* because Lieutenant Eliza needed Narváez to draw charts and help draft the report to Bodega.

Second, Eliza issued new orders. "On the 25th of July, I determined to depart from the strait and take my course for Nuca as I had nine sick [crew members] and no fresh meat to give them,"[25] wrote Eliza. This seems to contradict the fact that forays ashore by hunters actually had yielded some meat from elk, deer, and a variety of mammals. Also, the large inlet offered a plentiful supply of wildfowl and fish. Furthermore, hardly any of the wild berries or fruits that grew in the area had been gathered.[26] The problem, therefore, appears to have been Eliza's failure to organize the supply of food responsibly and distribute it effectively. As a result, some crewmen were suffering from scurvy and others were plagued by colds, rheumatic pains, and dysentery.

Eliza was also anxious to send his report to San Blas, complete the challenging assignment that had proved daunting and unwelcome, and return to his wife and family in Cadiz as soon as possible. Despite his wife's persistent appeals to the naval department for her husband's re-assignment, he would have to remain in San Blas twelve more years.

"On the 25th both vessels [the *San Carlos* and the *Santa Saturnina*] set sail [from Puerto de Quadra] for the outside of the strait," wrote Carrasco "but on account of calms [they] came to anchor the same day." With little wind from the east, the officers were forced to wait for falling tides twice a day, and catch the outflowing current in which under-nourished, tired, demoralized oarsmen could use the schooner and longboats to tow the packetboat slowly from one anchorage to the next. Unfortunately, the strongest ebb tides tended to occur during the night.[27]

Working in shifts, the Mexican sailors, most of whom were conscripted peasants, endured the monotonous, back-breaking, gut-busting labour hour-after-hour. Their one motivation was the prospect of surviving this seemingly hopeless ordeal and eventually reaching Cala de Los Amigos, where they might have a half-decent meal. Working their way gradually westward about 140 kilometres in Juan de Fuca Strait toward the open sea, it took the expedition fifteen days to reach Bahía de Núñez Gaona (today's Neah Bay) at the south side of the entrance. Neverthe-less, the slow progress had two advantages. First, it gave Carrasco time to update the working draft of his chart, which had evolved throughout the expedition, and to consult with Narváez. The latter's working draft seems to have represented a more restricted initial naming of places, which the two explorers may have deliberately kept unchanged to show how their findings developed. Secondly, the delay resulted in the dis-covery of a harbour that Quimper had overlooked in 1790, and they named it Puerto de Nuestra Señora de los Ángeles (now Port Angeles). Carrasco marked it on his chart, and also inserted an inset of the "new" port. After stopping at Bahía de Núñez Gaona to prepare for the longer trip northwest to Nootka Sound, the two vessels finally departed on August 11.[28]

Although Eliza did not realize it at the time, he had missed his opportunity for recognition as an accomplished explorer twice in a period of one month. If, in late June, the unassertive commander had overruled the advice of his senior *pilotos*, and followed his original plan to accompany Narváez's expedition with the *San Carlos*, he could have kept the smaller vessels better supplied and thereby supported a longer expedition into one or more of the waterways that Narváez was unable to explore. These are now known as the Inside Passage to the north, the extension of Burrard Inlet to the east, and Puget Sound to the south. Since Eliza did not accompany the expedition into the Gran Canal, he could have used the time to at least investigate the nearby Ensenada y Boca de Caamaño. Then he probably would have personally discovered what soon became known as Admiralty Inlet and at least some of the extensive waters beyond. Eliza's brief, superficial reports and lack of initiative as an explorer would not go unnoticed by his superiors, because his ineffectual leadership caused the Spaniards to miss a golden opportunity to make two major European discoveries one year before Captain George Vancouver sailed these waters in similar vessels, finished mapping what is now the entire Salish Sea, and gained most of the credit.

Nevertheless, thanks entirely to the Narváez expedition, in mid-1791, Spain finally possessed the first picture of the size, shape, and possible extensions of the inland sea that so many European navigators had sought for more than two centuries. As designated commander of the expedition, Lieutenant Eliza would receive credit for its findings. As a prolific, albeit self-promoting chronicler, Pantoja would draw the most official attention because his long journal survived. Yet it was Narváez and his team of competent, dedicated *pilotos* who accomplished all of the investigation, hydrography, chart work, and 90 percent of the initial reports related to this pioneering exploration. Some Spanish government officials of the era recognized the importance of Narváez's discoveries and saw the urgent need for further inquiry, but they failed to act swiftly enough. Many historians who subsequently assessed Narváez's three-week-long voyage failed to recognize its full significance. Fortunately, those evaluations have begun to change as contemporary researchers revisit the historical record.

For written documentation of the Narváez expedition, we have to rely mainly on two sources: the brief summary report submitted by Eliza and Pantoja's extensive comments. Yet neither man conveyed first-hand information about the voyage, nor did they participate in any part of it. English translations of their reports along with three charts (by Carrasco, Pantoja, and López de Haro) are contained in two books by Henry R. Wagner.[29] Carrasco's map is the primary document. Although we also have Narváez's chart, we do not have a written record of his direct observations, because, as noted earlier, his diary of what became known as the Eliza expedition of 1791 has disappeared. In the process of translating, editing, and researching the sources of Narváez's original journal about his voyage to Alaska in 1788,[30] the author uncovered information that indicated this mariner definitely wrote a similar journal about his expedition in 1791. A continuing search for this document, however, has proved fruitless.[31]

A few contemporary historians in both North America and Mexico have realized that Narváez's voyage of 1791 was one of the most impressive pioneering European explorations in early Pacific Northwest Coast history, and it was critically important for Spain. Furthermore, it produced one of the most valuable nautical charts that was made during this period. Nevertheless, the significance of Narváez's achievements remained largely obscured until the late twentieth century for three reasons. First, except for Carrasco's remarkably informative chart, there was limited first-hand documentation. Second, the admirable achievements of the low-ranking *pilotos* who conducted the assignment would soon be overshadowed by the arrival of three rising, highly acclaimed captains, who had mastered more sophisticated methods of exploration. Third, the narrative of Pacific Northwest Coast history was about to shift from a largely Spanish point of view to an English perspective.

CHAPTER 10

The Super-Explorers Arrive

IF 1791 CAN BE VIEWED as the first act of a European operetta about the Salish Sea in which a few ordinary Spanish *pilotos* held centre stage briefly, the second act in 1792 would see three maritime all-stars dominate the performance. First, a pair of up-and-coming Spanish naval captains would outshine Narváez to the extent that the audience would shift its attention to their acclaimed deeds. Then, an ambitious English naval commander — would win so much worldwide recognition that his name nearly erased that of the humble *piloto*. Nevertheless, Narváez had led the way, and all three of these famous explorers would actually end up either relying on or verifying his findings. Meanwhile, Narváez would remain near the centre of the simmering Nootka Crisis.

Before this second act began, however, Narváez remained focused on tying up the loose ends of his nautical investigations during the last thirteen weeks. As the packetboat *San Carlos* and the schooner *Santa Saturnina* beat their way north from Juan de Fuca Strait along the outer coast of Vancouver Island on August 11, 1791, both vessels encountered heavy northwest winds. During the night of August 14, the commanders of the two vessels — Lieutenant Eliza on the packetboat and veteran *piloto* Carrasco on the schooner — lost sight of each other.

Eliza — accompanied by Narváez, Verdía, and Pantoja — pressed on northward aboard the *San Carlos* and managed to reach the outpost of Cala de Los Amigos in Nootka Sound on August 30, nineteen days after leaving Juan de Fuca Strait. Eliza was surprised to learn from acting commandant Saavedra that, in his absence, the ambitious scientific expedition headed by Alejandro Malaspina had visited the Pacific Northwest Coast, stopped briefly at Cala de Los Amigos between August 14 and 16, reconnoitred the inland channels of Nootka Sound from August 18 to 26 to make sure none of these led to a cross-continental passage, and then left for Monterey, California, the next day.

During his thirteen-day visit, Malaspina made astronomical observations to fix the location of Nootka Sound and calibrate the expedition's new chronometers. He linked his survey maps of the area to the baseline established by Captain Cook in 1778, which finally allowed for more accurate calibration between Spanish and British charts. Learning about some of these accomplishments, Eliza became even more eager to report Narváez's significant new discoveries and thereby gain recognition for the work that had been done during the past four months, although he had contributed almost nothing to the actual investigation. Unfortunately, the rather passive commander would have to wait four months before he could convey this information to his superiors. For his own reasons, Pantoja was also keen to advertise the expedition's accomplishments, as if he too had been involved in every aspect of the exploration.

Carrasco, on the other hand, would deliver the latest news about what was still thought to be a potential Northwest Passage route much sooner. After losing sight of the *San Carlos* on August 14, he battled stiff headwinds round the clock for fourteen days, trying to reach Nootka Sound. Low on provisions and water, he was finally forced to abandon the effort and sail south, arriving at Monterey on September 15 or 16.[1]

Seeing two Spanish corvettes lying at anchor, he saluted their prestigious commander, Alejandro Malaspina, with seven guns and proceeded to report Narváez's discoveries to the renowned explorer.[2] Malaspina had arrived at New Spain's Alta California headquarters five days earlier and did not leave for Acapulco until September 27. He was impressed to learn that Narváez had probed deep into the northern arm of Juan de Fuca Strait to "a latitude of about 49°40' north," and that it seemed to continue a great distance. However, the experienced commander and his talented scientific officers reportedly were disappointed by the lack of detailed information provided by Carrasco, whose only documented information would have been the working chart that he carried.

"The lack of log books and the poor skills of *pilotín* Carrasco . . . prevented us from acquiring all the information we needed to include [Narváez's discoveries], so interesting to geography [and] to our own work in this area," wrote Malaspina condescendingly in his journal.[3] Although Carrasco was no mere junior mate, and his working chart had a certain beauty, evidently he and Narváez had not been sufficiently meticulous about taking bearings and recording their observations. Consequently, Felipe Bauzá — the best Spanish cartographer of the time — who was in charge of charts and maps on Malaspina's voyage, believed that whenever Eliza's *pilotos* turned in their finished charts, they would not have much value for increasing geographical knowledge. José Bustamante, Malaspina's co-captain, apparently agreed.[4]

One of several factors that might have made Malaspina and his assistants skeptical about the value of the somewhat ambiguous picture Narváez and Carrasco left for future explorers, was the mapping procedures they had used. As mentioned earlier, both *pilotos* worked from individual field surveys which they drew of different parts of the exploratory voyage. During the expedition, and after it finished, these tentative mini-charts would be patched together and adjusted in order to draft a larger chart of the entire voyage, which they would make as accurate as possible. If this rearrangement was not done precisely, however, errors occurred. Field charts not only had to be rescaled to match, but sometimes they needed to be reoriented. Normally a compass was

used to orient these drawings to magnetic north, which in the Gran
Canal was about twenty degrees east of geographic, or true, north. Because it is standard practice to have geographic north at the top of published maps, all the field charts which used compass north at the top had
to be twisted slightly to fit. As one perceptive researcher has noted, this
"confusion" about orientation seems to have contributed to the vague
geography that Narváez and Carrasco depicted in Boundary Bay.[5] On
his comprehensive chart, Carrasco inserted a note in this bay which
reads, "Declin. en Observ. a N.E.12°30'" (declination in observation to
N.E. 12°30'). In other words, the difference between compass north and
true north at this point in the Narváez expedition appeared to be 12°30'
to the northeast, whereas it should have been about 12°20' to the northeast. In fact, on the five inset charts on Carrasco's map, three indicated a
compass variation of 17°, one of 18°, and one of 16°. If Carrasco revealed
this sort of information to Malaspina's cartographers, it is not surprising
that they were dubious about the expedition's findings.

Between 1790 and 1792, the approach to maritime investigation on
the Pacific Northwest Coast evolved from the crude reconnaissance of
exploration to sophisticated scientific surveying. And the results of the
Narváez expedition in the Gran Canal marked a significant transformation in that process. The charts produced by Narváez and Carrasco
were remarkably more detailed and accurate than anything previously
produced about this particular area, and therefore both revealed new
information and confirmed previous hunches. At the same time, because these navigators lacked precision instruments, their cartography
was derived from latitudes and longitudes based on dead reckoning
with sextants, compass readings, direct observation, legitimate infer-
ence, incomplete data, and some speculation.[6] Nevertheless, the significant amounts of verified new information contained in those charts —
especially the two connections from Juan de Fuca Strait to a large inland
sea which might have one or two extensions of its own — would be
enough to whet the appetite of imperialists, fabulists, and scientists
alike.

Malaspina in particular was far more intrigued by Narváez's discoveries than he first indicated. When he finally returned to Madrid three

years later, he deleted the skeptical entries in his journal about what he learned from Carrasco. This led one reliable biographer to "suspect that [Malaspina] wanted the credit himself for mapping the only unexplored waters the [Eliza] expedition sailed through during the entire voyage."[7]

On October 6, Malaspina arrived in Acapulco, where he remained until early November while he concentrated on planning another comprehensive scientific exploration that would include Spain's final quest for the elusive passage. On October 12, Malaspina wrote a long letter to the viceroy, informing him about Carrasco's report. The importance of Narváez's reconnaissance must have impressed Revillagigedo to a considerable extent, because he proposed a proper follow-up expedition to the same waters by more accomplished navigators who would be accompanied by a naturalist and one or more artists. Malaspina knew he would be able to recruit top-notch officers who, having graduated from both the Academy of Midshipmen and the Astronomical Observatory School of Higher Studies, would be trained in the latest scientific methods and capable of using the new British chronometers for determining longitude accurately by means of regular astronomical observations. Knowing he could not lead the new reconnaissance because his more comprehensive expedition would soon sail to Asia, Malaspina looked "with envy toward those who achieve this important commission."[8]

After leaving Monterey on October 16, Carrasco continued south and arrived at his home port of San Blas on November 9.[9] Because Commander Bodega had been meeting with Revillagigedo in Mexico City to receive his orders for the new expedition and discuss their implications, Carrasco delivered the extract of his voyage to Salvador Fidalgo, who forwarded it to the viceroy three days later. Presumably he held on to his working chart. Carrasco's vessel also carried twenty-two Aboriginal boys and girls who had been purchased with copper sheets during Eliza's expedition. There is no documentary evidence concerning their actual condition when they arrived in San Blas or when they were taken elsewhere in Mexico. The authorities there were led to believe that the expedition's officers and some of the crew intended to educate and raise the youths. Carrasco returned thirty-seven untraded copper sheets.[10]

Meanwhile, at Cala de Los Amigos, Narváez, Verdía, and Pantoja laboured over two charts, which they completed by October 15 under Eliza's supervision. Narváez and Verdía collaborated in producing *Carta esférica que comprehende los interiores . . . Año de 1791*. It represents the original naming of places, which are recorded in Narváez's distinctive handwriting. This map shows the entire area investigated by the explorers. The route that was travelled can only be surmised in different locales by the order of the numbers for places that were discovered and named. Dotted lines clearly indicate places that were passed but not confirmed as well as shoals and sandbars, which are coloured light orange.[11]

Although Pantoja had remained at Puerto de Quadra with Eliza during Narváez's entire expedition, he produced the *Pequeña Costa que comprehende los interiores . . . año de '91*, which is a well-organized, carefully drawn duplicate of the primary chart produced by Narváez and Verdía. Meanwhile, Eliza had prepared other materials for the report he would send to Commander Bodega at San Blas and Viceroy Revillagigedo in Mexico City. Faced with spending a second winter in command of the garrison at Nootka Sound, Eliza confronted another critical problem: many of his men were sick, some were seriously ill, morale was at a low ebb, and food supplies were insufficient to sustain a large contingent of men.

Therefore, on October 15, Eliza ordered Ramón Saavedra to take command of the *San Carlos* and set sail for San Blas as soon as the weather and wind were favourable. His assignment had two purposes: to deliver Eliza's report about the expedition, which included the charts by Narváez and Pantoja rolled up in "well sealed . . . tin tubes," and to transport a maximum number of men back to Mexico as soon as possible. Given the unhealthy living conditions at Cala de Los Amigos, it is probable that some of the Indigenous children whom the Spaniards had purchased were on board as well. According to Pantoja, who was the only *piloto* assigned to this voyage, the packetboat carried sixty-four of the eighty-man crew that Eliza had brought with him eighteen months earlier, and "eight of them were unable to render any service, including the first boatswain" because of illness.[12]

Gran Canal

del Rosario

A Bahía à encontrar

Longitud occidental del meridiano de S. Blas.

Narváez's *Carta esférica ...*, of Gran Canal, 1791. (HONNOLD/MUDD LIBRARY)

Eliza Confronts Another Winter at Nootka Sound

Despite his abhorrence of remaining at Nootka Sound any longer than absolutely essential, Eliza recognized that, as commander of the remote outpost, he was duty-bound to endure a second winter at the port that he no longer considered "friendly" in any respect. Incapable of relating effectively with Maquinna and other local chiefs, the lieutenant assumed two caretaking roles: keeping an eye on the huge frigate *Concepción*, which rode at anchor in the harbour; supervising the small contingent of men left at the settlement. The latter included the *pilotos* Narváez and Verdía, Captain Pedro Alberni, and the surviving members of his Catalan volunteer soldiers. (Their sergeant, Miguel Zieras, had died from "an inflammation in his belly" nineteen days earlier.)[13]

This dispirited group of Spanish officers and Mexican soldiers may have been prepared to share cramped living quarters in the dank garrison and survive on limited, inadequate food supplies during the bitterly cold winter ahead. What they had not taken into account, however, was the prospect of remaining stuck in the isolated, inhospitable settlement for nine months, while their political masters in Europe debated ways to implement the Nootka Sound Convention of 1790, and their superiors in the navy discussed ways to follow up on the results of the so-called Eliza Expedition.

When the weather improved on October 18, Saavedra started transferring the small amount of food that remained stored aboard the *San Carlos* to keep it from being consumed by what Pantoja said was an "incredible number of rats" on the vessel. Although the men killed many of these vermin every day, the rodents "destroyed a set of sails and various strands of the cables" kept in the storeroom. Because the ropes had been made from agave plants, the rotten fibres had become a major food supply for the rats. In contrast, the only food on hand for human consumption was 794 kilograms of poor quality ordinary biscuits left at Cala de Los Amigos a month earlier by Malaspina. Despite the urgency to depart, inclement weather conditions forced Saavedra to remain in port six more days, while he and Pantoja stood watch every night.[14]

On October 24, the *San Carlos* finally warped out of Nootka Sound in a dense fog toward the open ocean, but Saavedra was unable to make sail until the next day, and then persistently "squally" weather and heavy seas made for slow progress for a week. When these conditions cleared up on the 31st, Saavedra was finally able to head southeast for Monterey, which they reached on November 9. After replenishing their pathetic food and medical supplies, mending two sets of tattered sails, and loading wood and water on the vessel, Saavedra set sail for San Blas on November 24. Twenty-eight days later they anchored in their home port.[15]

On December 22, 1792, Saavedra delivered Eliza's report to Commandant Bodega. It included Narváez's comprehensive chart of the 1791 expedition and the duplicate drawn by Pantoja. According to Pantoja, during the next seven days, he and Carrasco correlated "the plans and descriptions" that were on hand. [16] These consisted of Carrasco's working version of his *Carta que comprehende* . . . , which he had brought with him fifteen months earlier; Narváez's *Carta esférica que comprehende* . . . , which Saavedra had just delivered from Nootka Sound; the findings of the Quimper expedition in 1790; and Pantoja's *Pequeña costa que comprehende*. . . . This is when the detailed, comprehensive, final version of the *Carta que comprehende* . . . was drafted, which is in Carrasco's distinctive handwriting.[17] Although it does not show the exact route that the expedition took, it can be approximated by following two details: soundings that were recorded and tiny anchors. A note states that the latter indicate "good anchorages" and small "red squares at the edge of the coast are ranches [settlements] of Indians."

Comparing the original naming of most places shown on Narváez's *Carta esférica que comprehende* . . . and Carrasco's *working* version of his *Carta que comprehende* . . .[18] with those shown on Carrasco's final chart, it is clear that several place-name changes were made in San Blas, probably at Bodega's suggestion. For example, the point on the southern side of the entrance to Juan de Fuca Strait was named originally Punta de Martínez by Narváez in 1790, and he used that important toponym on his *Carta esférica*. Carrasco, however, has no name for this location on his working chart, but he restored it on his final chart. Although the temperamental, impetuous Martínez had become a political hot-potato

Carrasco's *Carta que comprehende . . .*, 1791. Often misattributed to Narváez, this map was the most revealing cartography about the Pacific Northwest Coast before 1792. It showed the first outlines of present-day Vancouver. (MUSEO NAVAL, MADRID) for Madrid, he was still admired in New Spain for two things: halting British expansionism in Nootka Sound without going to war, and formulating an economic plan that might have enabled Spanish trading companies to compete sufficiently on the Pacific Northwest Coast to maintain Spain's influence.

As soon as this cartographic work was completed, Pantoja immediately sent his chart and journal about the expedition — to which he had contributed in only minor ways — to his influential friend in Peru, Don José de Prados y Salbatierra. Never hesitant to take credit for the achievements of others, Pantoja created the false impression that his chart was the most comprehensive one that had been made and that he had participated in the entire expedition. "I have the pleasure of sending you," he wrote, "a long extract and *the* respective chart of, in my opinion, the splendid expedition which *we* have made from Noca to the Estrecho de Juan de Fuca, in the interior of which, *we* discovered the great Canal de Nuestra Señora del Rosario la Marinera, which is wider than the strait itself and whose limits up to now are unknown" [19] (emphasis added). Pantoja went on to say he believed that the information he was providing would significantly influence the balance of power between Spain and Britain on the Pacific Northwest Coast.

Eliza's report to Bodega and Viceroy Revillagigedo also stressed the need for further investigation of one of the two large channels Narváez had been unable to explore in the Gran Canal. After detailing the results of the expedition, Eliza made these comments about the Northwest Passage: "If there is anything of particular importance or consideration to be explored on this coast, it is this large canal. According to my method of thinking, and that of my *piloto* [Narváez], it promises much. . . . I assure your Excellency that the passage to the Atlantic Ocean, which foreign Nations search for with such diligence on this coast, cannot in my opinion, if there be one, be found in any other part; it is either, I think, by this great canal [in other words, behind the two 'islands' Narváez had sighted at the mouths of the Fraser River and Burrard Inlet], or it is a continent." [20]

When Viceroy Revillagigedo read this, his previously formulated plan to complete the survey — spurred primarily by Malaspina — took on new urgency. For commander and *piloto* of the expedition, Malaspina initially had professed great confidence in the ability of three veteran mariners: Francisco Antonio Mourelle, Jacinto Caamaño, and Juan Carrasco. Mourelle and Caamaño were experienced San Blas officers who had sailed northward several times and were familiar with all the maps and accounts collected over the years. Carrasco had sailed with both captains and he had recently drafted the most complete chart of the Narváez expedition, incorporating information from his chart and those of Pantoja, and López de Haro.

The latter had joined Carrasco in Spain's second exploration of Juan de Fuca Strait in 1790, which was headed by Quimper. Although he had not participated in the Eliza expedition, López de Haro was instructed to draw a chart that included findings from both voyages. His *Plano reducido que comprende parte* ..., finished at San Blas in January 1792, was almost an exact copy of the two charts made by Narváez and Pantoja, except that he added toponyms given by Quimper in 1790.[21] As previously noted, López de Haro also added the name Boca de Flórez for the opening that Narváez had left unnamed on his chart of the expedition. It is highly likely that Bodega would have suggested this insertion to draw the Viceroy Flórez's attention to the need for further investigation of this channel.

While all this information was being gathered, the viceroy had already placed Mourelle in charge of the expedition, which was ready to depart on December 1, 1791. Malaspina, however, soon changed the viceroy's mind. Before leaving Mexico in late December on a voyage to the Marianas and the Philippines, Malaspina convinced Revillagigedo to replace Mourelle with two of his recently promoted, most promising captains — Dionisio Alcalá-Galiano and Cayetano Valdés y Bazán. (In his letter of December 29 to José de Prados, Pantoja had reported that "in San Blas two small schooners have been built and sent to Acapulco" for these commanders.[22] The "small schooners" were the Spanish goletas[23] *Sutil* and *Mexicana*.) Despite Carrasco's demonstrated skills, impressive contributions, and direct knowledge of the territory, he was replaced by the more versatile José Cardero. This draftsman turned "proto-artist" was given the assignment of artist, scribe, journalist, map-maker, and *piloto*.[24] Felipe Bauzá, the best cartographer of the time, was also added to the team, which received its orders from Malaspina in December 1791 and Revillagigedo a month later.[25] Consequently, due to Malaspina's political connections in Madrid and his own assertiveness, the subsequent exploration by Alcalá-Galiano and Valdés was informally removed from the viceroy's direct jurisdiction and made part of Malaspina's widespread mission.[26]

Although the winter of 1791–1792 at Cala de Los Amigos may have been discouraging, unpleasant, and lethargic for Narváez, Spanish activities on the Pacific Northwest Coast would reach a peak in 1792, and the young mariner would find himself close to three of the four major developments that took place: Bodega's efforts to negotiate a boundary agreement with his British counterpart, Captain George Vancouver; Caamaño's explorations in Alaska; Fidalgo's establishment of an outpost at Núñez Gaona (Neah Bay); and the follow-up investigation of the Gran Canal by Alcalá-Galiano and Valdés.

Thoroughly prepared, confident, and determined to accomplish the objectives authorized by the viceroy, Bodega also intended to establish a stronger Spanish presence on the entire Northwest Coast. On February 29, three large vessels left San Blas: the giant frigate *Santa Gertrudis*, with Bodega in charge; the frigate *Princesa*, commanded by Salvador Fidalgo; and the 213-ton brigantine[27] *Activa*, commanded by Salvador Menéndez. After several months of refitting, the *Sutil* and the *Mexicana* finally headed north from Acapulco on March 8, with Alcalá-Galiano and Valdés carrying secret orders from Malaspina to "obtain complete knowledge" of the two openings in the Gran Canal sighted by Narváez and Carrasco, in the hope that one of these channels would lead to a northwest passage across the continent. Among the navigational maps that they carried was Carrasco's final hydrographic chart of Narváez's findings. The frigate *Aránzazu*, commanded by Jacinto Caamaño, was also sailing directly to Nootka Sound with more supplies for the dreary outpost that Bodega would soon transform into a bustling settlement. The *pilotos* on board were Juan Pantoja and Juan Martínez y Zayas.

For Eliza, Narváez, and the other winter-weary men who had been anticipating a resupply ship from San Blas for several weeks, Bodega's arrival in late April was a welcome sight. By the 13th of May, Cala de

Los Amigos was crowded with seven Spanish vessels — the six above as well as the huge frigate *Concepción*, which had been stationed there since 1790. It was the largest naval force that any nation had sent to the Pacific Northwest Coast during the eighteenth century. Operating separately or in pairs, each vessel would have a role to play in Bodega's coordinated plan.

LEFT: Dionisio Alcalá Galiano; RIGHT: Cayetano Valdés.

Straightaway, Bodega directed the unloading of supplies on the frigate *Aránzazu* that were desperately needed at Cala de Los Amigos. Then he had the remainder, which were destined for the California missions, transferred to the *Concepción*. This freed the shallower-draft ship for Caamaño to use for one of Bodega's primary objectives: completion of all coastal cartographic work from Nootka Sound to Bucareli Sound (well north of today's Dixon Entrance) in what is now southern Alaska. Bodega had named the sound in 1775 during his first voyage in the Pacific on Spain's second expedition to the Pacific Northwest Coast under the leadership of Bruno de Hezeta. Now, Viceroy Revillagigedo had instructed Bodega to chart the complex archipelagos along the coast from Bucareli Sound at the south end of today's Prince of Wales Island southward to Nootka Sound. The objective was to determine conclusively if there was an inlet that would lead to another legendary waterway — the Strait of Bartholomew Fonte — the existence of which continued to find some credence. (Narváez would soon find himself engaged in assisting with a large portion of this reconnaissance.)

Sailing from Nootka Sound on June 13, Caamaño was accompanied by the experienced Juan Pantoja (first mate), Juan Martínez y Zayas (second mate), and José María Maldonado (naturalist).[28] Caamaño explored Bucareli Sound, used longboats to penetrate the numerous channels and inlets in that area, and followed one large strait (today's Clark Trough) northward for more than 160 kilometres to about 55°05' north latitude before foul weather forced him to turn back. Nevertheless, he would continue surveying all uncharted coastal waters in this area throughout the summer, when Narváez would join the expedition in his own vessel.

Meanwhile, Bodega had launched a full-scale construction program in Cala de Los Amigos, where Narváez was stationed. He would see the small outpost transformed as it became, once again, the focal point of the most intense geopolitical action along the entire West Coast. The redevelopment project converted the old garrison and a few shacks into a functional settlement of numerous buildings surrounded by a palisade. Bodega fostered friendly relations with the Indigenous people, trade was lively, and chiefs were welcomed as visitors aboard Spanish vessels. Chief Maquinna, who had developed a knack for cultivating relationships with important European visitors, forged a strong working relationship with Bodega. The two men reportedly dined at the same table almost every day, and "amatory scenes" involving Indigenous women and the Spaniards were not uncommon.[29] Throughout the spring and summer of 1792, Cala de Los Amigos would be visited by a steady stream of vessels captained by key individuals who were familiar with the events of 1787–1789 that led to the Nootka Crisis and were responding to Bodega's request for eyewitness testimony so he could prepare for his negotiations with Captain George Vancouver, who had been designated as the British commissioner. Trading vessels from a variety of nations also frequented Nootka Sound.

The arrival on May 13 of Alcalá-Galiano and Valdés at Cala de Los

Amigos was another event that must have made a strong impression on Narváez. He was aware of their mission and the fact that a significant part of it would involve reconfirming many of the findings he had made the previous year and verifying others. Consequently, he had looked forward to meeting the two captains in person.

Initially, however, Alcalá-Galiano and Valdés concentrated on making critical repairs to their twin vessels, resupplying them as much as possible, and supplementing their crews with a few of Alberni's Catalan volunteers. During this period, Bodega undoubtedly introduced Narváez to the two captains so they could show him Carrasco's final chart — which Narváez had not yet seen — and ask questions related to their imminent investigation. On May 18 and 28, Alcalá-Galiano and Valdés also finely calibrated their new chronometers by making observations of Jupiter's moons, probably with Narváez and other officers standing by.

At Nootka Sound, the highly touted captains were primarily intent on carrying out one of their numerous specific cartographic assignments — reconfirmation of the exact location of Yuquot (in other words, Cala de Los Amigos or Friendly Cove), which Malaspina had calculated less precisely the previous summer.

At the same time, however, the two bright, forward-looking explorers were genuinely interested in demonstrating their expensive, new chronometers and explaining how to use the instruments. Narváez was familiar with using a quadrant and a sextant to take accurate sightings, and he had heard about the new chronometer. Nevertheless, he must have been fascinated by the opportunity to observe first-rate leaders of an important scientific expedition employ the instrument in the field. Along with the other skilled *pilotos* in the Pacific Ocean, Narváez had always struggled with the problem of knowing his actual longitudinal position.

To their credit, these early navigators carried out extensive explorations at the outer-reaches of the Spanish empire without the precise timekeeping instruments needed to determine longitude with certainty. They estimated their longitude by measuring the distance they travelled in a given period of time, using instruments such as a towing log and a pair of half-minute hourglasses, and then related this data to the meridian of San Blas which they arbitrarily set at 0°. (At that time, mariners could choose a variety of meridians as 0° because Greenwich had not yet been established as the universally accepted prime meridian.)[30]

Therefore, it would have been intriguing for Narváez to see how celestial observations with sextants combined with new astronomical tables could be used to calibrate an amazing timepiece that was only twelve centimetres in diameter, fix one's longitudinal position at any given moment, and finally produce more reliable charts. He looked forward to seeing how the follow-up examination of the Gran Canal by the two ascendant captains would compare with his earlier findings.

Early on June 5, the *Sutil* and the *Mexicana* left Nootka Sound and headed for Puerto de Núñez Gaona (Neah Bay), where Bodega had ordered Fidalgo to establish a base of operations that could control the vital waterway of Juan de Fuca Strait. From there, Alcalá-Galiano and Valdés would almost immediately launch their intensive investigation of the Gran Canal.

Although Narváez's brief encounter with the two mariners who would soon gain worldwide fame had to have been a memorable moment, the young *piloto*'s rewarding experiences did not end there. In recognition of his achievements during the Gran Canal expedition, Bodega promoted him on July 20 to *piloto de segunda clase* (second mate)[31] and commissioned him to complement Caamaño's expedition by using launches from the Concepción to make detailed explorations of "the lateral coasts . . . up to 50° latitude" north of Cala de Los Amigos, which included three large archipelagos: Nootka Sound, Esperanza Inlet, and Kyuquot Sound.[32] Malaspina had started the task, but he had concentrated on searching for a water passage across the huge land form, which had not yet been identified as an island. Consequently, he instructed Bodega to ensure that his initial survey was finished properly. Based on his proven skills, Narváez was an ideal selection. Presumably, Verdía went with him.

Four days later, Bodega ordered Narváez's former commander, Francisco Eliza, who had served on the Pacific Northwest Coast without respite since March of 1790, to take command of the *Concepción* and sail southward. The frigate was loaded with supplies, which Eliza was expected to deliver to the California missions en route to San Blas. Bodega also ordered Pedro Alberni to accompany Eliza to Mexico, and to return the remaining members of his Catalan volunteers to their garrison in Guadalajara.[33]

Meanwhile, Alcalá-Galiano and Valdés had left Puerto de Núñez Gaona on June 8, sailed eastward through Juan de Fuca Strait, and entered Fidalgo Channel three days later. Alcalá-Galiano's priority was finding any unexplored waters that extended east into the continent, in particular the existence of Boca de Bodega y Quadra, which Narváez had surmised, and Carrasco had renamed Boca de Florida Blanca on his final chart (quite possibly to catch the eye of Conde de Floridablanca, head of the King's cabinet until February 1792). Consequently, Alcalá-Galiano opted not to explore the southward trending Boca de Caamaño (Admiralty Inlet), which would have led the Spanish explorers into Puget Sound. Coincidentally, Captain George Vancouver had just finished exploring these waters when Alcalá-Galiano and Valdés were entering Juan de Fuca Strait. The celebrated encounter between Alcalá-Galiano and Vancouver, however, would not occur until June 22 near an anchorage in the Gran Canal marked on Carrasco's map off Islas de Lángara (Point Grey).

In an English translation of his journal, Alcalá-Galiano gave this account of the historic meeting: "At seven in the morning a boat was sighted, which we did not doubt would be that of the English. It set course to come alongside, and three officers came aboard this ship, being the commandant of the expedition, Mr. Vancouver, his lieutenant Mr. Puget, and a midshipman. They told us they had been engaged during the preceding days in exploring various inlets, and showed us [their] plans.... After seeing our map of the strait [Carrasco's], Mr. Vancouver reverted to the undertaking of joining the two expeditions."[34]

Vancouver wrote: "As we were rowing, on the morning of Friday the 22nd, we discovered two vessels at anchor under the land. These vessels, His Catholic Majesty's brig *Sutil*, under the command of Senor Don D. Galiano, with the schooner *Mexicana*, commanded by Senor Don C. Valdés, both captains of frigates of the Spanish Navy, had sailed from

Acapulco on the 8th of March in order to prosecute discoveries on this coast. Se. Galiano, who spoke little English,[35] informed me, that they had arrived at Nootka Sound on the 11th of April, from whence they had sailed on the 5th of this month, in order to complete the examination of this inlet, which had, in the preceding year, been partly surveyed by some Spanish officers [Narváez and his two colleagues] whose chart [Carrasco's] they produced.[36] I cannot avoid acknowledging that, on this occasion I experienced no small degree of mortification in finding the external shores of the gulf had been visited [by Narváez and Carrasco] and already examined a few miles beyond where my researches during the excursion had extended. . . . Their conduct was replete with that politeness and friendship which characterizes the Spanish nation; every kind of useful information they cheerfully communicated, and obligingly expressed much desire, the circumstances might so concur as to admit our respective labours being carried on together."[37]

That famous event has taken precedence as the official date of "discovery" of the city now known as Vancouver. In reality, three large groups of Central Coast Salish peoples — the Musqueam, Squamish, and Tsleilwaututh First Nations — had occupied the territory for many thousands of years before the European explorers arrived. And as has been seen, the first European vessel to sail upon the waters of English Bay and probe the mouth of Burrard Inlet was the *Santa Saturnina* in 1791, making the twenty-three-year-old Narváez and his crew the first non-Indigenous men to view the forest-clad north shore mountains that rose above what they thought might be the northern entrance to the Northwest Passage.

In the early 1790s, the impact of the Narváez expedition's findings were profound. To appreciate the magnitude of this exploration of what is now the largest portion of the Salish Sea, the Spanish navigator's twenty-one day voyage needs to be viewed from two perspectives.

The first one is geographical. By producing an informative map of the shores of two straits and several large bays that totalled approximately 7,000 square kilometres, Narváez and his first mate Carrasco gave European explorers their first knowledge of this region. Consequently, this reconnaissance triggered a transition from fable to fact

Aboard Capt. Galiano's *Sutil* off Point Grey on June 22, 1792, a "mortified" Capt.
George Vancouver learns that Narváez had surveyed the Gran Canal eleven months
earlier. Painting by Ian Bateson. (CITY OF VANCOUVER ARCHIVES)

concerning the long-held notion that an undiscovered passage across
the North American continent connected the Atlantic and Pacific
Oceans at this latitude. If it existed, Narváez and his fellow mariners
revealed two possible openings that warranted further investigation. If
these channels did not lead to the fabled waterway, then explorers could
save considerable time and money by searching for an Arctic route.
(Galiano, Valdés, and Vancouver had all been sent to the newly discovered Gran Canal to resolve the remaining geographical conundrum,
which would soon happen.)

The second way of assessing the importance of the Narváez expedition is to acknowledge its impact on local history. The fact that Spanish
mariners were the first Europeans to sail across the northern section of

the Salish Sea, make first contact with Indigenous peoples living there, and give colourful names to numerous locations could enrich our understanding and appreciation, to the extent that we are aware of this cultural heritage, which started to ebb all too soon.

One year after Narváez's expedition, the first wave of another European nation's imperialistic ambitions rolled across the same waters, left the pioneer explorers overshadowed in its wake, precipitated increasingly rapid intercultural change, erased hundreds of place names and substituted new ones (Vancouver Island, being just one). Soon, only echoes of the Spaniards' presence remained, but some of these remarkable men, the places they named, and those that were named after them are beginning to receive fresh attention. Today, as cultural diversity is celebrated and historic roots are re-examined, British Columbia's Spanish heritage is gradually regaining its well-deserved stature.

Whereas this part of the Narváez narrative has focused on restoring his place in local history, the next section will describe the navigator's ongoing connections with a wider scope of geopolitical developments that were taking place on the Pacific Northwest Coast as New Spain re-evaluated its colonial objectives.

PART III

New Spain
Changes Course

CHAPTER 11

Spanish Influence
Wanes

FOLLOWING THEIR CELEBRATED encounter in the Gran Canal on June 22, 1792, near Islas de Lángara (Point Grey), Captains Alcalá-Galiano and George Vancouver agreed to coordinate the rest of their investigations in this part of the Salish Sea on a few different tasks, exit the waterway by different routes, and meet at Cala de Los Amigos (Friendly Cove, to the English). Captain Vancouver and William Broughton left the inland sea by way of Juan de Fuca Strait and headed north for Nootka Sound to meet with Bodega. Captains Alcalá-Galiano and Valdés sailed northwest following Carrasco's chart and discovered the inside passage through Discovery Passage, Johnstone Strait, and Queen Charlotte Strait that led to the ocean.

Vancouver arrived at Cala de Los Amigos in command of the *Discovery* on August 28, 1792, accompanied by Broughton on the *Chatham*.

Maquinna entertains Bodega y Quadra and Vancouver at Tahsis, 1792,
in a drawing adapted by Atanásio Echeverría. (MINSTERIO DE ASUNTOS
EXTERIORES, MADRID)

That evening, the two British captains and several officers went on
shore to pay their respects to Commander Bodega. "We found him
[residing] at a decent house [that was] two story high, built of planks
with a balcony in the front of the upper story after the manner of the
Spanish houses," wrote Vancouver's surgeon Archibald Menzies in his
journal. "One end of the ground floor was occupied as a guard room
and the other as a kitchen and servants' hall, while the upper story was
divided into small apartments and occupied by [Bodega] and his officers, who were separated by a large hall in the middle where they commonly dined. On our landing, the guard was turned out in honor to
Capt. Vancouver, and [Bodega] and his officers received us at the door."[1]

As Narváez was still stationed at Cala de Los Amigos, he would have
been present on this memorable occasion unless he was busy charting
one of the nearby waters in conjunction with Jacinto Caamaño's assignment. As noted earlier, Malaspina had commissioned the latter to revisit the entire coast north of Nootka Sound up to 50° latitude and make

detailed, reliable charts. To assist in this project, Bodega had placed Narváez in command of the *Concepción*'s launches so he could remap Nootka Sound and then work his way up the coast to complement Caamaño's efforts. If Narváez was in port on August 28, the young explorer whose recent discoveries had triggered the high-profile follow-up investigation by Alcalá-Galiano and Valdés, had to be waiting expectantly to learn what these two men would report. What he could not have anticipated was that a famous English explorer would arrive first.

Three days later, however, Alcalá-Galiano and Valdés also arrived at Cala de Los Amigos, having proved once and for all, two important geographic facts: the huge landform they had circumnavigated for the first time was an island, and neither the eastern nor the northwestern extensions of the Gran Canal, which Narváez had discovered east of this island, led to a cross-continental waterway.[2] The former was closed, and the latter led westward to the open ocean. After reporting their findings to Bodega, the two Spanish captains headed south the next day.

Bodega and Vancouver — appointed by their respective governments as commissioners to settle specific territorial issues arising from the Nootka Sound Convention of 1790 — proceeded to take a couple of days to become acquainted with each other, and to discuss the current situation at Cala de Los Amigos in general terms. To conclude these introductory exchanges, Bodega proposed that a group of Spanish and English officers should make an excursion by boat about forty kilometres inland to pay a formal visit to Chief Maquinna at Tahsis, where he was living with his brother Chief Guadazapé. On September 4, two boats from the *Discovery*, one from the *Chatham*, and a large launch from the *Concepción* left Cala de Los Amigos and headed northwest in Tahsis Inlet, winding between steep, heavily forested mountains. Because Narváez had navigated this route a year earlier in the *Santa Saturnina* and had been recharting these waters as part of Caamaño's expedition, he was probably pointing the way in the lead vessel.

"We proceeded at an easy rate, with drums beating and fifes playing, to the . . . entertainment of the natives" wrote Archibald Menzies. "It gave a martial solemnity to our visit, highly gratifying to their feelings in thus imitating their own customs on similar occasions, for in their friendly visits their approach is always announced by vociferous songs and plaintive airs." As they approached Tahsis the next morning, Menzies said that "the boats made a kind of martial parade with our little musical band before . . . we landed amidst the noisy acclamations of the natives. Maquinna [and] his brother . . . received us on the beach and we were conducted to the Chief's House."[3]

As soon as everyone was seated, Bodega explained to Maquinna that he and Captain Vancouver had agreed informally that the Spanish probably would be leaving the Mowachaht's territory soon, and he assured the chief that the English officers could be relied upon to maintain "friendly intercourse with all [of] his tribe." Vancouver and Broughton gave presents to Maquinna, his brother, their wives, and Maquinna's thirteen-year-old daughter Apenas who had recently been named successor chief. In return, Maquinna gave his visitors some valuable furs. Then various Mowachaht performed several dances wearing intriguing masks, and, according to Menzies, Maquinna topped off the ceremony by "capering and dancing with great agility . . . to the satisfaction of the whole group." Vancouver responded by having some sailors "dance a reel or two to the fife."[4]

After spending two days visiting Tahsis, the "excursion" of Spanish and English officers returned to Cala de Los Amigos on September 7 to find that Maquinna and a large number of his people, who left Tahsis early, had arrived the previous day. To entertain the Mowachaht, Vancouver arranged an impressive display of fireworks.

With these important diplomatic preliminaries completed, Bodega and Vancouver began to address the primary purpose of their long-anticipated meeting: to secure Spain's compliance with the terms extracted from Madrid during the first Nootka Sound Convention of October 1790, which officially ended Spain's claims to a monopoly of settlement and trade on the Pacific Northwest Coast, but left several thorny territorial issues unresolved. Although the two naval officers established a friendly, mutually respectful relationship, they soon realized that the diplomatic task their respective governments had given them went far beyond settling specific issues related to Cala de Los Amigos. Because each of the two negotiators had received only general directives about arriving at a settlement that strengthened his nation's long-term interests in the region, the commissioners found themselves at loggerheads regarding implementation of political-military-economic power on the Pacific Northwest Coast.

Vancouver believed that he had to acquire complete control of Nootka Sound including all of Cala de Los Amigos, that Spain should withdraw its sphere of influence to San Francisco, and that British subjects should have free access to all territory north of that latitude. Bodega was willing to return a tiny portion of Cala de Los Amigos to the British as remuneration for offences that had caused the Nootka Crisis, but he was convinced that Spain's "legitimate right" to ownership of the rest of Nootka Sound remained inviolable, and that Madrid might consider withdrawing as far as Juan de Fuca Strait on the condition that the possibility of re-establishing its sovereignty at Nootka Sound in the future remained open. Recognizing that they were deadlocked, Bodega and Vancouver agreed to refer the issue back to Madrid and London for renegotiation. The stalemate postponed indefinitely the intended turnover of Nootka Sound to Britain, enabled the two conscientious and principled naval officers to break off discussions as good friends on September 20, 1792, and for three decades it left the major land mass that had been disputed with a bifurcated name — Isla de Quadra y Vancouver (the Island of Quadra and Vancouver).

Meanwhile, Caamaño had returned on September 8 from his three-month-long surveying expedition of the upper northwest coast, which had been complemented by Narváez's charting of three archipelagos closer to Cala de Los Amigos. While Bodega and Vancouver were focused on their high-level political negotiations, Caamaño and Narváez undoubtedly coordinated the cartographic work they were expected to submit to Malaspina. By mid-September, Bodega realized he was not going to achieve a satisfactory agreement with his British counterpart, and he was making plans to depart for Monterey. These included instructions sent to Fidalgo at Núñez Gaona (Neah Bay) to dismantle the base there and make preparations to load all equipment, animals, and personnel on the *Princesa* for transfer to Cala de Los Amigos as soon as he arrived.[5]

One day after negotiations with Vancouver collapsed, Bodega placed Caamaño in charge temporarily at Cala de Los Amigos, left Nootka Sound on the *Activa*, and headed south to Núñez Gaona. (Vancouver, however, remained in Nootka Sound.) By September 29, 1792, the Spanish establishment at the entrance to Juan de Fuca Strait had been dismantled completely, the *Princesa*, commanded by Fidalgo, sailed for Cala de Los Amigos carrying anything useful, and Bodega headed south to Monterey on the *Activa*. As soon as Fidalgo took over, Caamaño started preparing the frigate *Aránzazu* for departure to San Blas. Before he left, however, two memorable events took place that Narváez must have experienced. First, Caamaño hosted a grand party in the garrison's main room to acknowledge Fidalgo's role as New Spain's nominal commander at the outpost, and he invited Vancouver, his officers, and other captains in the port to attend. Unfortunately, when Maquinna and some of his relatives showed up, anticipating the same hospitality they had enjoyed with Bodega, Fidalgo turned them away. Understandably, the proud chief was offended. The second event was a farewell banquet that Vancouver held for all the Spanish officers on the eve of Caamaño's departure. It featured twenty-one-gun salutes and toasts to the British and Spanish sovereigns.[6]

On October 4, the *Aránzazu* left Cala de Los Amigos under Caamaño's command and sailed south for San Blas. Because Narváez had been working closely with Caamaño on a report to Malaspina, he was undoubtedly on board and finally headed for his home port. As the first winter storms rolled into Nootka Sound, Vancouver's two warships fought their way into the open sea on the 12th and headed for Monterey and then San Francisco.

At the end of October, Bodega was still in Monterey waiting for his vessels to be restocked and overhauled so he could return to San Blas. His health, however, had taken a turn for the worse. The challenging work that he had undertaken recently combined with long-standing physical problems had taken its toll. Forced to stay in Monterey and rest, he nevertheless used the time to "correlate in a [single] chart the results of the explorations undertaken since 1774," which indicated areas that needed further investigation.[7] Bodega was convinced this comprehensive map, drafted for Malaspina, would form the basis for a major expedition to survey the Pacific Northwest Coast from 50° to 60° N and prove that this area was a vast archipelago, as the recent explorations of Caamaño and Narváez had demonstrated. Bodega acknowledged that it would probably take six to nine months to prepare for such a voyage.

During the winter of 1792–1793, Madrid's policy regarding Nootka Sound changed from viewing Cala de Los Amigos as an indispensable outpost for maintaining a dominant Spanish presence on the Pacific Northwest Coast to recognizing it had become a geopolitical albatross. When Revillagigedo retired in November 1792, he advised that Spain could no longer sustain its claim to absolute possession of the entire Pacific Coast of North America. It lacked the military forces, the vessels, the interest in trade, and the money to compete with other ambitious nations, particularly Britain which seemed to be interested in extending its influence into Alta California. When France went to war against Britain and Spain in 1793, the ensuing Anglo-Spanish alliance opened the door toward resolving outstanding differences between England and Spain. This included settlement of financial claims at Nootka that had finally been resolved on February 12 of that year by a second Nootka Sound Convention. All that remained was the unresolved dispute over access rights and boundaries that had arisen between Bodega and Vancouver. Meanwhile, the viceroyalty in Mexico anticipated the probable necessity to withdraw New Spain's sphere of influence to the natural boundary of Juan de Fuca Strait (not San Francisco, as Britain was proposing), and it began to devote more of its limited resources to defending the settled coasts of Mexico and the two Californias — in other words, occupying, colonizing, and trying to control the territory from what is now Guatemala in the south to Juan de Fuca Strait in the north, and from the west coast to as far inland as possible.

Upon his return to San Blas from Nootka Sound, most likely aboard the *Aránzazu*, Narváez found that his former commander, Francisco Eliza, was still ensconced reluctantly as base commandant in Bodega's absence, despite his oft-expressed eagerness to gain a transfer to Spain.

When Bodega finally arrived from Monterey on February 1, 1793, after trying unsuccessfully to recuperate there for several months, he was worn out, disillusioned, seriously ill, and in debt. He soon went into semi-retirement in Mexico City.

Another Narváez–Malaspina Connection

Between December 1791 and November 1792, Alejandro Malaspina continued to pursue the ambitious goals of his voyage of exploration halfway around the world, which he believed would yield enough sound cartographic, ethnographic, and political information to enable Madrid to formulate a more progressive, functional foreign policy for governing its widespread colonies. On December 20, 1791, Malaspina and José Bustamante had sailed from Acapulco across the Pacific Ocean to Guam — the only stopping-off point in a three-month crossing — and the Philippines. Arriving in Manila Bay on March 25, 1792, the expedition spent nine months collecting scientific and geographical information. Although Spain had held the Philippine Islands since Miguel López Legazpi's conquest in the sixteenth century, little detailed information was known about the area. Consequently, Malaspina sent Bustamante to Macau on the *Atrevida* from April 1 to May 19 of that year, to perform gravitational experiments and evaluate the Portuguese government. The Malaspina expedition also conducted extensive, complex hydrographic surveys, one of which was a chart of the central part of the Philippines. Malaspina probably sent a copy of this back to San Blas on May 13, 1792, with Captain Emanuel Quimper aboard the *San José y Las Ánimas*,[8] to show subsequent Spanish captains the most direct routes through the complex Philippine archipelago to Manila Bay. Almost one year later, this chart apparently landed on Narváez's desk, because he would have a version of it with him when he sailed to Manila in the spring of 1793. The Malaspina expedition had left Manila on November 15, 1792.

On April 8, 1793, Narváez left San Blas on his first voyage to Manila. He was carrying Royal Services documents and serving as lieutenant of the frigate *San José y Las Ánimas*, which was commanded by Caamaño.

Narváez also seems to have carried the partially redrafted chart for the expedition mentioned above. Titled, *Plano de la zona central de las Islas Filipinas, que comprende Sur de la Isla de Luzón, parte de las Isla de Samar encierra esa zona, y el estrecho de San Bernardino*, it shows southern Luzon Island and the Sibuyan Sea in the north-central area of the Philippines. Although it was originally drafted by members of the Malaspina-Busta-mante expedition, it is signed in one corner by Narváez.[9] Delineations of certain features along the route may have been added by Narváez during his month-long visit, and the chart's worn condition indicates that it was probably used for navigational purposes. Narváez delivered government documents to both Manila and Macau.

By avoiding the monsoon season, Caamaño was able to make the round-trip voyage in seven months. Nevertheless, with only two other officers on board — Narváez, and a junior *piloto*[10] — he experienced daunting navigational challenges. The frigate battled tempestuous seas, encountered two tropical cyclones, and endured endless thunderstorms.

∾

By the time that Caamaño and Narváez returned to San Blas in No-vember 1793, negotiations between Spanish and English officials about settling boundary and sovereignty conflicts on the Pacific Northwest Coast had been going on for most of the year. Now these were close to being concluded, and Narváez soon would find himself involved — albeit peripherally — in another significant historical development: the closing scene of New Spain's five-year-long intense involvement in geopolitical tensions related to Nootka Sound.

On January 11, 1794, Spanish and English representatives meeting in Madrid signed the third Nootka Sound Convention. Spain formally renounced its rights to Nootka Sound, but a ceremonial handover still had to be carried out on site. Although Britain immediately dispatched a Lieutenant Thomas Pearce of the Royal Marines to confirm the pact, he would not reach New Spain on his way to the Pacific Northwest Coast for several months. Meanwhile, Bodega died in Mexico City in March 1794, and he was replaced in the autumn by Brigadier General

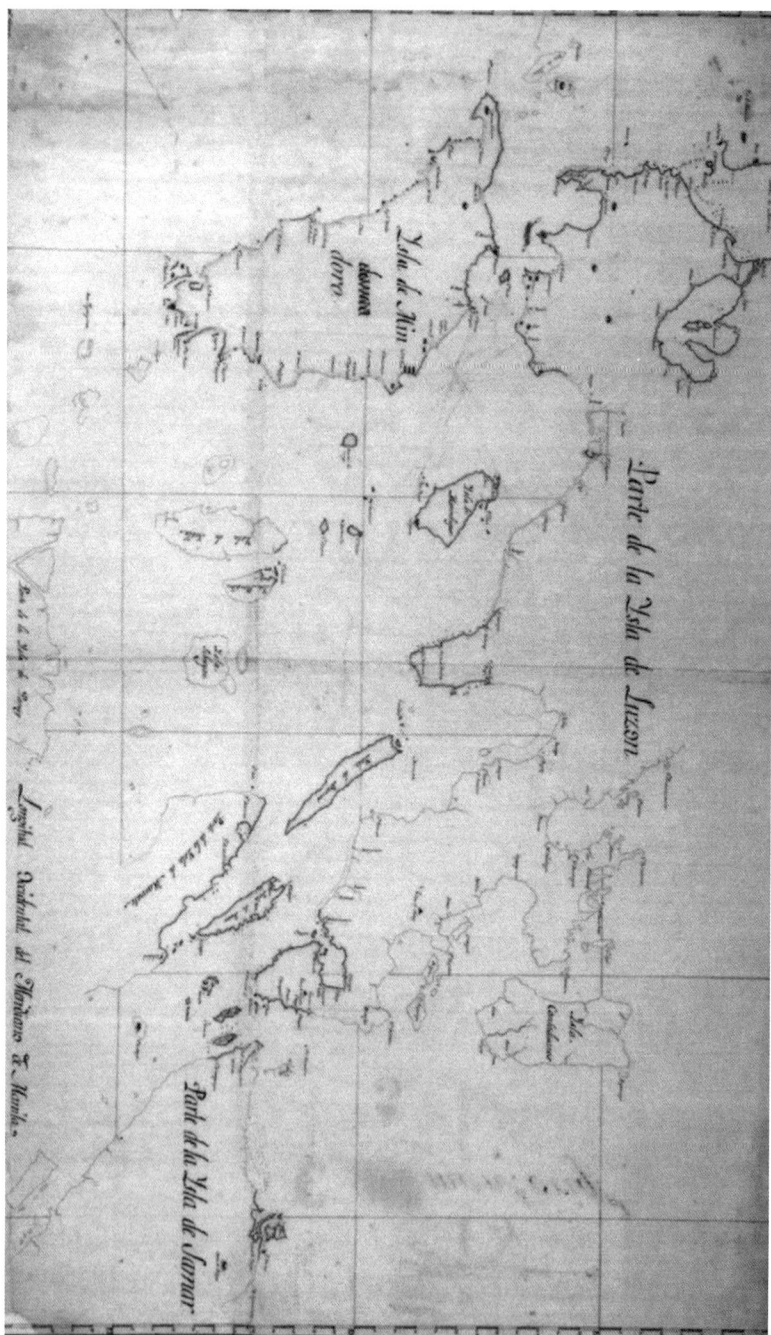

Chart of central zone of Philippines by Narváez et al., 1793. (MUSEO NAVAL, MADRID)

José Manuel de Álava as the new commandant of San Blas and commissioner for Nootka.

On June 23, 1794, Narváez was appointed *piloto havilitado de primera clase* (qualified first mate) — the rank in the Spanish Navy that he would hold for the next twelve years.[11] Less than a month later the 26-year-old mariner left San Blas in command of the frigate *Princesa* with the assignment of assisting the garrison at Loreto, near the southern tip of the Baja California peninsula. Soon after Narváez returned to San Blas in November, Lieutenant Pearce — the new British commissioner — arrived, seeking passage to Nootka Sound.[12] He was transported there on January 5, 1795, on the 213-ton brigantine warship *Activo*, which had been reconfigured in 1793 or 1794 from its earlier incarnation as the *Activa*. It was commanded by Frigate Lieutenant Cosme Bertodano, with Narváez serving as first mate and purser. When the brigantine reached Monterey, Brigadier General de Álava came aboard bearing the authority to represent the Spanish king during the subsequent handover ceremony. Narváez remained on the expedition as it continued north, carrying orders to assist in the evacuation at Cala de Los Amigos. The *Activo* sailed into the long-contested harbour on March 16, 1795.[13]

Assuming command at Cala de Los Amigos, Álava ordered the deconstruction of the entire Spanish outpost while he negotiated agreements with Pearce regarding these procedures and the official ceremony. Narváez helped supervise the actual work that was undertaken. Álava also faced the unwelcome task of confronting a controversial issue raised by the conduct of the man who had been serving as commander at Cala de Los Amigos, Lieutenant Ramón Saavedra. He had not only tolerated, but strongly encouraged the procurement of Aboriginal children — a practice that, as has been seen earlier, had been going on for years. Twenty-eight of these "purchased" youngsters were still living in the Spanish settlement when Álava arrived.[14] Álava found the practice objectionable, realized he could not address it satisfactorily in the present circumstances, and reported his concerns to Miguel de la Grua Talamanca, Marqués de Branciforte, Viceroy of New Spain (1794–1798).

On March 28, 1795, Álava and Pearce finally met to fulfill the last

Inset of Cala de Los Amigos from Carrasco's *Carta que comprehende* . . . , 1791, showing Spanish base. On shore, north to south, in first row: ship's warehouse, commander's orchard, carpenter and blacksmith, commander's house, hospital and food storage, bread oven. In second row: soldiers' quarters, captain of soldiers house, sergeant's house, captain's orchard. Battery on island.

requirement of the third Nootka Sound Convention: the reading of a Declaration and Counter Declaration by an official representative of each of the two nations. Spain was to recognize British claims and to restore lands which theoretically had been taken when the Spaniards established their outpost. The British representative would receive the lands, take possession by raising the Union Jack, and then both nations would depart. From that date forward, Nootka Sound was to be open to the citizens of both countries, who might construct temporary buildings but no permanent settlements. If a third nation attempted to establish itself on the Pacific Northwest Coast, both Spain and Britain would co-operate to defend the shared sovereignty.[15]

Because this ceremony marked the final settlement of the protracted Nootka dispute and corresponded with Spain's withdrawal from the arena of international competition north of Juan de Fuca Strait, it was one of the most significant events in Pacific Northwest Coast history. The shifting intercontinental plates of imperialism were generating a small, sharply focused geopolitical tremor.

On that Saturday morning in March, Narváez was part of the official group of commanders, officers, chaplains, and a few soldiers and sailors who heard Álava and Pearce read their declarations, saw the Spanish flag lowered at Cala de los Amigos, and watched the British flag run up and down. Then Álava, Pearce, Saavedra, Narváez, and a few other Spanish officers boarded a vessel and sailed about five kilometres away to bid farewell to the Mowachahts' three main chiefs, who welcomed Spain's withdrawal. For several years, Chief Maquinna had repeatedly asked when the Spanish planned to leave his favourite village site. Álava gave each chief gifts of copper and cloth that he had brought from Mexico. The Spanish general even let Pearce hand out some of these presents because the British officer had only his own flag to give away. Legend has it that Pearce gave the Union Jack to Maquinna, informing the Mowachaht chief that he was to hoist it whenever a vessel sailed into what was to be officially known as Friendly Cove. Álava also gave each chief one of the silver medals that had been dedicated by the merchant guild of Mexico City.[16]

Inclement weather kept Álava and Pearce from leaving aboard the *Activo* until April 2. Meanwhile, Narváez supervised the destruction of the buildings he had helped erect five years earlier. By April 16, Saavedra was ready to depart in command of the *San Carlos*. The former Spanish buildings were nothing but rubble, and the Mowachaht were already setting up makeshift houses. According to Saavedra, a persistent food shortage had prompted some of the Mowachaht to trade Indigenous clothes, masks, and other artifacts that they knew the crew members and soldiers valued as souvenirs.

The Mowachaht also offered to sell more children, and Saavedra encouraged his men to buy as many as possible.[17] Once Viceroy Branciforte heard about the large number of children that had been purchased, it appears that he made some "inquiries at Acapulco, San Blas, and Tepic [which] seemed to point out that most of the children were being raised as the sons or daughters of the soldiers or seamen." He did not say how the other boys and girls fared, nor did he address the possibility that some of these youth were being raised to become domestic servants, low-paid workers, or prostitutes. Although Branciforte was reportedly "satisfied by the morality of this traffic" in children, he "expressed some reservations," which prompted him to "inform the imperial government that he would investigate the numbers of Northwest Coast Indians resident in Mexico and whether there had been any complaints about poor treatment or sale of children."[18] Although the nature of the viceroy's "reservations" are clear, there is no indication that such an investigation was undertaken. If it was, it would have been difficult, if not impossible to locate all the youngsters who had been taken to Monterey, San Blas, or Tepic.

Furthermore, no effort was made at that time to examine how and why this type of human trafficking occurred. That would be left to future historians. One of them was Christon I. Archer, who analyzed the issue briefly when he assessed New Spain's impact at Nootka Sound as of March 1795. As explained in Chapter 8, it was Franciscan friars who initiated this sort of trade in children. Archer noted that, during the Franciscan's six-year-long stint at Cala de Los Amigos, they had been unable to establish a mission, as had been accomplished in the Californias. Consequently, Archer reasoned, they had failed to gain the total control of the daily lives of the Indigenous people that was necessary to achieve any degree of "spiritual conquest" over the Mowachaht. Instead, they actively engaged in purchasing Aboriginal children, which they justified with the notion that they were saving the boys and girls from slavery, sacrifice, and cannibalism.[19] Although Archer's explanation describes how this alleged missionary zeal may have gained widespread acceptance among the Spaniards on the Northwest Coast, it says nothing about the morality of the practice or the validity of the rationale used to justify it. Regrettably, we have no record of what Narváez thought about the issue.

Having fulfilled his orders at Cala de Los Amigos and observed most of the dramatic and disturbing events that occurred there between early 1789 and the spring of 1795, Narváez boarded the *San Carlos* and headed for San Blas. Spain's northernmost outpost on the Pacific coast had come to a quiet end, while the Mowachaht salvaged bits of metal, planks, and anything else left behind by the Spaniards. They even dug up the cemetery and removed nails from coffins for conversion to fish hooks.[20]

In December 1795, Narváez made his second voyage to Manila to deliver government documents. He sailed aboard the brigantine *Activo*, which was commanded by Salvador Fidalgo, with whom he was well acquainted. From Manila, Narváez was ordered to carry other documents to two warships in Macao. According to his service record, "he returned by the northeast past Hermosa Island [Taiwan] and the islands of Japan, a navigation [route] entirely unknown to the Spaniards" up to that time.[21]

On October 23, 1796, at age twenty-eight, Narváez married María Leonarda Aleja Maldonado, age sixteen, in the bride's hometown of Tepic, Mexico, about fifty kilometres east of San Blas. Narváez' fellow *piloto*, José Verdía, served as best man. For a time, the couple lived in San Blas before settling in the Indigenous city of Tepic, conquered by Spain in 1542, and now the capital city of the small province of Nayarit. Between 1802 and 1819, they would produce seven boys and two girls.

Now that New Spain had given up its effort to compete with Britain for control of the Pacific Northwest Coast, Narváez would find himself engaged in a series of challenging, new assignments both at sea and on land. In 1797, Francisco Eliza, still serving as commander at San Blas, commissioned Narváez to make a topographic map of the entire territory that comprised the first militia division on the southern coast of New Spain. The chart was sent to Viceroy Marques de Branciforte in Mexico City.

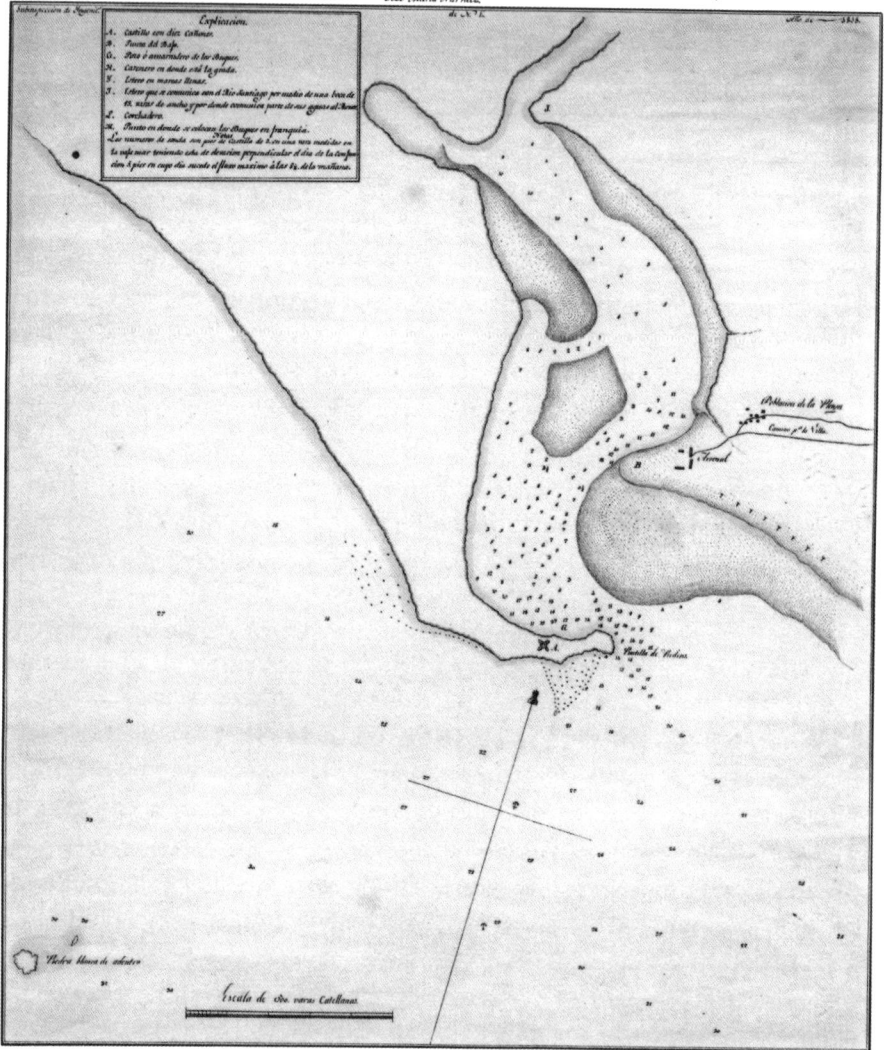

Narváez's plan of San Blas Harbour, 1803. (REAL ACADEMIA DE LA HISTORIA, DEPARTAMENTO DE CARTOGRAFÍA Y ARTES GRÁFICAS, MADRID)

During Narváez's first seven years of married life, his wife would give birth to four children in Tepic. Meanwhile, between February 1796 and December 1803, Narváez undertook military and diplomatic missions to Lima, Guayaquil, Panama, Loreto, and four garrisons in Alta

California. Because the port of San Blas had been gradually silting up for years, Narváez was ordered to make a detailed hydrographic survey. In addition to soundings inside and outside the harbour, his survey indicated several other noteworthy features: the fort with ten cannons at the entrance point (A); the cove where vessels were rigged (G); Shoal Point, where the sandbar threatened to choke off the mouth (B); the confluence of the Santiago River's two arms with the estuary where the water is only eleven metres wide (J); and the island of "white stone inside" offshore which was worshipped by the Wixarika people. (Although Narváez completed the chart in 1803, the Viceroy Juan José Ruiz de Apodoca (1816–1821) would not request a copy until 1818.) On June 17, 1804, Narváez left San Blas for San Francisco, Monterey, Santa Barbara, and San Diego in command of the *Activo*, which was armed for war with sixteen cannons. He carried orders to join the *Princesa* in halting "the contraband which strangers engage in on the coast."[22]

Narváez became an *alférez de fragata* (frigate ensign) on October 20, 1806. He would retain that rank for more than eleven years. Less than six weeks later, his wife María would give birth to their fifth child, Pedro Nolasco Antonio José María Narváez. Between 1805 and 1810, Narváez made at least six supply-and-support voyages to the garrisons in Loreto and the Californias. Sometimes he commanded a vessel, but he usually served as purser or captain's secretary.

In 1808, Narváez was commissioned to survey and construct a new road through the rugged mountains between San Blas and Tepic. After surveying the route that spring, he started overseeing construction of the route during the summer. The gruelling project forced him to endure blistering hot weather and a terrible infestation of insects. Road building continued throughout the next year, but the undertaking would soon be interrupted by a popular rebellion that was spreading throughout Mexico. It would test Narváez's allegiance in several ways.

CHAPTER 12

The Revolt of 1810
in New Spain

DURING THE NEXT thirty years, Narváez would witness momentous upheaval in New Spain, which would cause widespread political, social, and economic changes throughout the country. Confronting these developments would present the experienced seafarer with new challenges and gradually reshape his personal destiny.

By 1800, a pervasive desire to become independent from Madrid had been building up momentum in New Spain. The wellsprings of the rebellion were embedded in the caste system which the Spaniards had brought with them to this part of their far-flung empire.

Throughout the seventeenth and eighteenth centuries, this rigid socio-economic hierarchy had shown no signs of weakening. At the top were the *peninsulares* — those born in Spain. Their less fortunate countrymen called them *gachupines*, "wearers of spurs." They composed the smallest, richest, and most influential class. As a principle of colonial policy, Madrid tended to appoint these people to all the important positions of responsibility. Most of the *gachupines* lived in Mexico City, Veracruz, and the major provincial towns.

Although the first conquistadors did not bring women with them, Spanish women soon immigrated to New Spain, and almost all of them married *gachupín* men. Within two or three generations, their offspring — considered *criollos*, simply because they were born in Mexico, not Spain — outnumbered the *gachupines* and resented them deeply because of their lock on power. These ambitious *criollos* formed the second most important class in terms of social and financial prestige. Their broad geographic distribution gave them widespread influence among the masses of people. Their erudite leaders were in contact with worldwide liberal ideological currents. According to the rigid caste system, a *criollo* could have up to one-eighth Indigenous ancestry (in other words, one great-grandparent or the equivalent) without losing his or her social place.

The third group was called *mestizos*. Born of Spanish and Indigenous parents, they had almost no opportunity to rise socially or politically. Some of them managed to become merchants, however, and occasionally grew wealthy. Below them were eight or more castes, including *mulatos* — the offspring of Spaniards and Africans (who had been imported as slaves). At the bottom were *zambos* — the children of African and Indigenous persons.

Although their primary motivations were different, *criollos* and *mestizos* would lead the struggle for independence from Spain, which had been smoldering for years. The frustrated *criollos* had developed a strong sense of national identity and confidence in their collective future, and they yearned for access to power. Yet they had limited sympathy for a violent uprising among the oppressed masses of people. Widespread discontent among *mestizos* stemmed from the fact that the better paying employment opportunities were restricted to *gachupines* and *criollos*. *Mulatos* and other people at the bottom of the rigid, exploitive social order were demoralized, desperate, and angry enough to follow any leader who promised liberation from the unrelenting poverty and oppression they experienced every day.

The forty-two-year-old Narváez belonged to the *gachupín* class, his children were *criollos*, and throughout his naval career he had been a loyal supporter of the viceroyalty in New Spain. At the same time, he had many friends among the growing *criollo* population, he interacted with them in a variety of ways, and he understood their ambitions and long-term goals. As a conservative loyalist, however, he favoured gradual, peaceful change, not the violent revolutionary acts that were being advocated in many parts of the country.

On September 16, 1810, a full-fledged revolt broke out when the maverick Catholic priest Miguel Hidalgo launched a poorly organized armed movement about 240 kilometres northeast of Mexico City. The white-haired priest was joined by a young military officer named Ignacio de Allende. Both men were liberal *criollos*. Strong support for the spontaneous uprising came from large numbers of peasants and miners in the silver-rich fertile plateau surrounding Mexico City, which was known as the Bajío. Many of these people were trying to escape virtual slavery. The growing horde of insurgents carried the banner of the dark-brown Virgin of Guadalupe as their revolutionary symbol.

Hidalgo unleashed a highly charged rebellion against injustices. From the beginning, it took on the fervour and appearance of a religious crusade. The revolt spread rapidly and its untrained army expanded. When the rebel forces numbered 80,000, Hidalgo attacked Mexico City — the viceroy's seat of power. On the brink of capturing the city on November 3, Hidalgo inexplicably backed off. Temporarily the movement lost its momentum.

The desire to throw off the yoke of Spanish rule was not limited, however, to the people of the Bajío region around Mexico City. Resentment ran high in the province of what was then Nueva Galicia (which became Jalisco), especially in the capital city of Guadalajara, which was about 200 kilometres southeast of Tepic, where Narváez, his wife María, and five children were living while he served at nearby San Blas. To lead the revolt in Nueva Galicia, Hidalgo had managed to recruit José Antonio Torres, a *mestizo* administrator of a hacienda near Irapuato, 200 kilometres due east of Guadalajara. On November 11, Torres met little resistance as he crushed ill-prepared royalist forces between Lake Chapala and Guadalajara, where Hidalgo was viewed as a liberator.

Padre Miguel Hidalgo.

Hidalgo must have been encouraged by Torres' easy victory and reports of the revolt spreading to other parts of the country. On November 26, Hidalgo entered Guadalajara at the head of a triumphal procession of some seven thousand followers.

Some of the revolt's strongest support came from *criollos* in the lower clergy. Because of their superior education and intimate contact with Indigenous and African people, several priests of rural parishes became effective leaders of the peasant rebellion. In western Nueva Galicia, one of them was Padre José María Mercado, the priest in Ahualulco, a small town about eighty kilometres due west of Guadalajara. After Torres took over that city, Mercado joined the cause and was responsible for spreading the uprising into what became Nayarít. He occupied Tepic without a battle on November 23, 1810, and headed for San Blas, where Narváez remained stationed. The poorly defended naval base, commanded by frigate captain José Joaquín Lavayen, offered the rebels an easy target.

≈

Narváez had returned to San Blas from a voyage to the Californias on November 1 in command of the *Activo*.[1] By then, the long-debated relocation of New Spain's naval department to Acapulco had finally been completed.[2] Nevertheless, San Blas remained a strategic military outpost, and everyone was talking about the popular uprising. *Gachupín* officials, merchants, veterans, and ranchers from Guadalajara westward to the Pacific coast feared for their lives and property. As the revolt spread, they gathered up whatever they could carry and fled to the mil-

Padre Ignacio José de Allende.

itary garrison at San Blas, where they sought refuge and an escape route by sea. The frightened elite would soon include two of Guadalajara's most prominent citizens: Judge Juan Nepomuceno de Alva and Bishop Juan Cruz.[3]

On November 5, Commander Lavayen, who was in Tepic, ordered Narváez to arm the *Activo* for war and to load the vessel with all the supplies it could carry in case a rapid retreat was required. Three days later, Lavayen arrived in San Blas and placed Lieutenant Jacobo Murphy, commander of the *San Carlos*,

and Ensign Agustín Vocalán in charge of defending the establishment with the assistance of about 300 armed *gachupín* merchants, about twenty veterans, a number of ranchers on horseback, and about 200 unarmed sailors[4] from three vessels: the 300-ton frigate *Concepción*, the 213-ton brigantine *Activo*, and the *San Carlos*. Narváez estimated that, in total, the defenders had only about 110 rifles and flintlock muskets.[5]

According to Narváez, Lieutenant Murphy was reluctant "to compromise himself by defending the town with people who lacked discipline and subordination." Narváez said three poorly armed, under-manned batteries were activated but not fully armed with cannons — San José on one side of Cristobal Bay, Castillo at the entrance, and Guadalupe near the Caracol arsenal.[6] Narváez warned Lavayen that even if artillery fire could be maintained, most of it would come from the two batteries flanking the bay, providing little defence in the face of a land-based attack. He noted that the vulnerable Guadalupe battery, which had no cannons, could be taken by "any number of armed peo-ple."[7] Furthermore, the military had been able to cut off only one road with a trench.[8]

For about ten days the royalists sent out patrols to forage the sur-rounding area for food and supplies. The men returned, however, almost empty-handed, and the beleaguered royalists were running low on provisions. According to Narváez, about seventy water carriers and wood cutters had deserted the town. He said that Spanish sailors, mostly recruited from surrounding communities, were either not prepared or simply declined to perform these essential tasks. When a squad of fully armed veteran sailors was sent into San Blas on patrol, all the men fled to Tepic and joined the rebels. The *gachupín* volunteers constantly quar-relled among themselves. Their disorderly conduct and lack of disci-pline disgusted Narváez.[9]

One morning, the two companies of *gachupín* came close to waging a shootout because of a dispute over whether the Bishop of Guadalajara, Juan Cruz, who had taken refuge aboard the *Activo*, should be brought ashore or not. They feared he would sail off and abandon them to the rebels.

According to Narváez, "Their only interest was to save themselves and their possessions." He said one of the bishop's relatives, who had been pastoral priest of the cathedral of Guadalajara, had preached in San Blas about the need for the inhabitants to help defend the town from the rebels. But most of the townspeople had sided with Padre Mercado. Lieutenant Murphy, who had the thankless task of organiz-ing the royalists into an effective defensive force, ended up screaming at them in frustration: "We were better defended when we were alone, than now that you [*gachupín*] have come."[10]

By November 25, the royalists realized they were surrounded by two thousand to six thousand rebels from thirty-two different towns. The insurgent force was within six miles of San Blas.[11] Narváez said the rebels were armed with spears, bows and arrows, rifles, and six cannons. To make matters worse, the armed company of turncoat veterans had decided to use their guns against the royalists. Two days later, commander Lavayen shuffled his officers' responsibilities. He ordered Narváez to hand over command of the *Activo* to Lieutenant Antonio Quartara, and he replaced Murphy with Ensign Mateo Plowes as commander of the Guadalupe battery. On the 28th, Padre Mercado demanded that Lavayen surrender the Caracol arsenal to the insurgents. Ensign Vocalán, second in command to Lavayen, discussed the proposed terms with Mercado, but postponed a decision until he could present the options to his officers and key civilian supporters.

On November 30, Lavayen summoned Narváez, nine other naval officers, and leaders of the volunteers and veterans to two meetings. The commander told the men they had two choices. They could either surrender, or fight as long as possible and then retreat to the bay and board the two brigantines and two merchant vessels that were in port. Although the vessels would not be able to hold everyone, many of them could escape with their lives. After Lavayen read the four terms of surrender that Vocalán and Mercado had formulated, he asked his officers to voice their opinions. Only three men — Plowes, Ensign Felipe García, and a merchant named Carriaga — favoured sinking the brigantines and defending the camp. Faced with this minority view, Lavayen asked the men to cast written votes. All but one of them voted to surrender. Murphy abstained. Ensign Felipe García said those who voted for capitulation based their decision on the civilian volunteers' apparent insubordination, lack of discipline, and unwillingness to wage a united defence. Narváez said the royalist position was hopeless.[12]

At about eleven o'clock that night, Narváez retired to his quarters in San Blas, convinced that Lavayen would not take any final action until the next day. However, at one o'clock in the morning of December 1, Ensign García reported disturbing information to Narváez: Juan Echarte, captain of the civilian volunteers was preparing to escape by ship. García suspected that all three vessels would slip away before dawn. To find out where things stood, the two men rushed to the commander's residence, where they ran into Plowes and Vocalán. Lavayen said he had not ordered the vessels to leave. By then it was 2:00 a.m., and Narváez reckoned it was too late for him to reach the vessels. So he remained at the fort and waited for the inevitable surrender.[13]

Shortly after sunrise, Lavayen capitulated. According to Narváez, officers Plowes and Vocalán, along with civilian volunteers Francisco Pujadas (naval ministry administrator), José Monzón, and Marcelo Eroquer were all taken captive by the rebels to ensure that the surrender held.[14] Because of their intercessions on behalf of the rebels, Vocalán and Andrés Brillante, the customs house administrator in Guadalajara, apparently received preferential treatment.

After functioning as one of New Spain's two most strategic and active Pacific coast ports for forty-two years, San Blas had fallen into rebel hands. Narváez's fate appeared uncertain.

On January 17, 1811, Hidalgo's forces suffered a severe defeat near Guadalajara. Although the revolutionary army melted away, the rebellion was not over. Scattered insurgent forces would wage guerrilla warfare for the next decade.

Meanwhile, the royalist army was ready to regain control of territory that had been lost to the rebels. On January 26, Brigadier José de la Cruz, Commander of New Spain, left Guadalajara with a small force and set out to retake Tepic and San Blas. In Ahualulco, he issued a general pardon, then started hunting down rebels. At month's end Mercado was gunned down in a ravine near San Blas. One week later Tepic was under royalist control. Insurgents came in droves to seek pardons. By mid-February, western New Spain from San Blas northward was pacified.[15]

Narváez continued to serve the Spanish Navy. But now he was haunted by the spectre of possibly being found guilty of treason for his part in the surrender of San Blas. In February 1811, Commander

Lavayen, Narváez, and nine other indicted officers were brought before a nine-judge military tribunal, which had been called by Brigadier General José de la Cruz.[16] Narváez and his colleagues stood accused of failing to defend the San Blas establishment vigorously enough during the early stages of the rebellion.

In his testimony, Narváez declared he had fulfilled his obligation to the viceroy by demonstrating no sympathy for the rebels and by remaining in the service of the established government. "In my two assignments as commander of the brigantine *Activo* and as second in command of the battery commanded by Mateo Plowes, I always tried, in every way possible, to encourage naval personnel and other people to defend [the fort]," he said.

The tribunal cleared all ten officers of any responsibility for the base being undermanned and poorly defended and for surrendering it to the rebels. Lavayen was released from prison and restored to his post as commander at San Blas.

Following Hidalgo's disastrous defeat at Guadalajara, he and Allende went north toward what is now San Antonio, Texas, to reorganize the rebels. Pursued relentlessly by royalist soldiers, both rebel leaders were soon captured. Along with most of the revolutionists, Allende was executed by a firing squad in June. Nevertheless, he became a Mexican hero. Turned over to the bishop of Durango, Hidalgo was defrocked, excommunicated, and then returned to Spanish authorities for execution. On July 30, 1811, he was also shot by a firing squad. Although his revolutionary leadership had been brief, he became known as the father of Mexican independence.

CHAPTER 13

Narváez Adapts to Political
Change in Mexico

BETWEEN 1813 AND 1818, the popular uprising evolved in ways that would force Narváez to take one side or the other, demonstrate loyalty, and examine his conscience. For a forty-five-year-old man who had spent most of his life at sea, battling the elements and exploring un-known waters on behalf of a distant European-based nation, it repre-sented a major challenge. By training and experience, he was conven-tional, conservative, and respectful of authority. Now, his colonial homeland seemed to be engulfed in socio-political turmoil, radical change, and insurgencies that were difficult for him to understand and assess, let alone engage constructively.

In 1813, Padre José María Morelos continued the rebellion by orga-nizing a successful uprising in southern Mexico. Unlike Hidalgo, he was a talented military tactician. Instead of heading up a large, unorganized army, which the Spaniards knew how to crush, Morelos methodically trained guerrilla bands to carry out hit-and-run attacks.

Morelos's vision for Mexico after independence was summed up in his proposed constitution of 1814. It called for a democratically elected representative congress, a bureaucracy staffed by Mexicans, and equality under the law. It also abolished slavery, titles of nobility, government monopolies, sales taxes, and all forms of tribute. Morelos proposed a per capita income tax of 5 percent and an import duty of 10 percent. The *gachupines* and most of the *criollos* opposed these reforms, which were aimed at loosening their collective grip on political and economic power.

Narváez had set down roots in New Spain and, like many Spaniards, he had developed an increasing interest in the general aims of the more progressive *criollos* who advocated greater independence from Spain. Nevertheless, he remained a royalist and continued to represent Span-

Padre José María Morelos.

ish interests in the Pacific. When the Cadiz Cortes, Spain's first sovereign assembly, drafted the Constitution of 1812 — Spain's first written law of the land — the viceroy placed Narváez in charge of delivering it to Manila. Regarded as the leading document of liberalism in Spain, the constitution's primary aim was prevention of arbitrary and corrupt royal rule. It provided for a limited monarchy which governed through ministers subject to parliamentary control. It was also designed to pacify colonial unrest. Unfortunately, it was never fully implemented. This important administrative assignment would take Narváez away from Mexico from 1813 to 1814.

Meanwhile, in New Spain, the popular rebellion spread, and Morelos gained control of most of the southern part of the country. Brigadier General Cruz was determined to smash the insurgency. Widespread support for the rebellion throughout the region convinced royalist commanders that the Indigenous population had to be repressed. To combat the rebels' guerrilla tactics, General Cruz turned to draconian counterinsurgency measures and employed a wide range of coercive policies.

In 1815, Morelos was defeated, convicted of treason, and executed. Allende had triggered rebellion, Hidalgo had inspired the revolutionary movement, and Morelos had given it purpose. Other guerrilla leaders carried on the struggle. Two of them were José Santana and the *criollo* reformer Padre Marcos Castellanos. From 1813 to 1816, this pair spearheaded remarkably effective collective action by Indigenous people living around Lake Chapala at the head of the Santiago River, which runs northwest and empties into the Pacific Ocean just north of San Blas. The rebellion had come too close to home for Narváez to avoid getting involved, and the colonial government needed his naval skills to help quell the insurgents.

This part of the popular struggle centred on the fortification and courageous defence of Mezcala Island, a craggy, inhospitable volcanic island located about eight kilometres into Lake Chapala near the hamlet of Tlachichilco, on the lake's north shore. With an area of about 1,100 square kilometres, Lake Chapala is Mexico's largest freshwater lake. It is about eighty kilometres long and eighteen kilometres wide. In deciding to build a strong garrison on Mezcala Island, the rebels created a

defensible base for launching effective guerilla raids, gave them a strategic advantage, and unified insurgent forces throughout the region.
Nevertheless, the rebels' tenacious defence of the island fortress pitted
untrained, poorly equipped Indigenous freedom fighters against the
overwhelming firepower of disciplined, organized units of the royalist
army, which was backed by Spain's resources. Despite the royalists'
military superiority, their inability to capture the island base had inspired the rebel cause during more than three years of bloody conflict.[1]

Helping Cruz crush this intense phase of the Indigenous rebellion
was the last service Narváez would perform for the Spanish Navy. In
1815, he was sent more than 300 kilometres inland to the royalist garrison at Tlachichilco,[2] where he joined five other experienced marine
officers as launch skippers engaged in blockading Mezcala Island and
obstructing rebel raids. Captain-Colonel José Navarro assigned each
mariner two infantry officers. These officer teams and troops served
eight-day rotations, with half of the soldiers in patrol boats and the
other half at Tlachichilco as a reserve division.[3] With the royalist forces
considerably strengthened, Cruz launched a final campaign of merci-
less, brutal repression.

Having seen his troops fail to storm Mezcala Island at least four times
at significant cost of men and equipment, Cruz was determined to
starve out the island defenders by combining a tighter blockade with an
uncompromising scorched earth counter-insurgency policy around the
entire lake. It proved successful, and the two guerilla leaders, Santana
and Castellanos, finally surrendered the island fortification on November 25, 1816. Nevertheless, the widespread rebellion continued throughout the region.

During the next year, whenever Narváez was not harassing Indigenous guerrillas and bandits or supplying royalist outposts around Lake
Chapala, he was expected to chart the lake and make a survey for a new
road to Guadalajara, about fifty kilometres to the north. His *Plano del
lago de Chapala* was the earliest scientific map of the lake, and it was
used for many years with only minor changes. In recognition of his service during the Lake Chapala military campaign, Narváez received his
stripes as *alférez de navío* (ship's ensign) on March 20, 1818. At the time,

he was in the midst of mapping the entire province of Jalisco — a task that would take three more years.

By 1818, the royalists had pacified almost all of New Spain. But the viceroy's army was too fragmented, demoralized, and scattered among widely separated garrisons to quell another, determined, sustained insurgency. Fortunately for the royalists, none occurred. The rebellion collapsed because the influential *gachupín* and *criollos* elites failed to support it. Both classes saw their status, safety, and livelihoods were threatened if uprisings of oppressed Indigenous and *mestizo* masses continued. However, eight years of brutal war had plundered the land, forged permanent enemies, and sowed seeds of chaos that would plague the country for generations.

Meanwhile, Narváez was still chafing from the affront to his self-esteem that he felt he had suffered nine years earlier during the military trial that stemmed from the surrender of San Blas. He had written one letter after another to various officials pleading for documentation that would remove any stain on his reputation that was, or might have been, left by the tribunal. After receiving little or no satisfaction, in early 1820 Narváez finally petitioned Juan Villavicencio, Director General of the Armada in Cadiz, asking that he be given the Cross of the Royal and Military Order of San Hermenegildo for his performance during the fall of San Blas.[4] Saint Hermenegildo had become the patron saint of Spanish armed forces because he was the Visigoth King of Seville who was martyred defending the Christian faith in the sixth century. Beginning in 1815, the Cross was given to recognize soldiers who exemplified extraordinary bravery by exceeding their military obligations and continuing to fight despite suffering in battle. Although Narváez had conducted himself prudently and professionally during the San Blas episode, the criteria for granting the exclusive award did not come close to matching either his performance or the importance of the event. The fact that he even sought such an honour reveals the man's pride, and a seemingly unwarranted sense of shame.

The Spanish crown had been devoting most of its attention to defeating France and then trying to stabilize political control in the homeland after the war. With no direction coming from Madrid, factions in New

Spain began to look for leadership at home. The man who emerged was Agustín de Iturbide, a young *criollo* royalist captain who had helped defeat Morelos. This enthusiastic, spellbinding orator managed to convince General Vicente Guerrero that winning independence was more important than achieving the aims of any single group. In February 1821, the two men agreed on a plan that guaranteed independence from Spain, equal rights for Spaniards and *criollos*, and supremacy of the Catholic religion. Then they formed a common army. On September 28, 1821, Iturbide marched into Mexico City, proclaimed Mexico's independence, instituted the Regency of the [ancient Aztec] Empire, and declared himself president. It would turn out to be a brutal, but short-lived government.

With the end of Spanish rule, Narváez decided to retire from the Royal Navy, remain in Guadalajara with his family, and seek a position in the Mexican Navy that Iturbide was forming. Madrid agreed to grant him "retirement without gain of salary," but the Spanish Navy would not discharge him officially until May 25, 1825.[5] Meanwhile, Narváez was named speaker of Guadalajara's auxiliary consultative junta. Although Narváez supported the need for Mexican independence, as a former royalist he favoured development of a conservative approach to self-government. For this reason, he was soon elected by popular vote as Provincial Deputy to Iturbide's provisional government.

According to Narváez's great-great-granddaughter, Edelmira Trejo de Meillón, one of the first things Regent Iturbide did was to secretly commission Narváez to make an urgent survey of navigable west coast ports. Writing in 1935 about "The Founding of Manzanillo," Ms. Meillón did not credit her great-great-grandfather with discovering the original natural harbour at this location, but she asserted that he named the contemporary commercial port Manzanillo "because he saw an African tree of the same name there" when he made his survey. More revealing is Meillón's allegation that Iturbide (whom she called "the false independence advocate") had anticipated that the current struggle might result in decisive defeat of his plans," and he needed a secret escape route for himself and his followers. Meillón characterized her great-grandfather as "a true proponent of independence" whose support came from "a Spanish and Mexican brotherhood struggling for genuine national independence."[6] This conservative faction recognized the need for independence, and acknowledged that Iturbide's leadership had been essential for moving in that direction. However, as proponents of a more representative, stable republic, they did not fully trust the strong, wily, authoritarian leader.

Iturbide also undertook immediate reorganization of the Mexican Navy. In December 1821, on Iturbide's recommendation, Narváez was appointed *teniente de fragata* (frigate lieutenant). This must have been gratifying to Narváez because, if he had still been in the Spanish Navy, it was a rank achieved by very few former *pilotos*. In May of the following year, Iturbide ordered Lieutenant Narváez to take command of the packetboat *San Carlos* in San Blas and sail to Baja and Alta California with Canon Don Agustín Fernández de San Vicente of Durango. As the emissary of Emperor Agustín I, Fernández had been commissioned to set up a new national administration in Monterey that would replace Spanish authority with Mexico's sovereignty throughout the two California's.[7] Narváez helped to install commissions, councils, and local governments in both provinces. This was the first of several important assignments that he would carry out for successive Mexican governments.

While Narváez was in Monterey, he met Kiril Khlebnikov, historian-administrator of the Russian-American Company (RAC), and Narváez recounted some of the experiences he had with the Russian fur trader Kuzmich Zaikov during his voyage to Alaska in 1788.[8] Khlebnikov was using his diplomatic skills to protect the RAC's control over trade in Russia's American possessions. The monopoly had been established by charter in 1798 and renewed with few changes in 1821. At that time, Russia decided to ban all trade by foreigners in Russian America, the southern boundary of which it fixed at 51° north latitude near the northern end of Vancouver Island.[9] Khlebnikov also may have been seeking covert intelligence for the czar who, intent on fostering Russian expansion along the Northwest Coast, had indicated a willingness to assist Spain in recovering its former colonies in Latin America in exchange for Madrid's support.

While Narváez was still in the Californias, Iturbide stunned even his most ardent supporters when he declared himself Emperor Agustín of Mexico, on May 15, 1822. His reign did not last long, because eight months later, he was overthrown by a liberal revolt and exiled. Iturbide's successor was the even more devious General Antonio López de Santa Anna. Although Mexico would adopt a constitutional government, General Santa Anna found extra-legal ways to influence governmental decisions.

On March 9, 1823, following Lieutenant Narváez's return from his extensive work in the Californias, he was made commandant of the Department of San Blas, which was still a significant port on Mexico's western coast. (Although he would be engaged in other temporary assignments, Narváez would remain in this position until October 30, 1827, when the post was suspended due to funding cuts.) The new commandant's first task was to draw an important general map of Alta California, Baja California, and Sonora. This map remained in manuscript form and unavailable until the mid-twentieth century. Titled *Carta esférica de los territorios de la Alta, Baja Califórnia(s) y estado Sonora: construido por las mejores noticias y observaciones propias de Teniente de Navío D. José María Narváez 1823*,[10] it could have corrected many errors that plagued accurate determination of the international boundary after the Mexican-American war, but it was unknown to American cartographers at the time. It showed the land route to Monterey and San Francisco explored by Juan Bautista de Anza from 1774 to 1776, accurate delineation of communities in New Mexico, and the absence of any boundary along the southern side of New Mexico.

In late 1824 and early 1825, Narváez was engaged in two other significant mapping projects. In December 1824, Guadalupe Victoria, a distinguished jurist, became Mexico's first president. Narváez was ordered to take command of the schooner *Mexicana* so he could reconnoitre and map the coast between the ports of San Blas and Manzanillo. When Narváez finished this task, José Joaquin de Herrera, General Commandant of Jalisco, sent him to Colima so he could correct the locations of some towns between that city and Guadalajara on the map of Jalisco, which Narváez had all but completed. His *Carta Corográfica de los Estados de Jalisco*, dated 1824, gave the state, which was divided into eight cantons, its first scientifically drafted map. Narváez's statistics indicated that the canton of Tepic had a total population of 66,413, whereas only 46,592 people lived in the canton of Guadalajara, where the capital city was located. The state's total number of inhabitants was about 656,660. According to the renowned Mexican historian Manuel Orozco y Berra (1816–1881), Lieutenant Narváez had worked largely on his own, made remarkably few errors, and "determined principal points by astronomical means, linking them to others by geodetic and topographic surveying operations."[11]

By April 1825, Narváez had worked his way up to *capitán de fragata* (junior captain), and he returned to his post at San Blas. That same year, Captain Narváez supplied the government with maps he had drawn of the border areas with Louisiana and Texas. He also completed another survey of the port of San Blas, which constituted a post-mortem for the ill-conceived naval base. Narváez found that sandbars at the entrance and in the middle of the bay had doubled in size since 1803. Despite constant dredging, relentless erosion had actually ended the harbour's life as an anchorage for large vessels in 1809. In addition to his cartographic work, he supervised construction of schooners for Mexico's mail service to the Californias. In 1826, he became a founding member of the Institute of Science, Literature and the Arts.

At the end of October 1827, funding cuts in the Mexican Navy caused Narváez to lose his command at San Blas, but he continued living in Tepic as a civilian. On November 3, he wrote to President Guadalupe Victoria, saying he could not support his family on the skimpy navy pension he had been allotted. He was granted permission to work at half pay on coastal merchant vessels. Nevertheless, two years later, he was writing the president again requesting back pay that he was owed from his last year as commandant at San Blas. At the time, he had insisted that all the local day labourers be paid first, and the government had run out of money before it could pay Narváez.

In 1830, Narváez drew the earliest map of Alta California,[12] which showed the coastal area between "Estableamiento Ruso" (Fort Ross)[13] in the north and Mission San Miguel in the south divided into four districts:

Portion of Narváez's map of Jalisco showing area around San Blas and Tepic, 1824.
(MAPOTECA MANUEL OROZCO Y BERRA, COLECCIÓN OROZCO Y BERRA)

San Francisco, Monterey, Santa Barbara, and San Diego. According to Narváez, about 20,000 Indigenous "converts" inhabited nineteen missions and approximately 4,500 troops and unconverted people were scattered around presidios, towns, and ranches. He estimated that the total population was 23,676. Writing about California place names, geographer Erwin G. Gudde said that Narváez's *Plano del territorio de la Alta California..., 1830* was "probably the most valuable of the Mexican maps, especially for the missions and other settlements." Gudde also noted that, unlike previous maps that were devoid of topography, "it was the first map to show the three mountain ranges," fairly correctly but not labelled. Of particular interest was the fact that, east of the coastal range of mountains, Narváez's map showed the vast "Cienegas ô Tulares" — seasonal wetlands that in years of heavy rain sometimes covered the Mexican province's large central valley with what appeared to be a great, extremely shallow inland lake which covered more than 1,813 square kilometres. At that time, it was reputed to be the largest body of intermittent fresh water west of the Great Lakes. According to Gudde, however, "the hydrography is mainly imaginary."[14] Because Narváez had not actually traversed Alta California's entire vast interior, he had based some of its natural features, such as this one, on verbal reports.

Following a total of forty-nine years of naval service for two countries, Captain Narváez retired completely on April 20, 1831, at the age of sixty-three, and settled in Guadalajara. He was granted a meagre pension of 141 pesos, six reales, and eight granos. During his retirement years, the former mariner associated with academic scholars, politicians, and business leaders who were actively involved in local affairs. At home, he spent long hours in his room working on his various projects. The house was maintained by María del Carmen Narváez, a great-granddaughter of the family patriarch. According to Narváez family lore, María Narváez later told her niece, Carolina Narváez, that she often watched the elderly cartographer drafting a map of the world toward the end of his life. María told her niece that Narváez "rolled up the unfinished map around a wooden rod and left it standing upright in one corner of the room." Later, Carolina passed this information on to

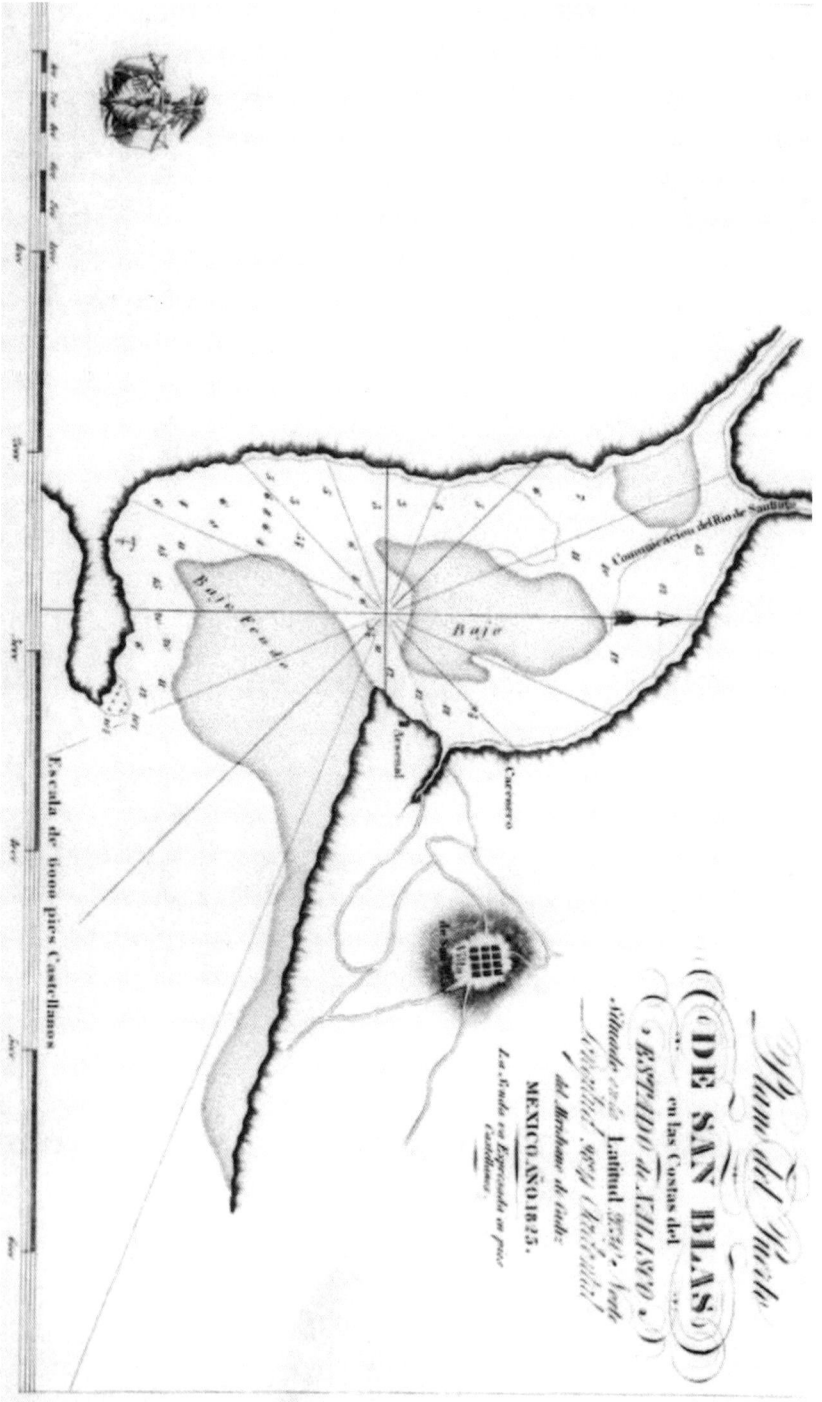

Narváez's *Plano del Puerto de San Blás en las costas del Estado Xalizco*, 1825. An updated revision of the chart first drawn by Jean-François de Galaup in 1777 and revised by Juan Pantoja in 1797. (PORTAL TO TEXAS HISTORY)

Edelmira Trejo Narváez (1868–1950), who developed a strong interest in her great-great-grandfather's life story. When she visited Guadalajara for the first time in 1909, she searched high and low for this map without success.[15]

Narváez's "Error"

By 1991, twentieth-century Mexican geographers had become convinced that Narváez had made one major mistake on his historic map of Jalisco, which they believed had been repeated for more than 150 years. During that time, confusion about the location of the border between Jalisco and Colima had led to a variety of problems and disputes at various levels of government. Finally, on February 26, 1991, an official convention was held in Guadalajara to determine if the border needed to be realigned. Professor Genaro Hernández Corona, a commission member for Colima, presented a biographical sketch of Narváez and testified that, despite Narváez's "great qualifications as a navigator and mapmaker," he was not sufficiently familiar with the coastal zone of Manzanillo and consequently made an "error" in "establishing the boundary of Colima and Jalisco," which "was repeated without major reflection in countless documents." Almost all the commission members from both states seemed to agree with Corona's assessment.

José María Murià, however — a history professor and commission member for Jalisco — presented Narváez's original version of his *Carta Corográfica de Jalisco, Zacatecas y Territorio de Colima, 1824*, and pointed out that it did not include the alleged "error" that had caused so much controversy for so many years. Murià had located the map in the Mapoteca "Manuel Orozco y Berra" of the Secretaría de Agricultura y Recursos Hidráulicos in Mexico City. Somehow, during the years of dispute no one had taken the trouble to find it. Presenting a number of maps made in Colima, Murià demonstrated that map-makers in Colima were responsible for introducing a mistake that Narváez never made, and then reproducing it for decades.[16]

Evidently, a small section of the border had been redrawn numerous times to accommodate various economic interests that were competing for mineral rights. Following the convention, Narváez's original map was published for the first time in the newspaper *El Informador, Diario Independiente*, in Guadalajara, Jalisco, on February 26, 1991, as part of an insert that summarized the conference.

Narváez's *Plano del territorio de la Alta California* . . . , 1830.
(CALIFORNIA STATE LIBRARY, SACRAMENTO)

In early 1840, Narváez produced a scaled-down version of the map of Jalisco that he had completed earlier. It included what are now the states of Jalisco, Nayarit, Colima, Zacatecas, and Aguascalientes. Antonio Escobedo, Governor of Jalisco, sent the map to Europe for engraving. Two years later, it became Jalisco's first official map. According to Manuel Orozco, all future maps of Jalisco were derived from Narváez's seminal work. In 1852, it was published in New York. Unfortunately, Narváez was already dead.

After navigating wooden sailing vessels across an estimated 165,000 kilometres of the Pacific Ocean on more than a dozen voyages between 1788 and 1840, the distinguished mariner, who had adopted Mexico as his homeland, died on August 4, 1840, in Guadalajara at age seventy-two. Writing an authoritative history of geography in Mexico forty-one years later, Manuel Orozco would conclude a short biographical summary of Narváez's career by praising the mariner-cartographer for having "constantly advanced the geography of the country until his death, [and] leaving a name dear to all who love the progress of science."[17] Unfortunately, it soon would become evident that this sentiment had not yet permeated the minds of government officials.

Narváez's family members possessed several original maps, charts, and notes, which they assumed would be valuable. These materials probably included Narváez's journal of the Gran Canal (Salish Sea) expedition of 1791. One authority claims to have seen the journal during the last year of Narváez's life. In 1839, Eugène Duflot de Mofras, a member of the French embassy in Madrid, was given the assignment of surveying New Spain and the Pacific Northwest for France. In the English translation of his book *Travels on the Pacific Coast*, he mentions that "in 1840 Don José Narváez brought out his Journal and the original charts of his interesting voyage for our inspection."[18] Duflot de Mofras seems to have been referring to the Mexican mariner's exploration of Juan de Fuca Strait in 1789, although Narváez discussed several voyages with him, including the one in 1791.[19] The reference to more than one chart is also noteworthy. Most important, this confirms that Narváez, unlike most officers, kept these important documents and possibly many others.

Narváez's family offered to give the noted hydrographer's historic documents to the Mexican government in exchange for about six thousand pesos in back pay. Their offer fell on deaf ears. Narváez died unappreciated and poor.[20] Today there are no monuments in either Nayarit or Jalisco to recognize this mariner, nor has his gravesite been located. In two instances, however, streets in major cities bear his name. In Guadalajara, the capital of Jalisco, Calle José María Narváez is a one-way street that runs south to north about 800 metres in an eastern section of the city. In Santiago Ixcuintla, Nayarit — located about twenty kilometres northeast of San Blas on the north shore of the Santiago River — a 300-metre-long-street in the middle of a six-street grid is named after Narváez. Located in the 1 de Enero ("First of January") section of the city, this grid commemorates several Latin American heroes including Ernesto Che Guevara, the Niños Héroes,[21] twentieth-century labour leader Vicente Lombardo Toledano, and Narváez.

Although history left Narváez in its wake, historians in Mexico continued to acknowledge his contributions. For example, in 1978, Gabriel Agraz García de Alba delivered a lecture at the Real Academia Hispanoamericana de Ciencias, Artes y Letras in Mexico City about the sixty-page monograph he had written titled, *Un Gaditano Insigne en América* ("A Cadizian Famous in America"): *José María Narváez*. García enumerated Narváez's achievements and pointed out that Mexico's president at that time, José López Portillo, was one of the naval officer's direct descendants — a great-great-great grandson, who held the seat from 1976 to 1982.[22]

To "perpetuate the memory of the illustrious mariner, chart maker, explorer of our Pacific coasts, and discoverer [sic] of the great archipelago of San Juan [de Fuca] and the Rosario Canal," García urged the federal government to take two steps: reconsider the Jalisco senate's refusal to recognize Narváez by giving his family a piece of vacant land, and purchase the mariner's valuable maps and papers from his relatives for the sake of posterity. Teodoro Amerlinck y Zirión, president of the academy, supported García's plea and petitioned the Republic's "First Magistrates" to name "a ship of the National Armada . . . *Don José María Narváez*."[23] There is no record of either being accomplished.

Narváez was a classic example of a reliable, deferential non-commissioned naval officer of considerable talent, versatility, courage, and determination who occupied key positions at one of the unforeseen crossroads of Pacific Northwest Coast history. What he thought about his experiences, and what he learned from them, we may never know.

We do know, however, that his achievements as the first European to explore a major portion of the Salish Sea are finally receiving long-overdue recognition in both Jalisco and British Columbia. Therefore, it would be appropriate for people in both provinces to urge an enterprising cruise ship line to name one of its vessels that regularly visits major ports along the Pacific coast of North, Central, and South America: *José María Narváez*. (British Columbia might lead the way by using this name on a BC Ferries vessel that plies the Salish Sea.) As an informative, constructive, cross-cultural, educational venture it could not only generate business but also bring history to life and promote understanding and appreciation of our collective inheritance. At the centre of this legacy stands an unsung mariner whose life, regardless of his modest rank in the Spanish and Mexican navies, expressed the uniquely human characteristic of man the explorer — the energetic, inquisitive, curious, searching species that is eager to see what is beyond known boundaries of understanding and awareness.

The Local Geographic Legacy of Narváez's Expedition of 1791

ALTHOUGH NARVÁEZ'S exploration of the Salish Sea in 1791 was brief, it marked an important turning point in the way such expeditions were conducted at the end of the eighteenth century, and it left a colourful array of Spanish place names that might have had long-term cultural impact if history had taken a different course in the following decade. Nevertheless, some Spanish names remain in British Columbia to remind us of this definitive phase of Pacific Northwest Coast history.

In surveying the Salish Sea one year after Narváez made his reconnaissance, Captain Vancouver — assisted by Captains Alcalá-Galiano and Valdés — depended heavily on charts made by the Narváez expedition. The most important one was the final *Carta que comprehende . . .* drafted by Juan Carrasco. Almost all of his toponyms were Spanish. Before Captain Vancouver renamed most of the places that were first

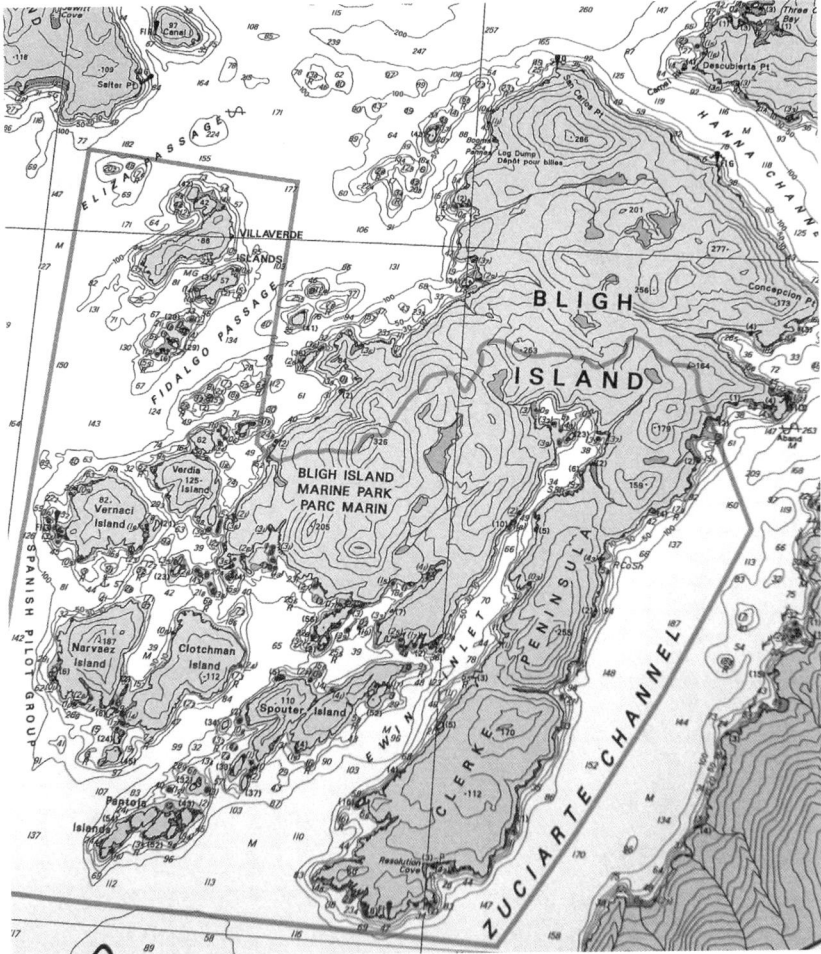

Narvaez Island, at the southwest corner of Bligh Island
Marine Park, B.C. (CHS #3675)

named by Spanish mariners, there were two geographic locations that
bore Carrasco's name. In 1790, the island in Juan de Fuca Strait, which
the Indigenous people called Chachanecuk and is now known as Protection Island, was named Isla de Carrasco. For a short time, the Spanish
also named Barkley Sound, on Vancouver Island, Boca de Carrasco.

The same English wave of renaming would soon erase many other
Spanish toponyms along the Pacific Northwest Coast. Today, eleven

relatively inconspicuous or remote locations remind British Columbians of Narváez's discoveries. In addition to the two monuments described in Chapter 8, the city of Vancouver memorializes the actual European founder of where it now stands with only one place name — the one-block-long Narvaez Drive, named in 1941 — and indirectly by one institution and another toponym: Langara College and Langara Golf Course, which acquired their names from the two Islas Lángara that the Spaniards observed along the shore, one of which was later named Point Grey.

Beyond the city of Vancouver there are eight other places that recognize Narváez directly or indirectly. There is a single geographic location in the Strait of Georgia commemorating its discoverer: tiny Narvaez Bay[1] at the south end of Saturna Island — the southernmost of the Gulf Islands. Appropriately, the road leading to this bay is Narvaez Bay Road. Furthermore, Saturna Island itself was named after the explorer's vessel, the *Santa Saturnina*. In that regard, the first large island southeast of Saturna in the San Juan Islands is now called Orcas Island, a name that may have been derived from *Horcasitas* — the alias of Narváez's vessel — which paid tribute to Viceroy Revillagigedo by using one element of his fourteen-word name. At East Point on Saturna Island, local volunteers have converted the former Fog Alarm Building into a Saturna Heritage Centre, which displays a model of the *Santa Saturnina* and interpretive information about the Narváez expedition. A small plaque nearby correctly indicates that Narváez sighted this point of land on June 15, 1791, but mistakenly suggests that he named it "Punta de Santa Saturnina" at that time. (See Chapter 9 regarding details of the actual naming.) On the Sechelt Peninsula, realtor Gary Little was instrumental in erecting an information panel about "The First European Explorer of the Sunshine Coast" at the south end of the Davis Bay seawall near the mouth of Chapman Creek.[2]

On Vancouver Island there is one street and a small island that bear Narváez's name. In the Gordon Head section of Greater Victoria there is a short street named Narvaez Crescent. A remote site of more historic interest is Narváez Island, the southwesternmost island in the Spanish Pilot Group of islands that are included in what is now the 4,455-hectare Bligh Island Provincial Park in Nootka Sound.[3]

Rosario Strait — the relatively short channel that separates mainland Washington State from the San Juan Islands — derived its name from the huge body of water which members of the Narváez expedition dubbed El Gran Canal de Nuestra Señora del Rosario la Marinera ("The Great Canal of Our Lady of Rosary the Seafarer") because they considered it their "most important" discovery. When Captain Vancouver replaced this colourful Spanish name with "Georgia Strait" in 1792, and demoted a single part (Rosario) of its ornate and pious symbolism to the comparatively minute waterway (now in United States territory), the general public became increasingly unaware of its connection to Narváez.

Narváez's Missing Journal
of 1790–1791

IN THE PAST 224 YEARS, historians have searched in vain for the journal that Narváez wrote on his important voyage of exploration in 1791 at age twenty-three. Although it is not needed to confirm the young navigator's remarkable achievements, it would clarify significant details of the expedition. It is also a key document for gaining a full understanding of that pivotal period in Pacific Northwest Coast maritime history when political and military control shifted from Spain to England, and then involved the United States of America.

Following the leads of previous investigators, the author has made the most intensive search to date for this document. It is not catalogued in any library in Mexico, Spain, the United States, or Canada. It seems to have been in Narváez's possession at the time of his death in 1840.[1] The Mexican government apparently did not purchase Narváez's journals, charts, and other papers at that time. Because his family was eager to sell these documents, it is highly probable that they were purchased by a private collector. If that happened, this individual probably purchased both the journal Narváez wrote in 1788 and the one he wrote in 1791.

To investigate that possibility, the author traced the route by which Narváez's journal of 1788 was obtained by the William Andrews Clark Memorial Library, where it was located, examined, and translated for the first time by the author in the early 1990s. This archive was founded by William Andrews Clark, Junior, and bequeathed in 1934 to the University of California Los Angeles as a memorial to his father, W. A. Clark (1839–1923) — the wealthy, influential Montana copper-mining magnate and United States senator.

The author found an interesting letter in W. A. Clark, Junior's correspondence files, dated December 1, 1933, from Henry R. Wagner — the American historian who did most of the seminal research about Spanish exploration of the Pacific Northwest Coast. The letter indicates that Clark purchased the 1788 manuscript and several other Mexican documents as a small block from Dr. Abraham S. W. Rosenbach "a few years ago" (in other words, the early 1930s). During the first half of the twentieth century, Rosenbach was the leading North American book and document seller.

David Szewczyk — owner of The Philadelphia Rare Books and Manuscripts Company in Philadelphia, Pennsylvania — once worked as a curator for the Rosenbach Foundation and was in charge of Rosenbach's Mexican collection. In 1980, Szewczyk wrote *The Viceroyalty of New Spain and Early Independent Mexico: A Guide to Original Manuscripts in the Collections of the Rosenbach Museum Library.*

According to Szewczyk, Rosenbach probably obtained the set of Mexican manuscripts that he sold to Clark from a Philadelphia lawyer by the name of George H. Hart, whose collection was sold in 1922. Lot 801 in that sale was titled: *Mexico: An extensive collection of official manuscript documents relating to Mexico, the Inquisition, legal cases, etc. from the late eighteenth century up to the period of the Mexican War.*

Szewczyk believed that Hart probably obtained this larger block of

Mexican manuscripts at a Bangs & Company auction held June 19–23, 1893, in New York City, during which 3,005 lots of Mexican materials collected by Henry Ward Poole were sold. Lots 1–2939 contained books and manuscripts.

"Poole was one of the least known but most colourful and important nineteenth-century collectors of Mexicana," wrote Szewczyk. In 1856, Poole landed in Veracruz as a surveying engineer for the Mexican Pacific Coal and Iron Mining and Land Company. The following year he returned to the United States. In 1858, Poole went back to Mexico to teach at the College of Mines. He worked there until his death in 1890. When not teaching, Poole collected books, manuscripts, and historical paintings.

In 1869 or 1870, Poole decided to sell his library. He shipped it to Boston, where it was auctioned in 1871. The sale catalogue listed 973 lots.

From 1874 to 1882, Poole built another enormous Mexican collection containing about ten thousand *legajos* (dossiers). "The bulk of the Rosen-bach Mexican manuscripts comes from this second collection," wrote Szewczyk in 1980.[2]

After Poole died, his brother William Frederick Poole arranged for the sale of Poole's second collection at the 1893 auction mentioned above. W. F. Poole was librarian of the Boston Athenæum and the Newberry Library and president of the American Historical Association and of the American Library Association.

As an annotated copy of the sale catalogue for the Bangs & Company auction has not been located, the identities of the buyers remain a mystery. Szewczyk believes W. F. Poole probably acquired some items for the Newberry Library or for collector Edward E. Ayer. However, *A Checklist of Manuscripts in the Edward E. Ayer Collection* by Ruth Lapham Butler does not list either of Narváez's journals.

Szewczyk also believed that dealers such as Lathrop C. Harper purchased most of the manuscript lots at the Bangs & Company auction. The author, however, was unable to find either of Narváez's journals listed in the Lathrop Harper catalogues after 1920.

"Most of the Poole manuscripts disappeared," wrote Szewczyk. "A portion re-emerged in the library of George H. Hart."[3] According to

Szewczyk, Rosenbach may have removed certain documents that he acquired in the Hart auction and sold these separately. We now know that it was exactly in this manner that Clark obtained Narváez's journal of 1788. In December 1993, however, responding to an inquiry from the author, Szewczyk said he could not find any record of the purchase of this journal from Rosenbach or "any evidence that Narváez's 1791 manuscript was part of Poole's collection."

In January 1994, at the author's request, Elizabeth Fuller, curator at the Rosenbach Foundation, made an extensive search of the foundation's catalogues and of Rosenbach's correspondence. Ms. Fuller reported finding isolated references to different lots of Mexican documents, but no itemization of either of the Narváez manuscripts.

Consequently, the author reached another dead end in the quest for the original of Narváez's missing journal. If the document exists in North America, it may be buried among the acquisitions of some private collector who obtained it in the early 1900s. Or it could be lost forever.

Nevertheless, this does not mean that the search must end. If the original manuscript cannot be located, the possibility remains that a copy might be found. During the exploration period, the Spanish Navy was strict about requiring all captains and *pilotos* of expeditions to file their original journals or copies thereof with the viceroy in New Spain and with Madrid. This means that an official copy should still reside in one of the Mexican or Spanish archives. Although other researchers have probed the catalogued materials in these archives for the manuscript in question without success, the large number of uncatalogued materials that are located in the Archivo General de la Nación and the Biblioteca Nacional in Mexico City require further investigation.

The Three Identities of an Historic Schooner (1788–1796)

THE COMPLEX HISTORY of the *Santa Saturnina* was examined in the greatest detail by Warren Cook in *Flood Tide of Empire*. A few of the key sources that he cited, however, left some room for different interpretations. The following appears to be the most probable chronology of its construction and reconstructions. (For clarity, the author has designated the outpost in Nootka Sound as Friendly Cove, not Cala de Los Amigos, as it was called by the Spanish.)

DATE	EVENT
Mar. 30, 1788	Chinese carpenters aboard English merchant captain John Meares' vessel prepare "moulds and model for a sloop of fifty tons that was designed to be built immediately on our arrival in [Nootka Sound]."[1]

DATE	EVENT
June 5, 1788	Meares had the keel laid for construction of a "vessel of 40 or 50 tons" at Friendly Cove.[2]
Sept. 20, 1788	*Northwest America* launched at Friendly Cove by Meares.[3]
Sept. 24, 1788	Meares leaves English fur trader Robert Funter in command of *Northwest America* at Friendly Cove and instructs him to winter in the Sandwich (Hawaiian) Islands and rendezvous at Friendly Cove in the spring.[4]
Oct. 27, 1788	Funter sails for Hawaii in command of *Northwest America*.[5]
Apr. 19, 1789	Funter returns to Friendly Cove in command of *Northwest America*, sails northward one week later in search of pelts, and returns June 8.[6]
June 9, 1789	Spanish captain Esteban José Martínez seizes *Northwest America* from Funter at Friendly Cove.[7]
June 19–20, 1789	The confiscated *Northwest America* is reconditioned at Friendly Cove and rechristened *Santa Gertrudis la Magna* by Father Severo Patero.[8]
June 21, 1789	Martínez sends José María Narváez in *Santa Gertrudis la Magna* to reinvestigate Clayoquot Sound, Barkley Sound, and Juan de Fuca Strait.[9]
July 5, 1789	Narváez returns to Friendly Cove on the *Santa Gertrudis la Magna*.
July 29–Aug. 1, 1789	Martínez starts using unfinished pieces of a new schooner under construction near Friendly Cove and unassembled parts of the *Jason* (seized aboard the *Argonaut* from the English captain James Colnett on July 2–3) to make *Santa Gertrudis la Magna* more seaworthy.[10]
Oct. 20, 1789	Alterations of *Santa Gertrudis la Magna* completed: planks replaced, ribs added, gunnels raised, and length increased 91.4 cm (three feet).[11]
Oct. 30, 1789	Martínez places José Verdía in command of *Santa Gertrudis la Magna* and it leaves Friendly Cove for San Blas.[12]

DATE	EVENT
Dec. 6, 1789	*Santa Gertrudis la Magna* arrives in San Blas.[13]
Feb. 3, 1790	Bodega has *Santa Gertrudis la Magna* dismantled at San Blas and returned in pieces to Friendly Cove by Francisco Eliza, new commandant at Nootka Sound.[14]
May 1790	Captain Pedro Alberni supervises laying of keel for new schooner at Friendly Cove.[15]
Sept. 1790	New schooner launched at Friendly Cove.[16]
Nov. 1, 1790	New schooner christened *Santa Saturnina*, alias *La Orcasitas*, at Friendly Cove.[17]
Dec.–Jan., 1790–91	*Santa Saturnina*, *Concepción*, and *Princesa* ride out the winter months unrigged at Friendly Cove.[18]
Jan. 4, 1791	Captain Colnett finds *Santa Saturnina*, *Concepción*, and *San Carlos* [actually *Princesa*] riding at anchor in Friendly Cove.[19]
Mar. 1, 1791	Colnett nearly recovers *Santa Saturnina* from Eliza, commander at Friendly Cove.[20]
Apr. 3, 1791	Eliza orders Narváez to use *Santa Saturnina* to scout entrance to Nootka Sound for five English or Russian vessels.[21]
May 4, 1791	Major expedition, with Eliza in command of the *San Carlos* and Narváez in command of the *Santa Saturnina*, leaves Friendly Cove to explore inside Juan de Fuca Strait.[22]
June 11, 1791	Both vessels rendezvous at Puerto de Córdova (Esquimalt).
June 14–24, 1791	Narváez commands *Santa Saturnina* to explore southern Gulf Islands from Juan de Fuca Strait.
June 28, 1791	*Santa Saturnina* and *San Carlos* anchor at Puerto de Quadra (Port Discovery) on south side of Juan de Fuca Strait.
July 1–22, 1791	Narváez commands *Santa Saturnina* to explore El Gran Canal (the Salish Sea).

DATE	EVENT
July 26, 1791	*Santa Saturnina*, with Juan Carrasco in command, and *San Carlos* leave Puerto de Quadra and head north for Nootka Sound.
Aug. 14, 1791	*Santa Saturnina* and *San Carlos* become separated.
Aug. 28, 1791	Headwinds force Carrasco to sail *Santa Saturnina* south to Monterey.
Sept. 15, 1791	Carrasco arrives at Monterey on *Santa Saturnina*.
Oct. 16, 1791	Carrasco leaves Monterey on *Santa Saturnina* and heads for San Blas.
Nov. 9, 1791	Carrasco arrives at San Blas on *Santa Saturnina* and delivers results of Narváez's explorations to acting commandant Salvador Fidalgo, prompting a follow-up expedition.
June 1792	Carrasco sent from San Blas to Monterey in command of *Santa Saturnina* with urgent instructions advising Bodega to hang on to Nootka Sound as long as possible.[23]
Sept. 1792	Carrasco reaches San Francisco on *Santa Saturnina*, but cannot deliver the instructions by hand to Bodega because he is in Monterey. Therefore, he may have sent the information overland to Monterey.[24]
1796	The *Santa Saturnina* continues serving coastal ports in various ways from the San Blas naval base until the vessel requires an "extensive overhaul."[25]

APPENDIX D

Dimensions of the
Santa Saturnina

I HAVE FOUND TWO SETS of information about the *Santa Saturnina*'s dimensions. These use different units of measure for length and beam, yet they appear equivalent. Henry R. Wagner, quoting both Francisco Eliza and Juan Pantoja, refers to *codos* ("elbows").[1] The manifest for the *Santa Saturnina*, located in the Museo Naval, Madrid,[2] uses *pies* (feet) and *pulgadas* (inches). I have used metric dimensions in the text, and shown the conversions below.

MEASUREMENTS	WAGNER	MANIFEST
Length on keel	18 *codos*	36 *pies*
Beam	6.5 *codos*	13 *pies*
Draft aft	5.5 *pies*	5 *pies*, 6 *pulgadas*
Draft at bow	4 *pies*	4 *pies*

The precise length of a *codo* — a crude elbow to finger-tip measurement that was used only by shipbuilders — is uncertain. According to Wagner, it was either 33/48 of a standard *vara* (yard) or 27.5/40 of the shipbuilder's *vara*. According to the *Diccionario Marítimo Español*, these equivalents (0.6875 of a *vara*) are equal to 24.75 *pulgadas* (inches).

According to Malcolm H. Kenyon,[3] the *pulgada* was 0.912 of an English inch. That would make a *pie* (12 *pulgadas* or 12 x 0.912) equal to 10.944 English inches. Consequently, a *codo* was equal to 21.888 English inches or about 1-foot-10-inches, and a *vara* was 32.832 English inches or about 2-feet-9-inches.

TABLE OF EQUIVALENCES:

	of a *vara*			*pulgadas*	*inches*	*feet*	ft. & in.
vara	40/40	48/48	1.0000	36.000	32.832	2.736	2' 9"
codo	27.5/40	33/48	0.6875	24.000	21.888	1.824	1'10"
pie	12.5/40	15/48	0.3125	12.000	10.944	0.912	11"
pulgada	1.04/40	1.25/48	0.0260	1.000	0.912		

Applying these figures first to Wagner's Spanish dimensions and then to those of the schooner's manifest, the English equivalents would be the same in both instances.

WAGNER'S DIMENSIONS:

Length on keel	18.0 *codos* x 21.888 in. = 393.984 in. = 32.83 ft. = 32'10"
Beam	6.5 *codos* x 21.888 in. = 142.272 in. = 11.86 ft. = 11'10"
Draft aft	5.5 *pies* x 10.944 in. = 60.192 in. = 5.02 ft. = 5'
Draft at bow	4.0 *pies* x 10.944 in. = 43.776 in. = 3.65 ft. = 3'8"

MANIFEST'S DIMENSIONS:

Length on keel	36.0 *pies* x 10.944 in. = 393.984 in. = 32.83 ft. = 32'10"
Beam	13.0 *pies* x 10.944 in. = 142.272 in. = 11.86 ft. = 11'10"
Draft aft	5.0 *pies* x 10.944 in. = 54.720 in.
	6.0 *pies* x .912 in. = 5.472 in.
	60.192 in. = 5.02 ft. = 5'
Draft at bow	4.0 *pies* x 10.944 in. = 43.776 in. = 3.65 ft. = 3'8"

APPENDIX E

Manifest of the *Santa Saturnina*

MANIFEST[1] showing the state of the four-cannon schooner *Santa Saturnina*, alias *Horcasitas*[2], commanded by Second *Piloto* of the Royal Fleet Don José Narváez, when he sailed from this Port of the Holy Cross of Nootka.

Officers	Infantry	Petty Officers	Gunners	Seamen	Boys	Servants	Total
2	5	2	5	5	2	1	22

Anchors	Cables	Rank & Number of Officers	Sails	
1: 6 *quin.*	1: 5 *pul.*	Captain & Second *Piloto*:	Mainsails	2
	2: 3 *pul.*	Don José Narváez	Foresails	2
Small Anchors:		*Pilotín* & Second Officer:	Square Sails	2
1 iron. 2 *aroba*		Don Juan Carrasco	Staysails	2
1 iron: 3 *aroba*			Jib	1

Dimensions & Stores of Vessel			Guns, Munitions, Firearms	
	pies.	*pul.*		
Keel (oakum to oakum)	36		Cannons, bronze 3 lb.	2*
Beam	13		Swivel Guns	3
Length (perp. to perp.)	39		Roundshot 3 lb.	100
Depth of hold	5	6	Bags of Grapeshot	130

Dimensions & Stores of Vessel

	pies.	pul.
Plan (width of hold)	5	
Draft – aft	5	6
Draft – foreward	4**	
Drag	1	6
Ballast	60 quin.	
Burden	32 tonales	

Guns, Munitions, Firearms

Roundshot 2 lb.	200
Muskets	9
Bayonets	9
Pistols	12
Swords	4

Flintlock	Quantity
Pikes	5
Musket balls of lead	1 aroba
Gunflints	42
Powder	116 lbs.
Cartridges for Cannon	69

Victuals & Water

Rations at the standard rate:
800 units for 40 days per
20 persons

Barrels of Water	24

Attestation — This vessel sailed seaworthy, with masts, spars, and standing and running rigging in good order and with the standard spare spars.

Explanations of Measurements:
Quin.: Quintal = 112 English lbs.
Pul.: Pulgada (Spanish inch) = 0.912 of English inch
Small anchors: grapnels with 4 flukes
Aroba = 1/4 *quintal* or 28 lbs.
Pie de Burgo = 0.912 English feet
Perp. to perp.: between perpendiculars
Tonal: tonelada or Spanish ton = 1.016 kg (U.K.) or 907 kg (U.S.)
* According to Eliza: 4
** According to Pantoja: 4-1/2

Notes:
1 Translated from the original Spanish document by Museo Naval.
2 Narváez used *Horcasitas*, Carrasco used *Orcasitas*. In Spanish, the letter "h" is not pronounced; consequently it is often omitted in writing. As explained in the text, this schooner was actually christened *La Orcasitas*. A sloop named *Orcasitas* (alias *Adventure*) was built in Clayoquot Sound in 1791–1792 and served briefly on the Pacific Northwest Coast.

A Brief History of the
San Carlos One and Two

ALTHOUGH THE *SAN CARLOS* was dwarfed by the huge 300-ton warship *Concepción* — the largest Spanish vessel to sail in Pacific Northwest coastal waters until about 1793 — this smaller workhorse had a much more varied and colourful career. Because a vessel bearing this name was involved in so many important historical incidents, those who have written about Spain's late eighteenth-century activities in the Pacific have not always understood that there were actually two such vessels named *San Carlos*, and that they had different histories.

Between 1768 and at least 1821, two packetboats named *San Carlos* operated out of New Spain's naval base at San Blas, but not simultaneously. Both of them were about 22 metres long on the keel and weighed about 193 to 196 tons. When referring to these smaller, faster vessels that were used for delivering supplies and dispatches, the Spanish commonly used the term "paquete" or "paquebote" — the equivalent of "pacquetbot" in French or "packetboat" in English. Rigged as a snow (a vessel with a trisail that had its own mast installed behind the main-mast), with square sails on both masts, each of these two packetboats was similar to a brig.

The first *San Carlos* (alias *Toisón de Oro* or "Golden Fleece")[1] was built near San Blas in 1767, before a naval department and shipyard were officially established there in May 1768. In early 1767, José de Gálvez, inspector general of New Spain, appointed Lieutenant Alonso Francisco Pacheco, an experienced naval shipbuilder from Veracruz, to supervise the construction of two packetboats at the above site near San Blas, where Gálvez intended to set up a naval base. By early spring, Pacheco had constructed a temporary shipyard on the banks of the San-tiago River, which enters the ocean about thirty kilometres north of San Blas. The site offered direct access to the cedar trees that would be used exclusively in all the vessels built at San Blas in the next seventeen years. Pacheco launched the vessels in the fall of that year and delivered the first *San Carlos* and its sister ship to San Blas by November.

By the time Gálvez arrived in San Blas in May 1768, the first *San Carlos* had been in active service for five months. Under the command of Colonel Domingo Elizondo, it was transporting supplies and soldiers northward to Guaymas in support of a campaign to subdue the Indig-enous Seri rebellion in Sonora.[2]

The first *San Carlos* left San Blas September 26, 1768, and headed 600 kilometres northwest across the mouth of the Gulf of California for La Paz, which was ordinarily a fifteen-to-twenty-day trip. Battered by heavy winds and rough seas, the *San Carlos* took almost three months and arrived in severely damaged condition on December 25, 1768.[3] On January 9, 1769, Gálvez sent the fully repaired *San Carlos* north as flag-ship of a "Sacred Expedition" aimed at planting the first settlements in Alta California.[4]

In the autumn of 1779, rumours of war with England caused the viceroy to send two local transport vessels — the first *San Carlos* (alias *Toisón de Oro*) and the *San Antonio* (alias *Príncipe*) — to Manila to warn of the danger and to deliver $300,000 for war preparations. Both ships remained at Manila as part of the royal naval operations.

In 1781, these vessels were replaced at Manila by two other vessels:

the frigate *Aránzazu* and a packetboat named *San Carlos* (alias *El Fili-pino*).[5] This second *San Carlos* was built in Manila,[6] possibly as early as 1763,[7] and it arrived in San Blas in 1783.[8] It was this vessel that Narváez interacted with, first on the Pacific Northwest Coast and later in San Blas.

Lineage of José María Narváez

NARVÁEZ MEANS "dweller of a plain in the mountains." Although the name is now found in all Spanish-speaking regions of the world, it might have appeared first in the Navarra-Basque areas of northwest Spain and southwestern France. According to Luis G. Marmolejo-Meillón, who is a direct descendant of José María Narváez, the family name had its origin in the town of Saint-Jean-Pied-de-Port (in French) or San Juan Pie de Puerto (in Spanish), meaning literally "Saint John at the foot of the mountain pass." Today, this small settlement lies in the Pyrenees foothills at 43°09'54" N and 1°14'08" W in southwestern Aquitaine on the Nive River, about eight kilometres north of the French-Spanish border with Navarra. It is the starting point for the "Way of Saint James," the most popular option for making the pilgrimage over the mountains to Santiago de Compostela.

At one time, San Juan Pie de Puerto was the capital of the traditional Basque province of Lower Navarra. Prior to 1512, Navarra was an independent European kingdom located on both sides of the Pyrenees Mountains. At that time, it encompassed a portion of present-day Aquitaine in southwestern France and four areas in northwestern Spain: Navarra, Aragón, La Rioja, and Basque country (*Euskadi*). Luis Marmolejo-Meillón — a sixth-great-grandson of José María Narváez — believes the Narváez name probably was used to identify someone from early Navarra. (Today, Navarra consists of three chartered communities: Navarra, western Aragón, and northeastern La Rioja. The Basque country has been designated a separate autonomous community.

In the Americas, the first explorer named Narváez who left his mark on history was the Spanish soldier-conquistador Pánfilo de Narváez (1470–1528). During the so-called age of "discovery" he participated in the conquest of Cuba in 1511 and named the city of San Cristóbal de la Habana (Havana), but he is more famous as the leader of two failed expeditions, one of which resulted in an extraordinary cross-continent exploration.

In 1520, the Governor of Cuba sent Narváez to New Spain to stop the unauthorized invasion by Hernán Cortés. Although Narváez's 900 troops outnumbered Cortés' men three to one, he was defeated, taken prisoner, and jailed in New Spain for two years before being returned to Madrid. Meanwhile, one or more members of Narváez's expedition had brought smallpox to New Spain, and the deadly disease devastated the vulnerable Indigenous population.

In 1527, King Carlos V dispatched Narváez on a mission to explore and colonize Florida with five vessels and 600 men. All the vessels were sunk, however, in a storm off Cuba. Somehow, Narváez and about 300 survivors landed in Florida among hostile Aboriginals. The Spaniards marched north and then west along what is now the Gulf of Mexico, trying to reach the west coast of New Spain. During a storm, Narváez and several men were swept out to sea on a raft and were never seen again. Only four members of the ill-fated expedition survived an eight-year-long trek to what is now Sinaloa, and then on to Veracruz. Led by Álvar Núñez Cabeza de Vaca, they became the first Europeans to cross the continent — 258 years before the celebrated Scottish explorer Alexander Mackenzie (1764–1820) accomplished the feat in 1793.

Portrait of Don José María Narváez with
signature (1768–1840), ca. 1835. (GARCÍA)

On the Pacific Northwest Coast, the most notable person to bear the
Narváez surname was the Spanish-Mexican mariner, navigator, and
explorer José María Narváez (1768–1840). While Narváez's extended
ancestry remains a mystery, his list of descendants is growing. Although
his accomplishments were known to at least one of his most recognized
descendants — the controversial José López Portillo, President of Mexico from 1976 to 1982 — many other Narváez relations are also beginning to investigate his legacy. José Narváez and his wife María had nine
children and seventeen grandchildren that we know of. At least two of
Narváez's seven sons served in the Mexican Navy. As noted in Chapter
13, endnote 7, his second son, José María Miguel Narváez, sailed with

him to Monterey in 1822, when Mexico replaced Spain's sovereign control of Alta California.[1] Narváez's fourth son, Pedro Nolasco Antonio
José María Narváez, served as captain of the port at Monterey from
1839 to 1842, and he was the naval captain who arranged the terms of
surrender of Monterey to the United States on October 19, 1842.[2] The
author has tried to verify the following information, but he does not
claim that all of it is correct. Corrections will be welcomed online at
jemcdowell@shaw.ca.

DESCENDANTS OF ANTONIO NARVÁEZ AND ÚRSULA GERVETE

1 Antonio Narváez
   +Úrsula Gervete
   2 José María Narváez b: 1768 in Cadiz, Spain
      d: August 4, 1840 in Guadalajara, Mexico
      +María Leonarda Aleja Maldonado b: July 16, 1780
      m: October 23, 1796 in Tepic d: Aft. 1847
      3 José Narváez b: 1797 d: September 1, 1802
      3 José María Miguel Narváez b: September 30, 1798
      3 Francisco de Paula Guadalupe de Jesús Narváez
         b: April 3, 1801 in Tepic d: September 15, 1880 in Tepic
         +Josefa Labastida y Bravo b: November 3, 1815 in Tepic
         m: June 23, 1835 in Tepic d: November 15, 1887 in Tepic
         4 José Francisco Julio Ataulfo Narváez b: April 13, 1836
         4 Rosa Blanco Leonarda Abraham Narváez b: March 16, 1837
         4 María Margarita Sixta de Refugio Narváez
            b: March 26, 1838 in Tepic d: May 23, 1884 in Tepic
            +Edward Weber b: 1831 in Germany
            m: April 24, 1859 in Tepic d: September 9, 1863 in Tepic
            5 Margarita Weber b: January 19, 1860 in Tepic
               +José López Portillo y Rojas b: 1850
               m: April 24, 1884 in Guadalajara d: 1923
               6 María de los Ángeles López-Portillo Weber
               6 José López-Portillo Weber b: April 19, 1889 in Guadalajara
                  d: 1975
                  +María del Refugio Pacheco y Villa-Gordoa
                  b: 1892 m: October 13, 1913 in Guadalajara

      7 José López-Portillo b: June 16, 1920 in Mexico City
        d: February 17, 2004 in Mexico City
        +Aleksandra Acimovic Popovic
        8 Nabila López Portillo y Acimovic
        8 Alexander López Portillo y Acimovic
        *2nd Wife of José López-Portillo:
        +Carmen Romano y Nolk b: 1926 in Mexico City
        m: October 20, 1951 in Mexico City d: May 9, 2000
        8 José Ramón López Portillo y Romano
        8 Carmen Beatriz López Portillo y Romano
        8 Paulina López Portillo y Romano
     7 Alicia López-Portillo
   6 Jesús Eduardo López-Portillo Weber b: 1894 d: 1949
   6 Guillermo López-Portillo Weber b: 1895 d: 1963
    +Esther Vernon Galindo b: 1906 d: 1978
   6 Manuel López-Portillo Weber b: 1900 d: 1976
5 María Weber Narváez b: 1862 d: 1911
+Carlos Fernando Landero Castaños b: 1858 m: 1883 d: 1930
   6 Gabriela Landero-Weber b: 1884 d: 1897
   6 Margarita Landero-Weber b: 1886 d: 1956
   6 Pedro Antonio Landero-Weber b: 1888 d: 1943
    +María Guadalupe Pacheco Villa-Gordoa b: 1890
   6 María Landero-Weber b: 1890 d: 1937
    +Richard Hedley Ludlow Thomas b: 1874 m: 1913
   6 Mercedes Landero-Weber b: 1893 d: 1937
    +Manuel Chávez Hayhoe b: 1895 m: 1916
   6 Luz Carlota Landero-Weber b: 1895 d: 1895
   6 N Landero-Weber b: 1896 d. 1896
   6 José Vicente Landero-Weber b: 1900
   6 Luz Landero-Weber b: 1902
4 María Nieves Josefa Narváez b: August 5, 1839
+Julio Bertrand m: September 28, 1864 in Tepic
4 Josefa Dolores Narváez b: March 19, 1841
4 Rito José María Narváez b: May 22, 1842
+Ramona Jiménez m: 1866
4 Leonides Dolores Narváez b: August 8, 1843
4 Eugenio Narváez b: June 24, 1844
4 Pedro Eugenio Narváez b: June 30, 1845

4 Manuela Narváez b: October 29, 1847
+Karl Johan Heinrich Kofahl m: 1875
  5 Manuela Kofahl Narváez b: 1880
  5 Blanca Kofahl Narváez b: Abt. 1880
    +Luis Labastida Izquierdo b: 1873 m: 1904
    6 Luis Eduardo Francisco Labastida Kofahl b: 1905
    6 José Eduardo Labastida Kofahl
      +Gloria Ochoa Sánchez
    6 Julio Labastida Kofahl
      +Alicia Martín del Campo Dunn
      7 Julio Labastida Martín del Campo Kofahl
    6 Blanca Labastida Kofahl
    *2nd Husband of Blanca Kofahl Narváez:
    +José Francisco Labastida Izquierdo b: 1874 m: 1915
4 Julio Narváez b: 1854
4 María Narváez Labastida b: November 10, 1857
3 María Simona de los Ángeles Narváez b: October 27, 1803
3 Pedro Nolasco Antonio José María Narváez b: November 30, 1806
+María Rita Estrada Vellejo b: March 30, 1828 in Monterey, Alta California m: 1843 in Monterey, Alta California d: August 9, 1848 in Tepic, Nayarit, Mexico
4 Alberto Edward Narváez b: November 16, 1843 in Monterey, Alta California
4 Adolfo Narváez b: May 23, 1845 in Monterey, Alta California
4 Josefa Edelmira Narváez b: August 17, 1846 in Monterey, Alta California
d: June 9, 1880 in Colima, Mexico
+Francisco E. Trejo m: January 13, 1868 in Colima, Mexico
  5 Edelmira Trejo Narváez b: October 22, 1868 in Colima, Mexico
    d: January 23, 1950 in Guadalajara, Jalisco, Mexico
    +José Carlos Augustín Meillón m: October 5, 1887
    6 María Edelmira Meillón b: October 19, 1899 in Colima, Mexico
      d: October 14, 1982 in Albuquerque, New Mexico
    6 Carlos Francisco Meillón b: 1891 d: 1968
    6 Jorge Meillón b: 1897 d: 1972
    6 Alfredo Enrique Meillón b: 1901 d: 1978
      +Pearl Carter

      7 Guillermo Armando Meillón b: November 6, 1906
          d: October 15, 1982 in Tampico, Mexico
          +Clementina Briz Ortiz
          8 Eva R. Mellión y Briz b: May 17, 1935 in Mexico City, Mexico
             +Raúl Marmolejo Martínez b: July 6th 1935 in Tampico Mexico m: 1961 d: July 3rd, 2000 in Reynosa, Mexico
             9 Luis G. Marmolejo-Meillón b: May 11, 1962 in Tampico, Mexico
               +María Yolanda Aguado de las Heras b: March 9, 1960 in Madrid, Spain
    5 Ysaura Trejo Narváez
    5 Belisario Trejo Narváez b: 1873 d: 1903 in La Paz, Mexico
    5 Francisco José Narváez b: 1873
  4 Carolina Narváez b: January 13, 1848 in Monterey, Alta California
  4 Belisario Narváez
3 José María Pedro de Jesús Narváez b: January 18, 1809
3 José Ramón Nepomuceno Narváez b: November 19, 1811
3 María del Carmen Narváez b: 1818
3 Miguel Narváez
   +Rufina Cota Mendaros m: 1837

NOTE: Bold numbering indicates José María Narváez's direct line of descendancy to José López Portillo, former president of Mexico.

ENDNOTES

AUTHOR'S NOTE (pp. xiii–xiv)

1 In nautical terms, *piloto* does not mean the same as "pilot." The term for a coastal pilot was *práctico* — the lowest rank of the *pilotos*. See Freeman M. Tovell, *At the Far Reaches of Empire* (Vancouver, British Columbia: UBC Press, 2008), 359–360.

INTRODUCTION: AN OVERLOOKED EXPLORER (pp. 1–7)

1 BC Geographical Names, geobc.gov.bc.ca/bcnames (accessed March 10, 2015).
2 Jim McDowell, *José Narváez: The Forgotten Explorer* (Spokane, Washington: Arthur H. Clark Company, 1998).
3 Samuel Bawlf, *The Secret Voyage of Sir Francis Drake, 1577–1580* (New York: Walker & Co., 2003). In 2008, however, amateur historian Garry David Gitzen identified Nehalem Bay at 45°41'N on the Oregon Coast as a much more realistic location for Drake's landing. His book, *Francis Drake in Nehalem Bay 1579: Setting the Historical Record Straight* (Wheeler, Oregon: Fort Nehalem Publishing, 2011 edition), presents considerable supportive evidence, and it does not have Drake circumnavigating Vancouver Island.
4 Bruce Hutchinson, *The Fraser* (New York and Toronto: Rinehart & Co., 1950), 13–14.

5 In 2013, *BC BookWorld* editor Alan Twigg travelled to the mariner's birth-
   place — the village of Valeriano on the Greek island of Kefalonia — and
   found a monument commemorating this intriguing fabricator. A brass
   plaque names him Ioannis Apóstolos Focas-Valerianos. According to André
   Gerolymatos, history professor at Simon Fraser University with a special
   interest in espionage, the old mariner "had many names possibly because
   he was a bit of a scoundrel, in a charming sort of way." Gerolymatos said
   the man's most common name in Greece is Ioannis Focas (or Phokas). In
   other words, John Focas in English or Juan de Fuca in Spanish. Twigg was
   not the first researcher from the Pacific Northwest to hunt for the "great
   fabricator's" roots. In 1859, *Hutchings' California Magazine* ran a biography
   of the man known as John Phokas (Fucas), which was authored by Alexander S. Taylor, who wrote about California and Oregon history. Based on
   information obtained from the American Consul in the Ioanian Islands,
   Taylor found that the seafarer Ioannis Phokas was born in the village of
   Valeriano on the island of Cephalonia (Kefalonia) near the beginning of the
   sixteenth century. His ancestors had fled Constantinople in the early 1400s
   and one of them, Emmanuel Phokas, found refuge on the island of Cephalonia in 1470. Emmanuel reportedly had four sons, one of whom was the
   father of Ioannis Phokas. Because he was living in Valeriano, he was given
   the name Ioannis Phokas Valerianos. The middle name Apóstolos may have
   been given at baptism to clarify that "John" was being named after John the
   Apostle, not John the Baptist.

6 For the most recent, thorough, and temptingly believable presentation of
   the Juan de Fuca story, see Barry Gough, *Juan de Fuca's Strait: Voyages in the
   Waterway of Forgotten Dreams* (Madeira Park, B.C.: Harbour Publishing,
   2012), 35–71. For a more whimsical approach, see Alan Twigg, "Finding
   Juan de Fuca in Kefalonia," *British Columbia History* 46 (4): 36–39. Gough
   treats the tale as alleged history; Twigg's historical fiction renders it factual.
   Both authors hang the credibility of this recycled legend on a single unsub-
   stantiated letter that was contained in a book published in 1625 by the Rev-
   erend Samuel Purchas, titled *Hakluytus Posthumus; or, Purchas His Pilgrimes*.
   It constituted a third-hand version of Juan de Fuca's fabricated yarn. In 1622,
   Purchas had inherited the missive from his dead brother-in-law, Michael
   Lok, who had flogged the fable unsuccessfully for more than two decades.

7 William Kaye Lamb, "The Mystery of Mrs. Barkley's Diary: Notes on the
   Voyage of the 'Imperial Eagle,' 1786–87." *British Columbia Historical
   Quarterly* No. 6 (1942), 43.

CHAPTER 1: A YOUNG MARINER'S JOURNEY
FROM CADIZ TO NEW SPAIN (pp. 11–27)

1 The author has been unable to confirm Narváez's official date of birth. The record presents conflicting years of birth, ranging from 1756 (Narváez's Naval record) to 1771 (*Apéndice al Diccionario Universal de Historia y de Geografía*). The year 1768 used herein is based on Narváez's testimony before a military tribunal held in Tepic, México, on February 13, 1811, when he stated that he was 43 years old. (See Enrique Cárdenas de la Peña, *San Blas de Nayarit*, Vol. 2, 117.)

Pronunciation of the mariner's surname seems to have puzzled some English speaking readers. Although Narváez may appear to have two syllables, in Spanish it actually is composed of three — the first is followed by a distinct pause, while the second and third are separated by a short (almost indistinguishable) gap: *Nar–vá-ez*. The grammatical reason for this is straightforward. In Spanish, the strong (or open) vowels are *a, e,* and *o,* and the weak (closed) semivowels are *i, u,* and *y.* The basic rule regarding vowel combinations and syllables is the following: usually two strong vowels cannot be in the same syllable. Therefore, when two strong vowels are adjacent as in Narváez, they belong to separate syllables. In this surname, the two vowel letters — *a* and *e* — have distinct sounds. The *a* appears twice and, in both instances, is pronounced as it is in "c*a*sa." The *e* is pronounced as in "m*e*sa." Although the gap between the last two syllables is often indistinguishable in everyday speech, this hiatus separates the two vowel letters into different syllables, and therefore two equal (nearly blended) vocal efforts are required to pronounce each of the vowels. In Spanish, when the final letter in a word is a vowel, *n, s* (or *z*), the stress usually is placed on the next to last syllable. The acute accent inserted in Narváez indicates where the stress occurs, and it reminds a reader that the word has three syllables.

2 John Harbron, *Trafalgar and the Spanish Navy* (London: Conway, 1988), 14.

3 Ibid., 42.

4 Marina de Guerra, *Estado de los méritos y servicios del Primer Piloto, Graduado de Alférez de Navío de la Real Armada Don José María Narváez, de edad de 63 años, estado casado y sus servicios los siguientes* (Madrid: Archivo–Museo Don Álvaro de Bazán, located in Museo Naval, 1825), Leg. 826, 1.

5 The *Triunfante* was launched in Ferrol, Spain, in 1756 and wrecked near Roses, Spain, in 1795. (See Harbron, *Trafalgar*, 169.)

6 More than three hundred years after Spain lost control of Gibraltar, it remains a bone of contention between Spain and Britain. In August 2013, the

centuries-old dispute over the seven-square-kilometre strip of land erupted again over a disagreement about Spanish fishing rights and an artificial reef installed by the local British-controlled government. Spain threatened to close the only border; the local mayor asked Britain to send in the Royal Navy. Paul Waldie, "Gloves dropped in fight for Gibraltar: 'Play time is over.'" *Globe and Mail* (August 7, 2013), 1.

7 From *piloto de segunda clase* (second mate), to *piloto de primera clase* (first mate), to *alférez de fragata* (frigate ensign), and *alférez de navío* (ship's ensign), a mariner aspired to *teniente de fragata* (frigate lieutenant). However, few former *pilotos* achieved that rank. Commissioned officers graduated from marine academies as *tenientes de fragata*. They aspired to the ranks of *teniente de navío* (ship's lieutenant), *capitán de fragata* (frigate captain), and *capitán de navío* (ship's captain). The chief officer of a Spanish vessel was the *comandante* (commander), regardless of rank. The *piloto* was the mate, the *pilotín* was the *piloto's* mate. See Warren Cook, *Flood Tide of Empire: Spain and the Pacific Northwest, 1543–1819* (New Haven & London: Yale University Press, 1973), 55n29. For a more complete, but slightly confusing, presentation of the rank and structure of the Spanish Navy, see Tovell, *At the Far Reaches*, 359–360. It should be noted that a *piloto's* rank and actual function during a particular assignment did not always correspond. For example, Narváez's rank during his exploration of the Salish Sea in 1791 was *piloto de segunda clase* (second mate), yet he functioned as *comandante* (commander) of that part of the larger expedition. Narváez held the same rank during the voyage of 1788, yet he functioned as López de Haro's first *piloto* (first mate).

8 See Appendix G.

9 Marina de Guerra, *Estado de los méritos y servicios*, 2.

10 Initially, only two were sent: Narváez and Juan Martínez Zayas. (See Tovell, *At the Far Reaches*, 172.)

11 Marina de Guerra, *Estado de los méritos y servicios*, 2.

12 Michael E. Thurman, *The Naval Department of San Blas: New Spain's Bastion for Alta California and Nootka, 1767–1798* (Glendale, California: Arthur H. Clark Co., 1967), 23, 56. Although the Spanish first arrived at San Blas in 1531, the official date of founding is 1768 when Don Manuel Rivera and 116 Spanish families arrived, on orders of the Viceroy of New Spain, Carlos Francisco de Croix, Marqués de Croix, and under the supervision of José de Gálvez, Visitador ("inspector") General of New Spain. Gálvez also established San Blas formally as a royal seaport on May 16, 1768.

13 Born in Lima, Peru, in 1743, Juan Francisco de la Bodega y Quadra's father was Tomás de la Bodega y de las Llanas, a Spanish-born official in the Peruvian bureaucracy. His mother, Doña Francisca de Mollinedo y Losada, was descended from one of Peru's most prominent aristocratic families. (See Cook, *Flood Tide*, 71.) Juan Francisco was descended through his father from both the Bodega and Quadra families of Spain, who were well established Basques of the minor landed nobility. (See Tovell, *At the Far Reaches*, 5.) Unfortunately, his full surname was incorrectly shortened to "Quadra" by British mariners such as Captain George Vancouver, and this mistake has been perpetuated frequently in Canada. Herein, the author has adhered to the standard convention of dropping distant patronymical references, and referred to the respected mariner as Bodega. Freeman Tovell, who has written the most authoritative biography of the man, followed the same practice.

14 The location indicated on the Chart of the Port of Santiago drawn in 1780 by José Camacho is 60°13' latitude. A small cross on an island in the middle of the bay marks the spot where the possession ceremony was held. (See Thurman, *The Naval Department*, plate 9, 186f.)

15 Blaise was a physician and bishop of Sebastea in Armenia (today's Sivas, Turkey), who was martyred in the year 316. In the Roman Catholic Church, his feast falls on February 3; in the Eastern Orthodox Church, the date is February 11.

16 Tovell, *At the Far Reaches*, 164.

17 Today an image of Nuestra Señora del Rosario la Marinera is located on the offshore islet of Piedra Blanca.

18 For background, see Thurman, *The Naval Department*.

19 José María Narváez, "Report about the Coasts of the South Sea" (*The Political and Literary Weekly of Mexico*, Vol. 4, Numbers 12 and 13, 1822) transcribed by Gabriel Agraz García, *Un Gaditano Insigne en América: Don José María Narbáes, explorador y cartógrafo de Alaska, de California y del primer mapa de Jalisco* (México: Real Academia Hispanoamericana de Ciencias, Artes y Letras, 1979), 36.

20 The papal bull and the treaty established Spain's rights of sovereignty in the Pacific as opposed to those of Portugal, but Madrid was never able to have it applied to other nations.

CHAPTER 2: INVESTIGATING THE RUSSIAN THREAT (pp. 28–42)

1 Maria Shaa Tláa Williams, *The Alaska Native Reader: History, Culture, Politics* (Durham: Duke University Press, 2009), 30; John L. Eliot, "Alaska's

Island Refuge" (*National Geographic*, November 1993), 53.

2 José María Narváez, *Diario el Navegación que espera hazer el 2nd Piloto de la Real Armada Don José María Narbáez en el paquebot el S.M. nombrado el San Carlos (alias el Filipino) al mando del Primer Piloto de [Marina] Don Gonzalo López de Haro . . . , 1788* (William Andrews Clark Memorial Library, University of California, Los Angeles). For this reference, and all subsequent references herein, to Narváez's *Diario el Navegación*, see the author's seminal translation of the original document: "Narrative of the Voyage, 1778," which constitutes chapter nine in Jim McDowell, *José Narváez: The Forgotten Explorer* (Spokane, Washington: Arthur H. Clark Co., 1998), 96–163.

3 McDowell, *José Narváez*, 102–111.

4 Ibid., 111–112.

5 Ibid., 112–113.

6 The Spaniards would not explore the sound completely until 1790.

7 McDowell, 111n32; 111n30; 114–118.

8 The Spaniards later learned that the Indians paid the Russians a three-ruble head tax and a 10 percent tax on trade. See Christon I. Archer, "Russians, Indians & Passages," *Explorations in Alaska* (Anchorage, Alaska: Cook Inlet Historical Society, 1980), 129–143.

9 Antonio Serantes, *Diario de Antonio Serantes, 1788* (México City: Biblioteca Nacional), June 28–30. Serantes' description is almost identical to the one recorded by Narváez. Between June 29 and July 1, Martínez apparently engaged in an even more devious exchange by trading the original tribute slips for substitute receipts, which he dated 1788 in the name of the King of Spain. See Antonio Palacios, *Diario de Antonio Palacios, 1788* (Mexico City: Biblioteca Nacional), June 30.

10 On June 27, Martínez met a single Russian lookout when he reached the southernmost point of the Trinity Islands, but he would not visit Potap Kuzmich Zaikov's large establishment in today's Dutch Harbor, Unalaska, until July 21 — three weeks after Narváez's first contact with Delarov at Three Saints Bay.

11 Jim McDowell, "Narrative of the Voyage, 1778," entry for June 30 to July 1, 1788.

12 The copied letter eventually was turned over to the viceroy. It now resides in the Spanish National Archives.

13 McDowell, "Narrative of the Voyage, 1778," entry for July 29 and 30, 137–138; 140n102.

14 Ibid., entry for August 3 and 4, 140.

15 Robin Inglis, *Spain and the North Pacific Coast* (Vancouver, British Columbia: Vancouver Maritime Museum, 1992), 29.

16 McDowell, "Narrative of the Voyage," entry for August 3 and 4, 140.

17 Kiril Khlebnikov, *Russkaia America v neopublikovannykh zapiskakh K.T. Khlebnikova* (Leningrad: Nauka, 1979), 94 (translated by Lydia Black).

18 Esteban José Martínez, *Diario de Esteban José Martínez, 1788* (Mexico City: Archives of the Gabinete de Historia Natural), Leg., 159.

19 Khlebnikov, *Russkaia America*, 94.

20 Narváez, *Diario el Navegación*, entry for June 1, 1788, 111n30.

21 Ibid., entries for August 4 and 5, 1788, 140n103; 141n104.

22 Ibid., entry for June 6, 1788, 111n30.

23 Manuel Antonio Flórez, "Flórez to Valdés, November 26, 1778" (Archivo General Interior del Estado, México), Leg. 20, Ramo 34.

24 Christon I. Archer, "Russians, Indians & Passages: Spanish Voyages in Alaska in the 18th Century," 129–130.

25 Christon I. Archer, "Seduction before Sovereignty: Spanish Efforts to Manipulate the Natives in their Claims to the Northwest Coast" (Paper delivered at the Vancouver Conference on Exploration & Discovery, Vancouver, B.C., April 1992), 21–25.

26 Inglis, *Spain and the North Pacific Coast*, 31–33.

27 Ibid.

28 Jim McDowell, *Father August Brabant* (Vancouver: Ronsdale Press, 2012), 65; *Hamatsa* (Vancouver: Ronsdale Press, 1997), 64. Gough mistakenly has the Pérez expedition (and Martínez) visiting Nootka in 1774. (See Gough, *Juan de Fuca's Strait*, 126.)

CHAPTER 3: CONFLICT AT NOOTKA SOUND, 1789–1790 (pp. 43–60)

1 William Kaye Lamb, "The Mystery of Mrs. Barkley's Diary," 31–48; 49–60.

2 Gough, *Juan de Fuca's Strait*, 95–96.

3 Ibid., 97–101.

4 Ibid., 112–116.

5 See Appendix C for a partial history of this vessel.

6 Although one historian cited Nitnat, most of the Spanish charts used Nitinat or a variation thereof. John Kendrick, *The Voyage of* Sutil *and* Mexicana: *The Last Spanish Exploration of the Northwest Coast of America, 1792* (Spokane, Washington: Arthur Clark, 1990), 241.

7 Henry R. Wagner, *Spanish Explorations in Strait of Juan de Fuca* (New York: Fine Arts Press, 1933, AMS Press, 1971), 20.

8 Esteban José Martínez, *Diario*, July 5, 1789, as translated by Wagner in *Spanish Explorations*, 4; James Colnett, *A translation of the Diary of Esteban José Martínez in The Journal of Captain James Colnett*. In *Juan de Fuca's Strait*, Gough neglected to give Narváez due credit for his achievement in exploring the strait, because he focused his narrative on Martínez's cunning efforts to win recognition for being the first European to "discover" the inlet.

9 Cook, 276, 276n; Wagner, *Spanish Explorations*, 141, 141n.

10 Juan Pantoja y Arriaga. (1791). *Extracto de la navegación que ha hecho el piloto Don Juan Pantoja y Arriaga en el paquebot de S. M. el San Carlos. . . desde San Blas el 4 de Febrero de 1791.* MS 332, Museo Naval, Madrid. Translations thereof are cited herein as Juan Pantoja y Arriaga, *Extract of the navigation* [of 1791], by Henry Raup Wagner in *Spanish Explorations*, 155–200.

11 Ibid., 161–162.

12 Ibid.

13 Cook, 276.

14 Wagner, *Spanish Explorations*, 106.

15 For a thorough description of Quimper's exploration, see Gough, *Juan de Fuca's Strait*, 138–143 with Quimper's chart shown on 140–141. Gough asserts that at some point Quimper "spied a pale blue hump that he named Lasqueti." It is, however, physically impossible to see this relatively small Northern Gulf Island feature from any sea-level location in Juan de Fuca Strait.

16 John Kendrick, *The Men with Wooden Feet* (Toronto: NC Press, 1990), 45.

17 Cook, *Flood Tide*, 276n; Wagner, *Spanish Explorations*, 141; Frederick William Howay, *Voyages of the "Columbia" to the Northwest Coast, 1787–1790 and 1790–1793* (Boston: Massachusetts Historical Society, 1941), 227n.

18 Christon I. Archer, "Eliza y Reventa, Francisco de," in *Dictionary of Canadian Biography*, Vol. 6 (Toronto: University of Toronto Press), 1987.

19 On pages 130–131 of *Juan de Fuca's Strait*, Gough presented a cursory analysis of the transformations that eventually produced the *Santa Saturnina*, which incorrectly implies that the vessel Narváez used at this stage was the *Santa Gertrudis la Magna*. Gough also inserted endnote 121, which stated that I gave "some of the details on this vessel [in my previous book about Narváez], which are not entirely finite or clear." In fact, Appendix B in that book presented (what was then) the most complete, accurate, and carefully

documented account of the schooner's complex origins and three lives between March 1788 and December 1792. That account is also updated in
Appendix C of this book.

20 Marina de Guerra, *Estado de los méritos y servicios*, 3.

CHAPTER 4: IN QUEST OF THE NORTHWEST PASSAGE, 1791 (pp. 63–70)

1 Michael W. Mathes, "The Province of Anian and its Strait: Myth, Reality,
and Exploration of the Pacific Northwest, 1542–1792," 19. It is also reproduced in Tovell, *At the Far Reaches*, 186f.

2 Robin Inglis, *Spain and the North Pacific Coast*, 58, 119, 184; Henry Raup
Wagner, *Spanish Voyages to the Northwest Coast of America in the Sixteenth
Century* (San Francisco: California Historical Society, 1929), 112.

3 For details of this expedition, see Gough, *Juan de Fuca's Strait*, 152–153.

4 Tovell, *At the Far Reaches*, 157.

5 Juan Pantoja y Arriaga, *Extract of the navigation* [of 1791], translated by
Wagner in *Spanish Explorations*, 157–158.

6 The first European to sight land in the area where Trinidad Bay, California,
is now located was the Portuguese navigator Sebastián Rodríguez Cermeño
(1560–1602). Returning from Manila in 1595 on the fully loaded 200-ton
Spanish galleon *San Agustín*, Cermeño had viceregal orders to locate a safe
port along the northern California coast where galleons could take refuge,
refit, and restock before continuing south to Acapulco. On November 4,
1595, Cermeño saw the continental shore somewhere between what are now
Point St. George (at Crescent City) and Trinidad Head, but he did not make
landfall. Another 180 years would pass before a European ship anchored in
Trinidad Bay. During the expedition of Pacific Northwest Coast waters by
Bruno de Hezeta and Bodega y Quadra in 1775, these mariners took shelter
in the protected harbour on June 9 of that year. On June 11, which was
Trinity Sunday, the Spaniards climbed the protective headland, planted a
wooden cross, conducted a formal act of possession, and named the area La
Santísima Trinidad. (See Tovell, *At the Far Reaches*, 21–22.) In 1913, the
Women's Club of Humboldt County installed a six-metre-high stone cross
at the site, which bears the inscription CAROLUS III DEI G. HYSPAN-
IARUM REX, June 9 [sic], 1775. (On-site research by author, 2014.)

CHAPTER 5: SURVEYING "PUERTO NARVÁEZ," MAY 1791 (pp. 71–81)

1 The chapel at their home base in San Blas was also dedicated to Nuestra
Señora del Rosario la Marinera — the name that these explorers would soon

give to what eventually became the northern section of the Salish Sea.

2　Inglis, *Spain and the North Pacific*, 85.

3　Warp: As a verb, it has (or had) several meanings. During the age of sail, seafarers were often faced with the question of how to make headway out of a harbour, through a channel, or even in open water when there was little or no wind. Such conditions often forced eighteenth-century mariners to *warp* out of a harbour using various methods. A longboat might take a kedge anchor ahead and drop it, attached to a *warp* line. Using a windlass to haul the rope in, sailors would inch the vessel seaward. Alternatively, one or more fixed objects (a tree, rock, or another vessel) could be used to secure the line or lines for *warping* the vessel. Another method involved oarsmen aboard one or more longboats, attaching *warp* lines to a large sailing vessel, and *warping* (or towing) the larger vessel. Unlike English terminology, the Spanish and the French commonly viewed towing as one form of warping. In Spanish, *espiar* means "to spy, observe, or discover." Among early Spanish mariners, however, it sometimes meant "to make a boat move by pulling it," in other words "to warp." More specifically, Spanish also has the word *remolcar*, "to tow." The French word *remorquer* also means "to warp," by pulling or towing a vessel by a boat or other small vessel with oars. See William Falconer, *An Universal Dictionary of the Marine* (London: Latimer Trend, 1780), 325, 397; Martín Fernández de Navarrete, *Diccionario Marítimo Español* (Madrid: Imprenta Real, 1831), 259–260; William Henry Smyth, *The Sailor's Word-Book* (London: Blackie and Son, 1867), 718; Dean King, *A Sea of Words* (New York: Henry Holt, 1995), 393.

4　See Appendix D for more exact measurements of the *Santa Saturnina*.

5　Tovell, *At the Far Reaches*, 159. Gough seems unduly perplexed by Eliza's decision, which he asserted has "never [been] properly explained." Gough also stated "we do not know the secret file on this" (Gough, *Juan de Fuca's Strait*, 145). Based on the information provided by Tovell and myself, Gough's concerns seem unwarranted.

6　John Meares, *Voyages Made in the Years 1788 and 1789 from China to the Northwest Coast of America* (Amsterdam: N. Israel; New York: Da Capo, 1967), 228–231.

7　Juan Pantoja y Arriaga, *Extract of the navigation* [of 1791], translated by Wagner in *Spanish Explorations*, 165.

8　Francisco Eliza, *Extract of the voyage, explorations and discoveries made under an order of His Excellency, the Conde de Revilla Gigedo, viceroy of New Spain, communicated by the captain of the royal fleet, Don Juan Francisco de la Bodega y Quadra, commandant of the department of San Blas, on the north coast of the* *Californias from 48°26' to 49°50' N. with the packetboat* San Carlos . . . *and* *the schooner* Santa Saturnina *alias* Las Orcasitas . . . , *the expedition being* *commanded by the lieutenant of the royal fleet and commandant of the establish-* *ment of San Lorenzo de Nuca Don Francisco de Eliza in the year 1791. Trans-* *lated by Henry R. Wagner, Spanish Exploration in the Strait of Juan de Fuca* (New York: Fine Arts Press, 1929), 144. To obtain quality furs for their copper sheets, the competitive British and American fur traders had been forced to adopt a one-pelt to four-coppers rate of exchange. The Spanish found this excessive, and tried to barter attractive sea shells, colourful beads, and fewer copper sheets.

9 Pantoja, *Extract of the navigation*, 165–166.

10 Ibid., 166.

11 Eliza, *Extract of the voyage*, 145–146.

12 Pantoja, *Extract of the navigation*, 167.

13 Eliza, *Extract of the voyage*, 145–146.

14 In 2014, the Tla-o-qui-aht First Nation used a previously exercised author-ity to manage areas of its traditional territory to unilaterally declare Tran-quil Valley a tribal park to protect it from mining. See Gordon Hoekstra, "Island First Nation declares 'tribal park' to protect land," *Vancouver Sun*, April 14, 2014, A4.

15 Based on these realities, the assertion by one aspiring historian that this incident illustrated Narváez's "youth and inexperience" and his tendency to "assume too much" in order "to avoid extra work when charting certain areas" seems totally unjustifiable. See Devon Drury, "That Immense and Dangerous Sea: Spanish Imperial Policy and Power During the Exploration of the Salish Sea, 1700–1791" (master's thesis, University of Victoria, British Columbia, 2007), 123–124.

16 Juan Carrasco, *Extract of the voyage with His Majesty's schooner the* Santa Saturnina *in company with the packetboat* San Carlos *from the Puerto de* *Santa Cruz de Nuca in the explorations of the coast to the south of the port, and* *arrival at the Department of San Blas during the present year of 1791.* Trans-lated by Henry R. Wagner, *Spanish Explorations in the Strait of Juan de Fuca* (New York: Fine Arts Press, 1929), 200. In Derek Hayes' impressive *British* *Columbia: A New Historical Atlas* (Douglas & McIntyre: Vancouver/Toronto, 2012), 33, the author mistakenly attributes this chart to Narváez and has Juan Pantoja helping him. Narváez may have been in command, but the

handwriting and cartographic style is definitely Carrasco's, and Pantoja was not present.

17 Pantoja, *Extract of the navigation*, 167–168.

18 Eliza, *Extract of the voyage*, 145.

19 Eugene Arima and John Dewhirst, "Nootkans of Vancouver Island," in William Sturtevant (ed.), *Handbook of North American Indians*, v. 7 (Washington: Smithsonian Institution, 1990), 392. This presents a map of territories and major settlements of the Nootkan tribal groups in the late nineteenth century. The author has slightly modified the orthography used there to conform with the *practical* orthography developed by ethnographer/linguist Randy Bouchard (see Chapter 6, note 3). The glottalized sonant "7" is unpronounceable by speakers of English. (A sonant is a voiced sound, belonging to the class of frictionless continuants or nasals, which is capable of forming a syllable.)

20 Pantoja, *Extract of the navigation*, 168–169.

21 Ibid., 169.

22 Eliza, *Extract of the voyage*, 146.

CHAPTER 6: CHARTING "ENTRADA DE NITINAT," JUNE 1791
(pp. 82–93)

1 Carrasco, *Extract of the voyage*, 200.

2 Eugene Arima and John Dewhirst, "Nootkans of Vancouver Island," 392.

3 In this chapter, the author has used the *practical* orthography developed in 1971 by ethnographer/linguist Randy Bouchard during the British Columbia Indian Language Project, Victoria, B.C. This orthography was designed to resemble the English alphabet and to be writable on an ordinary typewriter. See Alan D. McMillan, *Since the Time of the Transformers* (Vancouver: UBC Press, 1999), who used the same orthography in this area; Randy Bouchard *et al.*, *British Columbia Indian Language Project fonds AR019* (University of Victoria Archives, Victoria, British Columbia, 1973–1976); David W. Ellis and Luke Swan, *Teachings of the Tides: Uses of Marine Invertebrates by the Manhousat People* (Nanaimo, B.C.: Theytus Books, 1981); *Omniglot: the online encyclopedia of writing systems and languages* at www.omniglot.com/writing/nuchahnulth.htm (accessed January 24, 2014).

4 Eliza, *Extract of the voyage*, 149.

5 Why Carrasco did not erase the first series of islands is a mystery. Perhaps he simply wanted to draw attention to the need for resolving the correct location at a later date.

6 Eliza, *Extract of the voyage*, 149.

7 Ibid.

8 Alan D. McMillan, *Since the Time of the Transformers*, 64, 69.

9 Carrasco, *Extract of the voyage*, 200.

10 According to Luis Marmolejo, Carrasco used the symbols of the "floating man" and the letter "P" on different charts to indicate the type of sea floor. For example, "P" means *fondo de piedras* or "stone/gravel sea floor."

11 Robert T. Boyd, "Demographic History, 1774–1874," *Handbook of North American Indians*, Vol. 7, 145.

12 Eliza, *Extract of the voyage*, 148.

CHAPTER 7: RECONNAISSANCE OF AN UNKNOWN
ARCHIPELAGO, MAY–JUNE 1791 (pp. 94–118)

1 Eliza, *Extract of the voyage*, 148.

2 Wagner, *Spanish Explorations*, 106.

3 Named by Quimper in 1789 for his *piloto* Gonzalo López de Haro, whose surname was given to the adjacent strait. (See Wagner, *Spanish Explorations*, 117.)

4 Eliza, *Extract of the voyage*, 148–149 and Pantoja, *Extract of the navigation*, 171.

5 Pantoja, *Extract of the navigation*, 171.

6 Wagner, *Spanish Explorations*, 31. Not page 34 as cited by Gough, who also has this event happening on the July 31, not May 31. (See Gough, *Juan de Fuca's Strait*, 146.)

7 Tovell, *At the Far Reaches*, 159.

8 Robin Inglis, *Historical Dictionary of the Discovery and Exploration of the Northwest Coast of America* (Lanham, MD: Scarecrow Press, 2008), 115.

9 Eliza, *Extract of the voyage*, 149.

10 Ibid. Although Eliza's journal does not make it explicitly clear that he dispatched four *pilotos* on this exploration, a close reading of his instructions to Narváez, facts of the situation on June 14, and Pantoja's subsequent description of the expedition make it obvious that two *pilotos* (Narváez and Carrasco) were required on the schooner and two more (Pantoja and Verdía) were needed for the longboat.

11 Pantoja, *Extract of the navigation*, 173.

12 Ibid., 172.

13 Ibid., 172–173.

14 The feast day of San Antonio de Padua is June 13.

15 Pantoja, *Extract of the navigation*, 173. For details about eighteenth-century survey procedures, see Nick Doe, "Some Anomalies in a Spanish Chart of Vancouver Island 1791," *Lighthouse* 56 (Fall 1997), 7–20.

16 See National Oceanic and Atmospheric Administration Nautical Chart 18421 and Canadian Hydrographic Service Chart 3441.

17 Ibid., 174.

18 Ibid., 173.

19 Ibid., 173–74.

20 Ibid., 174.

21 Ibid., 175.

22 Ibid.

23 Ibid.

24 Ibid., 175–176.

25 Ibid. Pantoja, as he was inclined to do, gave himself credit for naming the inland sea, but it was undoubtedly arrived at jointly, based on the symbolic importance of the central figure to all mariners, especially those from San Blas. In fact, in a letter that he wrote after the expedition finished, he explicitly said "we discovered the great Canal" (see Wagner, *Spanish Explorations*, 198). Nevertheless, Wagner accepted Pantoja's use of "I" in his extract, and credited him with the discovery. Gough, in *Juan de Fuca's Strait*, 147, mistakenly credits Eliza with naming the large waterway. In the same paragraph, his grammatical construction incorrectly implies that Eliza and Narváez sailed at the same time in opposite directions. Gough neglects to describe any of these significant first European explorations made during this reconnaissance, which were done so thoroughly, and later charted so accurately, that Captain George Vancouver would rely on these findings rather than have his second in command, William Broughton, re-explore the area.

26 According to experienced mariner Captain Steve Mayo of Bellingham, Washington, the *Saturnina* had "hounds" near the top of the mast where the shrouds and stays were attached and a simple set of crosstrees. This served as a perch on which a lookout could stand or sit. "I think sending a man up the ratlines of the foremast to the hounds or crosstrees would have been a regular thing to do on the *Saturnina* whenever deemed necessary and even in fairly sloppy conditions," said Mayo. "I can also imagine the *pilotos* going up with a telescope often to satisfy their curiosity firsthand."

27 The Museo Naval in Madrid holds two versions of Carrasco's chart of the Narváez expedition of 1791. Carrasco's working chart is catalogued as MN

3-E-11. It is almost identical to MN 3-E-1 (13), which has been displayed and published consistently to show Carrasco's final chart, and it is shown in this book. The working chart is interesting in that it omits certain notations that were added later. It also includes other notations that do not appear on the final version, and it shows grid lines in several places which Carrasco used to draft insets. Differences between the two charts have been most thoroughly analyzed by Luis Marmolejo of San José, California — a direct descendant of José María Narváez. Marmolejo is developing a comprehensive e-book collection of the navigator's charts, titled *The Cartography of Frigate Captain José María Narváez (1768–1840)*. According to Marmolejo, this will be a "quantitative and qualitative analysis of the cartography of José María Narváez, including the Pacific Northwest (Alta California and Vancouver Island to Alaska), Mexico and the Philippines." It can be accessed online at groups.google.com/forum/#!forum/josemarianarvaez-cartographysanblas. Marmolejo also can be contacted at lgmarmolejo@gmail.com. Another researcher who has examined the differences in Carrasco's two charts is Nick Doe, of Gabriola Island, British Columbia.

28   This is the only anchorage shown on Narváez's chart. The small "x's" that he inserted at various places appear to be points at which sightings were taken, rather than anchorages.

29   Pantoja, *Extract of the navigation*, 176.

30   Ibid.

31   Ibid., 176–177.

32   In a letter, written from San Blas on December 29, 1791, to his "most venerated friend," Señor Don José de Prados y Salbatierra in Peru, Pantoja wrote: "I have the pleasure of sending you a long extract and respective chart of, in my opinion, the splendid expedition which *we* have made from Noca to the Estrecho de Juan de Fuca, in the interior of which *we* discovered the great Canal de Nuestra Señora del Rosario la Marinera, which is wider than the strait itself and whose limits up to now are unknown" (emphasis added). (Although Pantoja only participated in the first, small part of exploring the Gran Canal, this statement leads one to believe he was present throughout. On the other hand, he makes it clear that finding the inland sea was a collective discovery, not his alone, as he stated in his extract.) "In the general naming which we gave to everything discovered [at the end of the expedition], I had the glorious daring to cede the right which belonged to me [to name a small island and a point of land] to His Excellency Señor Don Francisco Gil y Lemus, the most worthy viceroy of your kingdom." (Francisco

Gil de Taboada Lemos y Villamarín was viceroy to Peru from May 17, 1790, to June 6, 1796.) See Wagner, *Spanish Explorations*, 198–200.

33 Pantoja, *Extract of the navigation*, 177; Eliza, *Extract of the voyage*, 149.
34 Eliza, *Extract of the voyage*, 149–150.
35 Ibid., 178.
36 Ibid., 150.
37 Pantoja, *Extract of the navigation*, 177–178.
38 Eliza, *Extract of the voyage*, 150.
39 Pantoja, *Extract of the navigation*, 178.

CHAPTER 8: EXPLORATION OF THE GRAN CANAL'S
EAST SHORE, JULY 1791 (pp. 119–145)

1 Eliza, *Extract of the voyage*, 150.
2 Pantoja, *Extract of the navigation*, 178.
3 Carrasco's journal indicates five soldiers. Most of the sailors and soldiers were Mexican.
4 Named by Manuel Quimper in 1790. See Henry R. Wagner, *Spanish Explorations*, 113.
5 Wagner consistently misrepresented this as "the Eliza chart." Although Eliza supervised creation of the penultimate draft of this chart at Nootka, the evidence clearly indicates that Carrasco prepared the final draft in San Blas with the assistance of his fellow *pilotos*.
6 Henry R. Wagner, *Spanish Explorations*, 16.
7 United States Hydrographic Office, *The Coast of British Columbia: Including the Juan de Fuca Strait, Puget Sound, Vancouver, and the Queen Charlotte Islands* (Washington, D.C.: Government Printing Office, 1891), 131–132.
8 Tom Dailey, "Coast Salish Villages of Puget Sound," http://coastsalishmap.org (accessed September 1, 2013); Wayne Precott Suttles, "Economic Life of the Coast Salish in Haro and Rosario Straits," *Coast Salish and Western Washington Indians*, Vol. 1 (New York: Garland Publishing, 1974).
9 Pantoja, *Extract of the navigation*, 180.
10 Alejandro Malaspina, *Viaje político-científico alrededor del mundo por las corbetas Descubierta y Atrevida, 1789–1794*, two vols. edited by Pedro de Novo y Colson, Madrid, 1885, translated by Carl Robinson, 1934, and titled *Politico-Scientific Voyage Round the World by the Corvettes Descubierta and Atrevida under the Command of the Naval Captains Don Alexandro Malaspina and Don José de Bustamante y Guerra from 1789–1794*, 361.
11 Warren Cook, *Flood Tide*, 313–314.

12 Wayne Suttles, "Central Coast Salish," in *Handbook of North American Indians, Northwest Coast*, Vol. 7 (Washington, D.C.: Smithsonian Institution Press, 1990), 453–455.

13 Barbara Huck, "The Beach Grove Site," *In Search of Ancient British Columbia*, Vol. 1 (Winnipeg: Heartland, 2006), 183–185.

14 Thomas Bartroli, *Discovery of the Site of Vancouver City by José María Narváez in 1791* (Vancouver: Bartroli, 1986), 17.

15 Pantoja, *Extract of the navigation*, 186.

16 Wayne Suttles, "Central Coast Salish," 453–455.

17 Eliza, *Extract of the voyage*, 152.

18 James Skitt Matthews, "Conversations with Khahtsahlano, 1932–1954" (Vancouver: City of Vancouver Archives, 1955), 8C, 8D, 24A, 43, 394. Matthews obtained his information from August Jack Khahtsahlano, born 1877, the grandson of Squamish Chief Khatsahlanough. Khahtsahlano was living on the Capilano Indian Reserve and his grandfather had lived at the large Squamish village in Stanley Park.

19 Pantoja, *Extract of the navigation*, 187. In this instance, Pantoja mistakenly reported that this and other events occurred at Isla de Zepeda, not Islas de Lángara. The latter location is confirmed by Warren Cook, *Flood Tide*, 305.

20 Wagner and others have mistakenly concluded that this settlement was located at today's Point Atkinson. See Wayne Suttles, "Central Coast Salish," 453–455.

21 James Skitt Matthews, "Conversations with Khahtsahlano," 24A, 40, 43, 123, 414. According to Wayne Suttles, the Musqueam may have resided here before 1850, but the Squamish used the site as a summer camp. See *Handbook of North American Indians, Northwest Coast*, v. 7, 453–455.

22 Eliza, *Extract of the voyage*, 151–152. Regrettably, Gough (147) overlooked Eliza's reference to Narváez's finding "drinkable" water at the mouth of Burrard Inlet, and only mentioned the water that was "more sweet than salt," which Narváez tasted earlier as he sailed past the southern mouth of the Fraser River. Also note that Eliza and Pantoja gleaned different information about "copious" rivers and "sweet water." Eliza referenced an event that occurred at one specific location, and Pantoja referenced a different one. Wagner seems to have missed this point (see Eliza, *Extract of the navigation*, 152n22.) Although it would be incorrect to credit Narváez with being the first European to find the Fraser River, it is not inaccurate to note that he was the first such explorer to come that close. Using Narváez's findings

in 1792, Captains Alcalá-Galiano and Valdés would become the first Europeans to enter the great river.

23 Matthews, "Conversations with Khahtsahlano," 24, 417, 422, 443.

24 Ibid., 40. Wayne Suttles used ciclxwiqw. See *Handbook of North American Indians, Northwest Coast*, v. 7, 453–455.

25 The British Captain George Vancouver would follow by water in 1792, and the celebrated Scottish explorer Alexander Mackenzie would arrive overland in 1793.

26 Wagner grasped the name swapping correctly, but left the impression that Eliza, rather than Carrasco, selected Lasquety [sic]. See Wagner, *Spanish Explorations*, 38–39. Captain John Walbran mistakenly attributed the naming of Lasqueti to Narváez. See John T. Walbran, *British Columbia Place Names, their Origin and History* (Vancouver: J. J. Douglas Ltd., 1971 reprint of 1909), 302. G. P. V. and Helen B. Akrigg also misattributed the naming to Narváez, but they correctly noted that the island was named "after Juan María Lasqueti, a prominent Spanish naval officer." See G. P. V. and Helen B. Akrigg, *British Columbia Place Names* (Vancouver: UBC Press, 1997), 150. Juan María Lasqueti y Roy was born in Cadiz July 24, 1743, and became a *Capitán de Navío*. See Vicente de Cadenas y Vicent (ed.), *Caballeros de la Orden de Santiago: Siglo 18*, Tomo 7 (Madrid: Hidalguia, 1995), Número 2.157, Año 1793, sig. 4.379, p. 79.

27 Gough has Eliza (not Narváez) leading the voyage at this stage, when he was actually anchored about 275 kilometres south at Puerto de Quadra, where he made no significant contribution to the expedition for three weeks. See Gough, *Juan de Fuca's Strait*, 148–149.

28 See Gonzalo López de Haro, *Plano reducido que comprende parte de la Costa Se[p]tentrional de California desde los 47 grados de latitud N. hasta los 50. Corregido y enmendado hasta la boca del Estrecho de Fuca; y levantado el Plano de el en las expediciones que se ejecutaron los años de 1790, y 91, desde el Puerto de S. Blas. Construido y delineado por el Primer Piloto de la Real Armada D. Gonzalo López de Haro, en el dicho Puerto en enero de 1792.* Henry R. Wagner, *Cartography of the Northwest Coast of America and Spanish Explorations in the Strait of Juan de Fuca.*

29 Nick Doe, publisher of *SHALE*, the Journal of the Gabriola Historical & Museum Society, has studied these locations intensively using various techniques, and he arrived at conclusions that are similar to mine. However, Doe assumes that Narváez would have been able to see certain islands,

which were neither drawn nor identified on any of the expedition's charts, and they were not mentioned as such in existing reports. From the approximate point that the *pilotos* looked northwest, I believe it is more realistic to assume that any land forms observed would have had to have been much higher than the small low-lying islands that became the focus of Doe's analysis. See Nick Doe, "Simón Gaviola's family connections — eighteenth-century place names in the Strait of Georgia," *SHALE* 26, November 2011, 10–18.

CHAPTER 9: EXPLORATION OF THE GRAN CANAL'S WEST SHORE, JULY 1791 (pp. 146–164)

1 One researcher has suggested the point of land may have been named after Juan de Araoz y Caro, a Spanish naval officer. See Nick Doe, "The Origin of Garbriola's Name," *SHALE* 13, June 2006, 18.

2 The K'ómoks First Nations had a large settlement inside the harbour and a burial ground on the spit, which they called *pélxwiḵw*, meaning "round in point." There is no record of the Spanish explorers sighting the K'ómoks, but it is quite likely that the Indigenous people observed the two sailing vessels.

3 Regional District of Nanaimo, Recreation and Parks, *Little Qualicum River Estuary Regional Conservation Area 2010–2019 Management Plan*, A23.

4 The old Qualicum Beach E&N railway station is located at 600 Beach Road, a short distance west of Old Island Highway #19A. Three plaques about local history face the station.

5 Jim McDowell, *The Story of Sidney Island's Three Names* (Richmond, British Columbia: JEM Publications, 2011), 32–37.

6 Lorraine Littlefield, "The Snunéymuxw Village at False Narrows," *SHALE*, 1, November 2000, 3–11.

7 To prove that the corruption of Gabriola Island's name did not begin with confusion between the spelling of *gaviola* (possibly Italian for "small topsail") and *gaviota* (Spanish for "sea gull") — which he found both absurd and offensive — local historian Nick Doe made an extensive study of the naming of Gabriola Island, and concluded that it stems from the aristocratic Basque surname Gaviola. See Doe, "The Origin of Gabriola's Name," 7–38.

8 In the first instance, see Derek Hayes, *Historical Atlas of Vancouver and the Lower Fraser Valley* (Vancouver, British Columbia: Douglas & McIntyre, 2005), map 11:11. In the second case, see Derek Hayes, *British Columbia:*

New Historical Atlas (Vancouver, British Columbia: Douglas & McIntyre, 2012), map 88:33.

9 Eliza, *Extract of the voyage*, 151.

10 Pantoja, *Extract of the navigation*, 178–179.

11 Eliza, *Extract of the voyage*, 151.

12 Ibid.

13 Juan Francisco de la Bodega y Quadra, "Secret Instructions to Lieutenant Don Francisco de Eliza, Commandant of the Puerto de Nutca and the Frigates *Concepción* and *Princesa*," February 4, 1791, as translated by Wagner in *Spanish Explorations*, 137–140.

14 Pantoja, *Extract of the navigation*, 188.

15 Ibid., 180.

16 Ibid., 188.

17 Tom Dailey, "Coast Salish Villages of Puget Sound," http://coastsalishmap. org (accessed September 1, 2013); Wayne Prescott Suttles, "Economic Life of the Coast Salish in Haro & Rosario Straits," *Coast Salish and Western Washington* Indians, Vol. 1 (New York: Garland Publishing, 1974); *Duwamish et al vs USA*, F-275 (Washington, D.C.: US Court of Claims, 1927).

18 Pantoja, *Extract of the navigation*, 181, 188.

19 For a thorough treatment of this issue, see Jim McDowell, *Hamatsa: The Enigma of Cannibalism on the Pacific Northwest Coast* (Vancouver, British Columbia: Ronsdale Press, 1997), 75–92.

20 Eliza, *Extract of the voyage*, 154, 154n.

21 Carrasco, *Extract of the voyage*, 201.

22 Eliza, *Extract of the voyage*, 180. Having confused leadership roles on the expedition, Gough mistakenly credits Eliza (not Narváez) with planning to extend the exploration southward. See Gough, *Juan de Fuca's Strait*, 149.

23 Ibid.

24 Carrasco, *Extract of the voyage*, 201.

25 Eliza, *Extract of the voyage*, 152.

26 The most well-known native berry plants in the area were wild blueberry, blackberry, and strawberry. Others included huckleberries, salmonberries, and thimbleberries. The wild fruits included crabapple, Oregon-grape, and rose hips.

27 Tidal estimates for this period are based on the author's investigation of tidal heights at Port Angeles, Strait of Juan de Fuca, Washington, for July 2000, which are equivalent to those of 1791.

28 Eliza, *Extract of the voyage*, 152.

29 *Cartography of the Northwest Coast of America and Spanish Explorations in the Strait of Juan de Fuca*.

30 Located in the William Andrews Clark Memorial Library, which is connected with the University of California, Los Angeles. The important historical information contained in this journal forms the content of Chapter 9 of the author's first book about Narváez: *José Narváez: The Forgotten Explorer*.

31 See Appendix B.

CHAPTER 10: THE SUPER-EXPLORERS ARRIVE (pp. 165–185)

1 Carrasco, *Extract of the voyage*, 201–202. Malaspina said Carrasco arrived on September 16. See Alejandro Malaspina, *Viaje político-científico alrededor del mundo por las corbetas Descubierta y Atrevida, 1789–1794*. (Two vols. edited by Pedro de Novo y Colson, Madrid, 1885), Vol. 1, book 2, 291–292. For more on the exact date see Donald C. Cutter, *Malaspina in California*, 32n51.

2 Alejandro Malaspina, "Letter to Revillagigedo, San Blas, October 12, 1791," in *Correspondencia relativa a la expedición de Malaspina*, Tomo A, (583), Museo Naval, Madrid. See Wagner, *Spanish Explorations*, 46; Cutter, *Malaspina in California*, 32n52.

3 Alessandro (sic) Malaspina, *The Malaspina Expedition 1789-1794, Journal of the Voyage by Alejandro Malaspina* (London: Hakluyt Society and Museo Naval, 2003), 210.

4 Felipe Bauzá, *Viaje alrededor del mundo, 1789–96* (MS 749, Museo Naval, Madrid); José Bustamante, *Viaje de las corbetas Descubierta y Atrevida a Montevideo, Chile, Perú, Acapulco y Filipinas — 1789*, MS 13 in Archivo del Ministerio de Asuntos Exteriores, Madrid, as cited by Donald C. Cutter, *Malaspina in California*, 33n54. Bauzá, a top-flight geographer who eventually became director of the Depósito Hidrográfico in Madrid, may have exaggerated his apparent disdain for the *pilotos*'s talents. However, it seems clear that Carrasco had not completed his chart at this time.

5 Nick Doe, "Fraudulent Bay — Spanish explorations of Boundary Bay," *British Columbia Historical News* 34 (4), Fall 2001, 27–28.

6 By 1788, for basic hydrographic work, a vessel was supposed to carry the following: two azimuth compasses to take exact bearings, observe variation, and take bearings on land; three sextants to observe latitude and longitude; a graduated semicircle with a radius of one foot and a plane table for surveying coastlines. To make the exact observations of latitude and longitude of

main points needed to chart longer coastlines, the following astronomical instruments were required: an astronomic pendulum, a quadrant with a two-and-a-half-foot radius and two telescopes with a 24-inch focus. See Luisa Martín-Merás, "The Evolution of Spanish Cartography on the Northwest Coast of America," *Spain and the North Pacific Coast* (Vancouver, British Columbia: Vancouver Maritime Museum, 1992), 19.

7 John Kendrick, *Alejandro Malaspina: Portrait of a Visionary* (Montreal & Kingston: McGill-Queen's University Press, 1999), 59.

8 Mercedes Palau-Baquero, *Nutka 1792* (Madrid: Ministerio de Asuntos Exteriores de España, 1998), 87–88.

9 Carrasco, *Extract of the voyage*, 202; Robin Inglis, *Spain and the North Pacific Coast*, 186.

10 Wagner, *Spanish Explorations*, 34.

11 An original fair copy is in Special Collections of the Honnold/Mudd Library, Claremont University Consortium, in Claremont, California. A clean photocopy is in Special Collections, Vancouver Public Library, Vancouver, British Columbia.

12 Juan Pantoja, *Extract of the navigation*, 195.

13 Eliza, *Extract of the voyage*, 154.

14 Pantoja, *Extract of the navigation*, 196.

15 Ibid., 197–198.

16 Juan Pantoja, *Letter to Señor Don José de Prados y Salbatierra, written in San Blas*, December 29, 1791, as translated by Wagner in *Spanish Explorations*, 199–200.

17 Although today it is often mistakenly referred to as the "Narváez Chart" or even more incorrectly the "Eliza Map," Carrasco was certainly the cartographer. Wagner, in his *Cartography*, lists this chart as #779 and attributes it "probably" to Carrasco. The original is located in the Depósito Hidrográfico, Madrid. A large, clear reproduction of Carrasco's chart can be found in *Northwest Coast of America*, edited by María Dolores Higueras. The author's full-size photocopy of the same chart is on file in the Special Collections section of the main Vancouver Public Library.

18 A colour copy of Carrasco's *working* chart can be found in the John Crosse Fonds, Rare Books and Special Collections Library, University of British Columbia.

19 Pantoja, *Extract of the navigation*, 199–200.

20 Eliza, *Extract of the voyage*, 152.

21 Henry Raup Wagner (*Cartography of the Northwest Coast of America*, 224)

was mistaken when he stated, "This is in many respects the most valuable map made, for the reason that we are able to trace by it quite accurately the course of the Narváez reconnaissance *by means of the dotted lines which are inserted at various places*" (emphasis added). In fact, these dotted lines only indicate the same soundings shoals, mudflats, and unobservable segments of land which were shown more clearly on Carrasco's chart. Small anchors on Carrasco's chart and the numerical order of places seen on Narváez's chart are better indicators of the course.

22 Pantoja, *Extract of the navigation*, 199, 199n.

23 The Spanish *goleta* was similar to a brig-rigged schooner.

24 Donald C. Cutter, *Malaspina and Galiano*, 111–112; Donald C. Cutter, "*José Cardero: Protoartist*, 14; Inglis, *Spain and the North Pacific Coast*, 186–189; María Dolores Higueras, *Northwest Coast of America*, 15–16.

25 Wagner, *Spanish Explorations*, 203–209; John Kendrick, *The Voyage of the* Sutil *and* Mexicana, 17–21, 39–54.

26 Kendrick, *Alejandro Malaspina*, 60.

27 The 16-gun, two-masted, 200-ton brigantines were the eyes and ears of the Spanish empire. They were small, fast vessels that carried messages and official correspondence back and forth among Spain's far-flung establishments.

28 Juan Francisco de la Bodega y Quadra, *Voyage to the Northwest Coast of America, 1792: Juan Francisco de la Bodega y Quadra and the Nootka Sound Controversy* (Norman, Oklahoma: The Arthur H. Clark Company, 2012), 58; Jacinto Caamaño, "The Journal of Jacinto Caamaño" as translated by Harold Grenfell, *British Columbia Historical Quarterly* (1938), 192.

29 Cook, *Flood Tide*, 353.

30 According to Luis Marmolejo, who has an extensive private collection of Narváez's maps, his preliminary results of analyzing errors in latitude and longitude indicate a regression fit of over 98 percent in distances of 100 kilometres and an absolute error in positioning from the latitude/longitude of Guadalajara of only about one minute.

31 Although Narváez had functioned unofficially as second mate, first mate, or even captain of a specific vessel on many different voyages, this was the first time that he had received the *official* rank of a full second mate.

32 Marina de Guerra, *Estado de los méritos y servicios*, 2–3, 11.

33 Cook, *Flood Tide*, 356–357.

34 John Kendrick (translator), *The Voyage of the* Sutil *and* Mexicana, 131.

35 Vancouver's chief lieutenant, Peter Puget, said "this gentleman spoke English with great ease and fluency."

36 Although Gough does not identify the chart that left Captain Vancouver "mortified," which Gough says "still exists," it had to have been Carrasco's *Carta que comprehende.* It was the only one available that constituted a complete summary of "the state of Spanish knowledge of these straits to the end of the year 1791" and it was "the first [comprehensive] cartographic record of these waters produced by the Spanish."

37 William Kaye Lamb (editor), *The Voyage of George Vancouver, 1791–1795* (London: Hakluyt Society, 1984), 591–592. Also see George Vancouver, *A Voyage of Discovery to the North Pacific Ocean, and Round the World* (London: G.G. and J. Robinson, 1798), 312.

CHAPTER 11: SPANISH INFLUENCE WANES (pp. 189–205)

1 Archibald Menzies, "Menzies' Journal of Vancouver's Voyage, April to October, 1792." Memoir No. 5, Archives of British Columbia (Victoria: Kings Printer, 1923), 110–111.

2 On June 14, 1792, they also became the first Europeans who actually entered the Fraser River.

3 Menzies, "Menzies' Journal," 116–117.

4 Ibid., 118–119.

5 Cook, *Flood Tide*, 384.

6 Ibid., 387–388.

7 Juan Francisco de la Bodega y Quadra, *Voyage to the Northwest Coast*, 163.

8 Alessandro (sic) Malaspina, *The Malaspina Expedition 1789–1794, Journal of the Voyage by Alejandro Malaspina* (London: Hakluyt Society and Museo Naval, 2003), 326, 358.

9 Narváez, Malaspina, y Bustamante. *Plano de la zona central de las Islas Filipinas, que comprende Sur de la Isla de Luzón, parte de la Isla de Samar encierra esa zona, y el estrecho de San Bernardino,* [1793]. Museo Naval, Madrid.

10 Marina de Guerra, *Estado de los méritos y servicios*, 3.

11 Ibid.

12 Ibid.

13 Ibid.

14 Christon I. Archer, "Retreat from the North: Spain's withdrawal from Nootka Sound, 1793–1795," *B.C. Studies*, No. 37 (1978), 31.

15 Convention signed at Madrid, 11 January 1794, transcript, British Columbia Provincial Archives.

16 Christon I. Archer, "Retreat from the North," 34.

17 Ibid., 34–35.

18 Ibid., 35.

19 Ibid, 21.

20 Christon I. Archer, "The Transient Presence: A Re-Appraisal of Spanish Attitudes toward the Northwest Coast in the Eighteenth Century," *B.C. Studies* No. 18 (Summer 1973), 31.

21 Marina de Guerra, *Estado de los méritos y servicios*, 3.

22 Ibid.

CHAPTER 12: THE REVOLT OF 1810 IN NEW SPAIN (pp. 206–214)

1 Enrique Cárdenas de la Peña, *San Blas de Nayarit* (Mexico City: Secretaria de Marina, 1968), Vol. 2, 117. Much of the following narrative is based on this source, which in part summarizes the testimony given by Narváez and other officers at a subsequent military tribunal.

2 Relocation was approved by Royal Order of King Carlos IV on September 24, 1794. See Tovell, *At the Far Reaches*, 180.

3 Cárdenas de la Peña, *San Blas de Nayarit*, 115.

4 Ensign Felipe García estimated 300 to 400 sailors. See Cárdenas de la Peña, *San Blas de Nayarit*, 105.

5 Cárdenas de la Peña, *San Blas de Nayarit*, 117, 119.

6 Ibid., 117.

7 According to Ensign Felipe García, the town was sufficiently fortified with cannons in each of four or five batteries and on three vessels in the bay.

8 Ibid., 118–119.

9 Ibid., 118.

10 Ibid., 118–119.

11 Ibid., 105, 118–119.

12 Ibid.

13 Ibid., 119.

14 Ibid.

15 Lucas Alamán, *Historia de México* (Mexico City, 1849–1852), 1st ed., Vol.1, 141–149.

16 Cárdenas de la Peña, *San Blas de Nayarit*, 104ff.

CHAPTER 13: NARVÁEZ ADAPTS TO POLITICAL
CHANGE IN MEXICO (pp. 215–231)

1 Christon I. Archer, "The Insurgents of Mezcala Island on the Lake Chapala Front, 1812–1816," in *Native Resistance and the Pax Colonial in New Spain*,

edited by Susan Schroeder, (Lincoln, Nebraska: University of Nebraska Press, 1998), 95–96.

2 Marina de Guerra, *Estado de los méritos y servicios*, 4.

3 Archer, "The Insurgents of Mezcala Island," 114, 120.

4 Marina de Guerra, *Estado de los méritos y servicios*, 16–17.

5 Ibid.

6 Edelmira Trejo de Meillón, "La Fundación de Manzanillo," *Ecos de la Costa*, Colima, México, July 8, 1935.

7 Narváez's instructions from Gonzalo de Ulloa, commandant at San Blas, were dated June 9, 1822, and the *San Carlos* probably sailed on the June 13. Narváez delivered Canon Augustín Fernández to Monterey on September 26. Narváez's second son, José María Miguel Narváez, was serving as captain's mate on the voyage. See Hubert Howe Bancroft, *History of California*, Vol. II, 1801–1824 (San Francisco: The History Company, 1886), 456–459.

8 In Chapter 2, see pages 36–39 and note 18.

9 Inglis, *Historical Dictionary*, 279–280.

10 José María Narváez, *Carta esférica de los territorios de la Alta, Baja Californias y Estado Sonora: construido por las mejores noticias y observaciones propias de Teniente de Navío D. José María Narváez 1823* (Washington, D.C.: Library of Congress, Geography and Map Division).

11 Manuel Orozco y Barra, *Apuntes para la Historia de la Geografía en México* (México: Imprenta de Francisco Díaz de León, 1881), 352–353.

12 José María Narváez, *Plano del territorio de la Alta California construido por las mejores noticias y observaciones propias del Capitán de Fragata D. José Ma. Narváez, año de 1830* (Bancroft Library, University of California, Berkeley), No. 392 M; Carl G. Thelander, *Life on the Edge* (Santa Cruz, California: Biosystems Books, 1994), 170. The manuscript map is also reproduced in Carl I. Wheat, *The Maps of California Gold Regions 1848–57* (San Francisco: Grabhorn Press, 1942), 398.

13 Fort Ross was established in 1812 by the Russian-American Company as a colonial outpost aimed at hunting sea otters and obtaining agricultural supplies for the joint-stock company's main base at Sitka, in what was then Russian Alaska. The fort was located on a promontory above a small cove about 25 kilometres north of Bodega Bay, California. This historically important site is now called Fort Ross State Historic Park. See Stephen Watrous, "Russian Expansion to America," *Fort Ross* (Jenner, California: Fort Ross Interpretive Association, 2001).

14 Erwin G. Gudde, *California Place Names: The Origin and Etymology of*

Current Geographical Names (Berkeley: University of California Press, 1998), 457.

15 Luis Marmolejo, *Letters*, August 19 and 27, 2014.

16 José María Murià, "Comentario sobre los documentos de carácter histórico aportados por la comisión de límites de Estado de Colima" and "Los mapas falseados de Colima," in an insert titled "Límites entre Jalisco y Colima," published in *El Informador, Diario Independiente* (Guadalajara, Jalisco, México, February 26, 1991), 7-E and 8-E respectively.

17 Manuel Orozco y Barra, *Apuntes para la Historia*, 352–353.

18 Eugene Duflot de Mofras, *Duflot de Mofras' Travels on the Pacific Coast*, trans. and ed. by Marguerite E. Wilbur (Santa Ana, California, 1937), 63n64.

19 Ibid., 63–64 and Eugene Duflot de Mofras, *Exploration du territoire de L'Oregon, des Californies, et de la mer Vermeille* (Paris, 1844), Vol. 2, 131.

20 Mariano Otero, *Obras del Sr. Licenciado Mariano Otero* (México: Tipografía de Nabor Chávez, 1859), Vol. 1, 62–63.

21 The Niños Héroes ("Boy Heroes") were six teenage Mexican military cadets who died defending Chapultepec Castle in Mexico City from invading United States forces on September 13, 1847, during the Mexican-American War. According to legend, after all the other Mexican troops had fled, these six young cadets remained, determined to defend the castle with their lives. The last of them, Juan Escutia, wrapped himself in the Mexican flag and jumped from the castle's roof to prevent the flag from being taken by the enemy. Other accounts suggest that, after the castle fell, large numbers of Mexican fighters were taken prisoner, including numerous cadets. In Mexico, September 13 is a national holiday that commemorates the Niños Héroes: Juan de la Barrera, Juan Escutia, Francisco Márquez, Agustín Melgar, Fernando Montes de Oca, and Vicente Suárez.

22 See Appendix G for Narváez's lineage.

23 Agraz García de Alba, *Un Gaditano Insigne en América: Don José María Narbáes, explorador y cartógrafo de Alaska, de California y del primer mapa de Jalisco* (Mexico City: Real Academia Hispanoamericana de Ciencias, Artes y Letras, 1979), 58, 61.

APPENDIX A: THE LOCAL GEOGRAPHIC LEGACY OF NARVÁEZ'S EXPEDITION OF 1791 (pp. 232–235)

1 Narváez Bay was named in 1905 by Captain John F. Pery, commander of the surveying vessel H.M. *Egeria*. See John T. Walbran, *British Columbia Coast Names* (Vancouver: J.J. Douglas, 1971), 351.

2 Most of the information for this panel was derived from Jim McDowell, *José Narváez: The Forgotten Explorer*.

3 GeoNameId: 6086111; N 49° 37' 58" / W 126° 35' 10" or 49.63289 / -126.58627.

APPENDIX B: NARVÁEZ'S MISSING JOURNAL OF 1790–1791 (pp. 236–239)

1 See the last two paragraphs of Chapter 7, pages 95–96.

2 David Szewczyk, *The Viceroyalty of New Spain and Early Independent Mexico* (Philadelphia: Rosenbach Museum and Library, 1980), xi.

3 Ibid., xii.

APPENDIX C: THE THREE IDENTITIES OF AN HISTORIC SCHOONER (1788–1792) (pp. 240–243)

1 John Meares, *Voyages Made in the Years 1788 and 1789*, 88.

2 Ibid., 116.

3 Ibid., 220–222.

4 Ibid., 222–225.

5 Ibid., 334.

6 Cook, *Flood Tide*, 146–147, 160.

7 Ibid., 160.

8 Esteban José Martínez, *Diario de la Navegación*, 78–79. (British mariners who had come from Asia considered the date to be June 20.)

9 Ibid., 79.

10 Ibid., 100–101; Colnett, *The Journal*, 204, 204n; Cook, *Flood Tide*, 188–189, 188n; Wagner, *Spanish Explorations*, 137, 141; Howay, *Voyages of the "Columbia,"* 227n.

11 Martínez, *Diario de la Navegación*, 131; Cook, *Flood Tide*, 192.

12 Ibid., *Diario de la Navegación*, 132; Cook, *Flood Tide*, 193.

13 Cook, *Flood Tide*, 194.

14 Ibid., 276, 276n; Wagner, *Spanish Explorations*, 192.

15 Cook, *Flood Tide*, 276.

16 John Kendrick, *The Men with Wooden Feet*, 45.

17 Cook, *Flood Tide*, 276n; Wagner, *Spanish Explorations*, 141; Howay, *Voyages of the "Columbia,"* 227n; n345.

18 Cook, *Flood Tide*, 294.

19 Colnett, *The Journal*, 204.

20 Ibid., 206–207.

21 Cook, *Flood Tide*, 297.
22 Wagner, *Spanish Explorations*, 142.
23 Cook, *Flood Tide*, 386–387; Tovell, *At the Far Reaches*, 270.
24 Cook, *Flood Tide*, 387. According to Tovell, "Carrasco hastened to join Bodega in Monterey to hand him" the orders. Tovell, *At the Far Reaches*, 270.
25 Michael E. Thurman, *The Naval Department of San Blas* (Glendale, California: Arthur H. Clark, 1967), 346.

APPENDIX D: DIMENSIONS OF THE *SANTA SATURNINA* (pp. 244–245)

1 Wagner, *Spanish Explorations*, 141, 141n, 182.
2 See Appendix E.
3 Malcolm Hall Kenyon, "Naval Construction and Repair in San Blas," master's thesis, University of New Mexico, 1972.

APPENDIX E: MANIFEST OF THE *SANTA SATURNINA* (pp. 246–247)

1 Translated from the original Spanish document by Museo Naval.
2 Narváez used *Horcasitas*, Carrasco used *Orcasitas*. In Spanish, the letter "h" is not pronounced; consequently it is often omitted in writing. As explained in the text, this *schooner* was actually christened *La Orcasitas*. A sloop named *Orcasitas* (alias *Adventure*) was built in Clayoquot Sound in 1791–1792 and served briefly on the Pacific Northwest Coast.

APPENDIX F: A BRIEF HISTORY OF THE *SAN CARLOS* ONE AND TWO (pp. 248–250)

1 Log and Manifest of the *San Carlos* (alias *Toisón de Oro*). The Orden del Toisón de Oro (Spanish) was established in 1430 by Philip the Good, Duke of Burgundy, when he married his third wife, Isabella of Portugal. He founded the institution "to honor and exalt the noble order of knighthood." Down through the centuries it became one of the highest orders of knighthood, the oldest in Europe, and it was given to kings and a limited number of high-ranking individuals. Today the prestigious award is given for diplomatic recognition. The order's insignia features an inert, apparently dead, golden-coloured sheep hanging from a jewelled collar of fire steels — each of which is in the shape of the letter "B" for Burgundy — which are linked by flints. Philip and Isabella had three sons, and the high-minded duke

fathered at least eighteen illegitimate children by his twenty-four docu-mented mistresses.

2 See Thurman, *The Naval Department*, 37–60 passim; Thomas E. Sheridan, *Empire of Sand: the Seri Indians and the Struggle for Spanish Sonora, 1645–1803* (Tucson: University of Arizona Press, 1999), 277, 284–287 passim; Hubert Howe Bancroft, *History of California*, Vol. I, 1542–1800 (San Francisco: A.L. Bancroft & Company, 1884), Chapter 4, 116–117.

3 Thurman, *The Naval Department*, 68–70; Bancroft, *History of California*, 120.

4 Bancroft, *History of California*, Vol. I, 120; Cook, *Flood Tide*, 52; Thurman, *The Naval Department*, 53. For a brief summary of the voyage, see Mark Allen, "So Extended and Painful a Voyage: A Narrative of the 1769 Journey of the *San Carlos* to San Diego," *Mains'l Haul*, Winter 2000, 4–13.

5 Bancroft, *History of California*, Vol. I, 329–330n.

6 Tovell, *At the Far Reaches*, 181.

7 Barry Gough, *Juan de Fuca's Strait*, 129.

8 Tovell, *At the Far Reaches*, 181.

APPENDIX G: LINEAGE OF JOSÉ MARÍA NARVÁEZ (pp. 251–257)

1 See Chapter 13, note 7.

2 Bancroft, *History of California*, Vol. XXI, 97n42, 307–308, 339n17, 357n14, 408n14, 431n19, 537n46, 650n1, 652, 653, 655n, 667n12.

NARVÁEZ PRIMARY SOURCES

■ Unpublished Manuscripts

Anon. (1791). *Estado que manifiesta en el que salió a navegar de este Puerto de la Santa Cruz de Nuca, la goleta* Santa Saturnina, *alias Orcasitas, del porte de 4 Cañones. Mandada por el Segundo Piloto de la Real Armada Don José Narváez.* MS 332. Museo Naval, Madrid.

Bauzá, Felipe. (1796). *Viaje alrededor del mundo, 1789–96.* MS 749. Museo Naval, Madrid.

Eliza, Francisco. (1791). *Extracto de la Navegación.* MS 332. Museo Naval, Madrid. Copy in John Crosse Fonds, Special Collections, University of British Columbia, Vancouver, B.C.

Flórez, Manuel Antonio. (November 26, 1778). "Flórez to Valdés." Archivo General Interior Estado, México, Leg. 20, Ramo 34, 29.

Marina de Guerra. (1825). *Estado de los méritos y servicios del Primer Piloto, Graduado de Alférez de Navío de Real Armada Don José María Narváez, de edad de 63 años, estado casado y sus servicios los siguientes.* Madrid: Archivo–Museo Don Álvaro de Bazán (located in Museo Naval), Leg. 826.

Martínez, Esteban José. (1788). *Diario de Esteban José Martínez, 1788.* Mexico

City: Archives of the Gabinete de Historia Natural, presently the Archivo del Museo Ciencias Naturales, Leg. 1529.

Narváez, José María. (1788). *Diario el Navegación que espera hazer el 2º Piloto de la Real Armada Don José María Narbáez en el paquebot el S.M. nombrado el San Carlos (alias el Filipino) al mando del Primer Piloto de [Marina] Don Gonzalo López de Haro vajo las órdenes de la frigate de la S.M. nombrada la Princesa su comandante el Alférez de la Navío y Primer Piloto de la Armada Don Esteban José Martínez con destinación ambos buques de la exploral la Costa Septemptrional de las Californias hasta los 61° latitud Norte, 1788*. William Andrews Clark Memorial Library, University of California, Los Angeles. (This is an original document in the handwriting of, and signed by, Narváez. It is the only one in existence: 32 leaves or 61 pages. Copies of author's original photocopy are located in the following places: B.C. Provincial Archives (BCPA), Victoria; Special Collections, Vancouver Public Library, Vancouver, B.C. The latter includes a translation from Spanish by Rose Esparza and Jim McDowell.)

Pantoja y Arriaga, Juan. (1791). *Extracto de la navegación que ha hecho el piloto Don Juan Pantoja y Arriaga en el paquebot de S. M. el San Carlos . . . desde San Blas el 4 de Febrero de 1791*. MS 332. Museo Naval, Madrid. Copy in John Crosse Fonds, Special Collections, University of British Columbia, Vancouver, B.C.

Palacios, Antonio. (1788). *Diario de Antonio Palacios, 1788*. Biblioteca Nacional, Mexico City.

Serantes, Antonio. (1788). *Diario de Antonio Serantes, 1788*. Biblioteca Nacional, Mexico City.

■ Published Journals of Voyages

Bodega y Quadra, Juan Francisco de la. (2012). *Voyage to the Northwest Coast of America, 1792: Juan Francisco de la Bodega y Quadra and the Nootka Sound Controversy*. Trans. Freeman M. Tovell. Norman, Oklahoma: Arthur H. Clark Company.

Caamaño, Jacinto. (1938). "The Journal of Jacinto Caamaño," *British Columbia Historical Quarterly*. Victoria, B.C.: BCPA.

Carrasco, Juan. (1929). *Extract of the voyage with His Majesty's schooner the Santa Saturnina in company with the packetboat San Carlos from the Puerto de Santa Cruz de Nuca in the explorations of the coast to the south of the port, and arrival at the Department of San Blas during the present year of 1791*. Trans. Henry R. Wagner, *Spanish Explorations in the Strait of Juan de Fuca*. New York: Fine Arts Press.

Colnett, James. (1940). *The Journal of Captain James Colnett aboard the Argonaut from April 26, 1789 to November 3, 1791*. Toronto: Champlain Society.

Eliza, Francisco. (1929). *Extract of the voyage, explorations and discoveries made under an order of His Excellency, the Conde de Revilla Gigedo, viceroy of New Spain, communicated by the captain of the royal fleet, Don Juan Francisco de la Bodega y Quadra, commandant of the department of San Blas, on the north coast of the Californias from 48°26' to 49°50'N. with the packetboat* San Carlos, *carrying sixteen reinforced cannon of four pounds, thirty-nine codos long on the keel, twelve beam, and fourteen feet draft aft and fifteen forward, and the schooner* Santa Saturnina *alias* Las Orcasitas, *constructed in Nutca, carrying four three-pound cannon and eighteen codos long on the keel, six and a half beam, with a draft five and a half feet aft and four feet at the bow, the expedition being commanded by the lieutenant of the royal fleet and commandant of the establishment of San Lorenzo de Nuca Don Francisco de Eliza in the year 1791*. Trans. Henry R. Wagner, *Spanish Exploration in the Strait of Juan de Fuca*. New York: Fine Arts Press.

Fernández de Navarrete, Martín. (1802). Introduction to *El Viaje de las Goletas Sutil y Mexicana*. A translation from the Spanish in 1911 by G.F. Barwick, Keeper of Printed Books in the British Museum, is available in manuscript form in the University of British Columbia Library, Vancouver, and in the Provincial Archives in Victoria, B.C. Trans. Josef Espinosa y Tello, *Account of the Voyage Made by Schooners Sutil and Mexicana in the Year 1792 to Survey the Strait of Fuca, with an Introduction Containing a Notice of the Expedition Previously Carried out by the Spaniards in Search of the Northwest Passage of America*. Madrid: Royal Printing Office. This document is located in Special Collections, Vancouver Public Library, Vancouver, B.C.

Kendrick, John, trans. (1991). *The Voyage of* Sutil *and* Mexicana, *1792*. Spokane, Washington: Arthur H. Clark Company.

Malaspina, Alejandro. (1885). *Viaje político-científico alrededor del mundo por las corbetas Descubierta y Atrevida, 1789–1794*. 2 vols. Ed. Pedro de Novo y Colson. Madrid. Trans. Carl Robinson. (1934). *Political-Scientific Voyage Round the World by the Corvettes Descubierta and Atrevida under the Command of the Naval Captains Don Alexandro Malaspina and Don José de Bustamante y Guerra from 1789–1794*. Located in Special Collections, Vancouver Public Library, Vancouver, B.C.

————, Alessandro [sic]. (2003). *The Malaspina Expedition 1789–1794, Journal of the Voyage by Alejandro Malaspina*. London: Hakluyt Society and Museo Naval, Madrid.

Martínez, Esteban José. (1964). *Diario de la Navegación que yo el Alf(ére)z de Navío de la R(ea)l Arm(a)da D(on) Esteban José Martínez voy a ejecutar al P(uer)to de S(a)n Lorenzo de Nuca, mandando la frag(a)ta Princesa, y paquebot S(a)n Carlos... 1789.* Ed. Roberto Barreiro-Meiro, *Colección de diarios y relaciones para la historia de los viajes y descubrimientos.* Madrid: Instituto Histórico de Marina.

———. (1900). *Diary of the Voyage* [of Esteban José Martínez], *in command of the frigate Princessa* [sic] *and the packet San Carlos in the present year of 1789.* Trans. William L. Schurz. Madrid. Located in Special Collections Library, University of British Columbia, Vancouver, B.C.

———. (1940). *A Translation of the Diary of Esteban José Martínez from July 2 till July 14, 1789 in The Journals of Captain James Colnett aboard the Argonaut from April 26, 1789 to November 3, 1791.* Trans. & ed. Frederick William Howay. Toronto.

Meares, John. (1967). *Voyages Made in the Years 1788 and 1789 from China to the Northwest Coast of America.* Amsterdam: N. Israel; New York: Da Capo.

Menzies, Archibald. (1923). "Menzies' Journal of Vancouver's Voyage, April to October 1792." Memoir No. V. Ed. C.F. Newcombe. British Columbia Provincial Archives. Victoria: Kings Printer.

Mourelle de la Rúa, Francisco Antonio. (1920). *Voyage of the Sonora in the second Bucareli expedition to explore the Northwest Coast, survey of the port of San Francisco, and found Franciscan missions and a presidio and pueblo at that port.* Trans. Daines Barrington. (Includes reproduction of Bodega's *Carta General . . .* , showing Spanish discoveries on the coast up to 1791.) San Francisco: Thomas C. Russell.

Moziño, José Mariano. (1970). *Noticias de Nutka, An Account of Nootka Sound in 1792.* Trans. & ed. Iris Higbie Wilson Engstrand. Seattle: University of Washington Press.

Pantoja y Arriaga, Juan. (1929). *Extracto de la navegación que ha hecho el Piloto Don Juan Pantoja y Arriaga en el paquebot de S. M. el San Carlos . . . desde San Blas el 4 de Febrero de 1791.* Trans. Henry R. Wagner, *Extract of the navigation made by the pilot Don Juan Pantoja Arriaga in His Majesty's packetboat* San Carlos, *under the command of the ensign of the royal navy Don Ramon Saavedra, which sailed from the department of San Blas February 4, 1791, destined to carry supplies to the establishment of San Lorenzo de Noca; and of the expedition in this vessel upon the northern coast of California under the command of First Lieutenant Don Francisco Eliza, the commandant of that establishment which is situated in latitude 49°35' N and longitude 21°20' W of San Blas by astronomical*

observation. See Wagner, *Spanish Explorations in the Strait of Juan de Fuca.*
New York: Fine Arts Press, 155–200.

■ Cartography

Alcalá-Galiano, Dionisio and Cayetano Valdés. (1792). *Carta esférica de los
reconocimientos hechos en 1792 en la costa N.O. de América.* BCPA: CM A176.

Alcalá-Galiano, Dionisio. (1792). *Carta esférica de la parte de la Costa N.O. de
América comprehendida entre la entrada de Juan de Fuca y salidas de las goletas
con algunos canales interiores.* U.K. National Archives: FO 925 1650 (13).

Bodega y Quadra, Juan Francisco de la. (1791). *Carta General de cuanto hasta
hoy se ha descubierto y examinado por los españoles en la Costa Septentrional de
California formada bajo unos conocimientos bien solidos con arreglo al Meridiano
de San Blas que dista 88°15' al O. del de Tenerife por Don Juan Francisco de la
Bodega y Cuadra de la órden de Santiago, Capitán de Navío de la Real Armada y
Comandante del Departamento de Marina.* Museo Naval, Madrid. See Wagner,
Cartography of the Northwest Coast of America.

Carrasco, Juan. (1791). *Plano Del Archipiélago de Clayocuat situada su boca mas
O. llamado Puerto de San Rafael por las 49°20' de latitud N. y en la Longitud de
20°55' y la mas E. nombrada de Clayocuat por los 49°07' de la misma especie. y
20°22' al O. del Meridiano de San Blas reconocidas sus bocas y descubiertos todos
sus Brazos e Yslas interiores por el Theniente de Navío de la Real¹ Armada Don
Francisco de Eliza Comandante del Paquebot de S.M. nombrado San Carlos, y
Goleta Santa Saturnina (Alias la Orcasitas) en este presente Año 1791.* See Wagner, *Cartography of the Northwest Coast of America,* map 797. Copies at: Library
of Congress, Washington, D.C., map 14; British Columbia Archives Cartographic Materials, map A1413; Historical Map Society of British Columbia,
map 431. (The Library of Congress, which has an atlas containing the original map, attributes authorship to "Eliza or a cartographer working under the
direction of Eliza, likely José María Narváez or Juan Carrasco." Although
Wagner credits Juan Pantoja, the record shows Narváez and Carrasco did
most of the work. Pantoja might have added finishing touches during the
twenty-one days his fellow pilots were exploring the Gran Canal. The handwriting is Carrasco's, not Pantoja's. Although the map is often ascribed to
Narváez, it is not in his handwriting either.)

———. (1791). *Carta que comprehende los interiores y veril de la costa desde los
48° latitud N. hasta los 50° examinados escrulosamente por el Teniente de Navío*

de la Real Armada Don Francisco Eliza . . . en este año de 1791. Original in Depósito Hidrográfico (now Museo Naval), Madrid, Atlas MS 11-13 or MN 3-E-1 (13). A copy of photostat from Honnold Library, Claremont, California, is on file in Special Collections, Vancouver Public Library, Vancouver, B.C. For the best published copy, see María Dolores Higueras, *Northwest Coast of America: Iconographic Album of the Malaspina Expedition*, 28–29. For Carrasco's preliminary working version see MN 3-E-11, Museo Naval, Madrid. For a reproduction of an imperfect copy made for the United States government, see Derek Hayes, *British Columbia: A New Historical Atlas*, map 117, 72–73.

López de Haro, Gonzalo. (1790). *Plano del Estrecho de Fuca reconocido por el Alférez de Navío de la Real Armada Dn. Manuel Quimper en la expedición que hizo con la balandra de S.M. de su mundo nombrada la Princesa Real en el año de 1790. Levantado por su Primer Piloto Don Gonzalo López de Haro.* U.K. National Archives: FO 925 1649 (a).

————. (1792). *Plano reducido que comprende parte de la Costa Se[p]tentrional de California desde los 47 grados de latitud N. hasta los 50. Corregido y enmendado hasta la boca del Estrecho de Fuca; y levantado el Plano de él en las expediciones que se ejecutaron los años de 1790, y 91, desde el Puerto de S. Blas. Construido y delineado por el Primer Piloto de la Real Armada D. Gonzalo López de Haro, en el dicho puerto en enero de 1792.* See Wagner, *Cartography of the Northwest Coast of America* and *Spanish Explorations in the Strait of Juan de Fuca*, map 813.

Narváez, José María. (1791). *Carta esférica que comprehende los interiores, y veril de la costa del NO de California desde los 48° hasta los 50° de latitud N. con el reconocimiento últimamente hecho en el Canal de Juan de Fuca por los pilotos de paqueuot San Carlos, y goleta Santa Saturnina mandados . . . Año de 1791.* Honnold Library, Claremont, California, Wagner map 784.

————. (1791). *Plano del Archipiélago de Carrasco situado en la latitud N. de 48° 51' longitud 20° al O. de Sn. Blas reconocido en los años de 89 y 91 por Don J.M. Narbáez.* Map Society of British Columbia: 1791-06B. A copy is located in John Crosse Fonds, Box 3, File 3-2 (not listed in inventory), Special Collections, University of British Columbia, Vancouver, B.C. An almost identical chart is shown on page 198 of Palau, *Nutka 1792*, where it is cited as MS 146, number 13. In each instance, the title seems to be in Narváez's handwriting, but in the latter case his surname is spelled Narváez not Narbáez. (This appears to be an initial, rough working chart because it contains no place names, no notes indicating entry point for the reconnaissance, no Indigenous settlements, and some sounding numbers. It also seems to be based on Narváez's explorations of this waterway in both 1789 and 1791.)

——. (1791). *Plano del Archipiélago de Nitinat ó Carrasco situada su punta más E. por los 48°48' de latitud N. y 19°15' al O. del Meridiano de San Blas y la más O. por los 48°53' de latitud, y 19°37' del mismo meridiano descubiertos sus interiores por el Theniente de Navío de la Real Armada Don Francisco de Eliza en este prescrito año de 1791.* Museo Naval, Madrid, map 7340.7. It can also be found in the following: BCPA, Maps Collection CM/A1415; Wagner, *Cartography of the Northwest Coast of America*, map 795; Hayes, *Historical Atlas of British Columbia and the Pacific Northwest*, map 118, p. 73, BCARS CM/A1415. (This appears to be a more refined working chart. Although there are no place names, no notes indicating entry point, and nothing to indicate the route that was travelled, there are small squares marking about five major Indigenous settlements, and some sounding numbers. This chart is commonly attributed to Narváez, and the title is in his handwriting.)

——. (c. 1792). *Plano del Archipiélago de Nictinac ó de Carrasco en la Isla de Quadra y Vancuber en la Costa No. de América.* John Crosse Fonds, Box 4, Files 5-23 and 5-24, Special Collections Library, University of British Columbia, Vancouver, B.C. (The source of this photocopy was MN 3-B-3, Museo Naval, Madrid. Although Crosse attributed the chart to Narváez, it was probably drafted for him by Carrasco, or it was produced jointly. The notations are in Carrasco's handwriting. It appears to be a final chart because it contains many more details than the preceding charts. Some place names are included, the entry point is identified, letters indicate the approximate route, the locations of several Indigenous settlements are marked, and several sounding numbers are shown.)

——, Malaspina and Bustamante. (1793). *Plano de la zona central de las Islas Filipinas, que comprende el sur de la Isla de Luzón, parte de la Isla de Samar encierra esa zona, y el estrecho de San Bernardino.* Museo Naval, Madrid: MN-69-16.

——. (1803). *Plano de Puerto de San Blas levantado el año de 1803 después del gran temporal acaecido en Octobre del mismo año por el Primer Piloto Don José Narváez.* Signatura: C-1a22. Real Academia de la Historia, Departmento de Cartografía y Artes Gráficas, Madrid. (Manuscript copy of chart published in 1818 by Manuel de los Reyes, Engineer for New Spain.)

——. (1823). *Carta esférica de los territorios de la Alta, Baja Californias y estado*

Sonora: construido por las mejores noticias y observaciones propias de Teniente de Navío Don José María Narváez 1823. Washington, D.C: Library of Congress, Geography and Map Division.

—————. (1824). *Carta Corográfica de los Estados de Jalisco, Zacatecas, y territorio de Colima con parte de los Estados Limitrofes, construida por las mejores noticias y manuscritos que se han ternido presente ye con precisa sujecion alas Latitudes ye Longitudes determinadas Astronomicamente en los principales Pueblos del Estado de Jalisco y sus Costas*. Mapoteca Manuel Orozco y Berra, Servicio de información Agroalimentaria y Pesquera; Colección Orozco y Berra, Parciales 723, Varilla OYBPAR72301, No. Clasificador 250-OYB-723-A.

—————. (1825). *Plano del Puerto de San Blas en las costas del Estado de Jalisco: situado en la latitud 21°30' Norte, longitud 98°41' occidental del meridiano de Cádiz, México*. The Portal to Texas History. Online at texashistory.unt.edu/ ark:67531/metapth298349. Accessed October 14, 2013.

—————. (1830). *Plano del territorio de la Alta California construido por las mejores noticias y observaciones proprias del Capitán de Fragata Don José María Narváez, Año de 1830*. Bancroft Library, University of California, Berkeley, California, map 392M. Also map 912 C15n 1830, image 2010-4977, California History Section, California State Library, Sacramento, California.

Pantoja y Arriaga, Juan. (1791). *Pequeña Costa que comprehende los interiores, y veril de la costa desde los 48 grados de latitud N. hasta los 50; examinados los expresados interiores con la prolijidad posible por los pilotos de paquebot de Su Majestad, el San Carlos y goleta Santa Saturnina . . . en este año de 91*. Bancroft Library, Berkeley, California.

Quimper, Manuel. (1790). *Carta reducida que comprehende parte de la Costa Septentrional de California, corrigida y enmendada hasta la Boca de Estrecho de Fuca . . . Don Maunel Quimper en el año de 1790. Construida por su primer Piloto Don Gonzalo López de Haro, 1790*. (Map 112, p. 70 in Hayes, *Historical Atlas of British Columbia and the Pacific Northwest*; map MPK 203 [2], Public Record Office, England.)

NARVÁEZ SECONDARY SOURCES

Agráz García de Alba, Gabriel. (1979). *Un Gaditano Insigne en América: Don José María Narbáes, explorador y cartógrafo de Alaska, de California y del primer mapa de Jalisco*. México: Real Academia Hispanoamericana de Ciencias Artes y Letras.

Akrigg, G.P.V. and Helen B. (1997). *British Columbia Place Names*. Vancouver, B.C.: UBC Press.

Alamán, Lucas. (1849–1852). *Historia de México desde los primeros movimientos que preperaron su independencia en al año 1808 hasta la época presente*. First ed., 5 vols. Mexico City.

Allen, Mark. (Winter 2000). "So Extended and Painful a Voyage," *Mains'l Haul*, 4–13.

Álvarez, José Rogelio. (1988). *Enciclopedia de México*. Vol. 10, 5715. Mexico City: Secretary of Public Education.

Anna, Timothy E. (1990). *The Mexican Empire of Iturbide*. Lincoln, Nebraska: University of Nebraska Press.

Anon. ed. (February 26, 1991). "Limites entre Jalisco y Colima," *El Informador, Diario Independiente*. Guadalajara, Jalisco, México, Sección E, 1–8.

Archer, Christon Irving. (Summer 1973). "The Transient Presence: A Re-Appraisal of Spanish Attitudes toward the Northwest Coast in the Eighteenth Century," *B.C. Studies* 18:3ff.

———. (Spring 1978). "Retreat from the North: Spain's withdrawal from Nootka Sound, 1793–1795," *B.C. Studies* 37:19–36.

———. (1978). "Spanish Exploration and Settlement of the Northwest Coast in the 18th Century," *Nutka*. Ed. Barbara S. Efrat and W.J. Langlois. Victoria, B.C.: Province of British Columbia, 33–53.

———. (1980). "Russians, Indians & Passages: Spanish Voyages in Alaska in the 18th Century," *Explorations in Alaska*. Ed. Antoinette Shalkop. Anchorage, Alaska: Cook Inlet Historical Society, 129–143.

———. (April 1992). "Seduction before Sovereignty: Spanish Efforts to Manipulate the Natives in their Claims to the Northwest Coast." Paper delivered at the Vancouver Conference on Exploration and Discovery, Vancouver, B.C.

———. (1998). "The Insurgents of Mezcala Island on the Lake Chapala Front, 1812–1816," *Native Resistance and the Pax Colonial in New Spain*. Ed. Susan Schroeder, 84–128.

Arima, Eugene & John Dewhirst. (1900). "Nootkans of Vancouver Island," *Handbook of North American Indians*. Washington: Smithsonian Institution, Vol. 7, 391–411.

Bancroft, Hubert Howe. (1884). *History of California*, Vol. 1, 1542–1800. San Francisco: A.L. Bancroft & Company.

———. (1886). *History of California*, Vol. II, 1801–1824. San Francisco: The History Company.

———. (1886). *History of California*, Vol. XXI. San Francisco: A.L. Bancroft & Company.

Bartroli, Thomas. (1986). *Discovery of the Site of Vancouver City by José María Narváez in 1791*. Vancouver: Bartroli. (Revised version of an earlier tentative account. Located in Special Collections, University of British Columbia Library, Vancouver, B.C.).

———. (1991). *Brief Presence: Spain's Activity on America's Northwest Coast (1774–1796)*. Vancouver: Bartroli.

Bateson, Ian, illustrator. (1984). *Vancouver, on the Move*. (Documentary film.) Vancouver, B.C.: Thomas Howe Associates.

Bawlf, Samuel. (2003). *The Secret Voyage of Sir Francis Drake, 1577–1580*. New York: Walker & Co.

Bolton, Herbert Eugene. (1913). *Guide to Materials for the History of the United States in the Principal Archives of Mexico*. Washington, D.C.: Carnegie Institution of Washington.

Bouchard, Randy et al. (1973–1976). *British Columbia Indian Language Project fonds AR019*. University of Victoria Archives, Victoria, B.C.

Boyd, Robert T. (1990). "Demographic History, 1774–1784," *Handbook of North American Indians*, Vol. 7, Northwest Coast. Ed. by Wayne Suttles. Washington, D.C.: Smithsonian Institution, 135–148

Cadenas y Vicent, Vicente de, editor. (1995). *Caballeros de la Orden de Santiago: Siglo 18*, Tomo 7. Madrid: Hidalguia.

Cárdenas de la Peña, Enrique. (1968). *San Blas de Nayarit*. Mexico City: Secretaría de Marina, Vol. 1, 134, 138; Vol. 2, 104, 117–120, 197–199.

Chapman, Charles E. (1916). *The Founding of Spanish California: The Northwest Expansion of New Spain, 1687–1783*. New York: Macmillan.

Chapman, Fredrik H. (1967). *Architectura Nalis Mercatoria 1768*. New York.

Clayton, Daniel W. (2000). *Islands of Truth: The Imperial Fashioning of Vancouver Island*. Vancouver, B.C.: UBC Press.

Clayton, Lawrence A. (1980). *Caulkers and Carpenters in a New World: The Shipyards of Colonial Guayaquil*. Athens, Ohio: Ohio University, Center for International Studies.

Collins, June M. (1974). *Valley of the Spirits: the Upper Skagit Indians of Western Washington*. Seattle: University of Washington Press.

Cook, Warren L. (1973). *Flood Tide of Empire: Spain and the Pacific Northwest, 1543–1819*. New Haven & London: Yale University Press.

Crosse, John. (May 1991). "Spaniards in the Gulf," *Boat World* 2 (5): 20–21.

————. (July 17, 1991). "Day the Spanish Came Ashore," *Vancouver Sun*. Vancouver, B.C., A11.

————. (1985–2006). *John Crosse Fonds*: Boxes 1–4, 9–11. Special Collections, University of British Columbia, Vancouver, B.C.

Cruz, Francisco Santiago. (1967). *Fronteras con Rusia*. Mexico City: Editorial Jus, S.A. [Anonymous Society], 83–85.

Cutter, Donald C. (1960). *Malaspina in California*. San Francisco: J. Howell.

————. (1991). *Malaspina and Galiano: Spanish Voyages to the Northwest Coast, 1791 & 1792*. Vancouver, B.C.: Douglas & McIntyre.

————. (April 1992). "José Cardero: Protoartist of the Pacific Coast." Paper delivered at the Vancouver Conference on Exploration & Discovery, Vancouver, B.C.

Dailey, Tom. (2013). "Coast Salish Villages of Puget Sound." Online at coast-salishmap.org. Accessed September 1, 2013.

Davis, Chuck. (March 30, 1980). "José María Narváez," *The Province*. Vancouver, B.C.

Doe, Nick. (Fall 1997). "Some Anomalies in a Spanish Chart of Vancouver Island 1791," *Lighthouse* 56: 7–20.

————. (Fall 2001). "British Columbia's Mexican Connection: The Naval Base of San Blas 1768–1810," *British Columbia Historical News* 34 (4): 4–7.

————. (Fall 2001). "Fraudulent Bay: Spanish explorations of Boundary Bay," *British Columbia Historical News* 34 (4): 23–28.

————. (June 2006). "The Origin of Gabriola's Name," *SHALE* 13: 7–38.

————. (September 2006). "George Vancouver Visits Gabriola," *SHALE* 14: 3–9.

————. (November 2011). "Simón Gaviola's family connections: 18th century placenames in the Strait of Georgia," *SHALE* 26: 10–18.

Drury, Devon. (2007). "That Immense and Dangerous Sea: Spanish Imperial Policy and Power during the Exploration of the Salish Sea, 1700–1791." Master's thesis, University of Victoria, B.C.

Dufolt de Mofras, Eugene. (1844, 1846). *Exploration de Territoire de L'Orégon, des Californies et de la mer Vermeille*. Paris.

————. (1937). *Duflot de Mofras' Travels on the Pacific Coast*, 2 vols. Trans. & ed. Marguerite Eyer Wilbur. Santa Ana, California: Fine Arts Press.

Duwamish et al vs USA, F-275. (1927). Washington, D.C.: US Court of Claims.

Eliot, John L. (November 1993). "Alaska's Island Refuge," *National Geographic*.

Ellis, David W. and Luke Swan. (1981). *Teachings of the Tides: Uses of Marine Invertebrates by the Manhousat People*. Nanaimo, B.C.: Theytus Books.

Fanon, Frantz. (1968). *The Wretched of the Earth*. New York: Grove Press.

Fernández de Navarrete, Martín. (1831). *Diccionario Marítimo Español que además de las definiciones de las voces con sus equivalentes en francés, inglés e italiano, contiene tres vocabularios de estos idiomas con las correspondencias castellanas; redacto por orden del Rey nuestro señor*. Madrid: Imprenta Real.

Galois, Robert, (2012). *Kwakwaka'wakw Settlements, 1775–1920*. Vancouver, B.C.: UBC Press.

Gitzen, Garry D. (2011). *Francis Drake in Nehalem Bay 1579: Setting the Historical Record Straight*. Wheeler, Oregon: Fort Nehalem Publishing.

Gonzalez-Aller Hierro, José Ignacio. (2014). "La milagrosa reconstrucción de la flota Española del siglo XVIII," *Revista Divulgativa de Historia Naval en Internet*. Online at www.todoababor.es.

Gooch, Anthony, et al. (1978). *Cassell's Spanish–English, English–Spanish Dictionary*. London: Cassell.

Gough, Barry. (2007). *Fortune's River: The Collision of Empires in Northwest America*. Madeira Park, B.C.: Harbour Publishing.

———. (2012). *Juan de Fuca's Strait: Voyages in the Waterway of Forgotten Dreams*. Madeira Park, B.C.: Harbour Publishing.

Governments of Jalisco and Colima. (February 26, 1991). "Límites entre Jalisco y Colima," *El Informador Diario Independiente*. Guadalajara, Jalisco, México.

Gudde, Erwin Gustav. (1998). *California Place Names: The Origin and Etymology of Current Geographical Names*. Berkeley: University of California Press.

Hamill, Hugh M. Jr. (1966). *The Hidalgo Revolt: Prelude to Mexican Independence*. Gainsville, Florida: University of Florida Press.

Habron, John D. (1988). *Trafalgar and the Spanish Navy*. London: Conway.

Hayes, Derek. (2005). *Historical Atlas of Vancouver and the Lower Fraser Valley*. Vancouver: Douglas & McIntyre.

———. (2012). *British Columbia: A New Historical Atlas*. Vancouver/Toronto/Berkeley: Douglas & McIntyre.

Henry, John Frazier. (1984). *Early Maritime Artists of the Pacific Northwest Coast, 1741–1841*. Vancouver: Douglas & McIntyre.

Higueras, María Dolores. (1991). *Northwest Coast of America: Iconographic Album of the Malaspina Expedition*. Madrid: Museo Naval.

Howay, Frederick William, ed. (1941). *Voyages of the "Columbia" to the Northwest Coast, 1787–1790 and 1790–1793*. Boston: Massachusetts Historical Society.

Huck, Barbara. (2006). "The Beach Grove Site," *In Search of Ancient British Columbia*, Vol. 1. Winnipeg, Manitoba: Heartland.

Hull, Raymond and Gordon and Christine Soules. (1974). *Vancouver's Past*. Seattle: University of Washington Press.

Hutchinson, Bruce. (1950). *The Fraser*. New York and Toronto: Rinehart & Co.

Inglis, Robin. (2008). *Historical Dictionary of the Discovery and Exploration of the Northwest Coast of America*. Lanham, Maryland: Scarecrow Press.

———, ed. (1992). *Spain and the North Pacific Coast*. Vancouver, B.C.: Vancouver Maritime Museum.

Kendrick, John S. (1985). *The Men with Wooden Feet*. Toronto: NC Press.

———. (June–July 1987). "Spaniards on the West Coast," *The Beaver* (now *Canada's History* Magazine) 67:3, 51–54.

——— ed. & trans. (1990). *The Voyage of* Sutil *and* Mexicana, *1792: The last Spanish Exploration of the Northwest Coast of America*. Spokane, Washington: Arthur H. Clark Company.

———. (1999). *Alejandro Malaspina: Portrait of a Visionary*. Montreal/Kingston: McGill-Queen's University Press.

Kenyon, Malcolm Hall. (1972). "Naval Construction and Repair in San Blas." Master's thesis, University of New Mexico.

Khlebnikov, Kiril. (1979). *Russkaia America v neopublikovannykj zapiskakh K.T. Khlebnikova*. Leningrad: Nauka.

King, Dean. (1995). *A Sea of Words: A Lexicon and Companion for Patrick O'Brian's Seafaring Tales*. New York: Henry Holt.

Lamb, William Kaye. (January 1942). "The Mystery of Mrs. Barkley's Diary: Notes on the Voyage of the 'Imperial Eagle,' 1786–87," *British Columbia Historical Quarterly* 6 (1): 31–48; related documents 49–60.

———. (1984). *The Voyage of George Vancouver 1791–1795*. London: Hakluyt Society.

Littlefield, Lorraine. (November 2000). "The Snunéymux[W] Village at False Narrows," *SHALE* 1: 3–11.

McDowell, Jim. (February 18, 1991). "'Spanish Columbia' Revisited: A museum exhibit pays tribute to pre-Vancouver explorers," *British Columbia Report* 2:25, 35.

———. (April 1991). "Europeans on the Gran Canal," *Pacific Yachting* 33: 24–29.

———. (1997). *Hamatsa: The Enigma of Cannibalism on the Pacific Northwest Coast*. Vancouver, B.C.: Ronsdale Press.

———. (1998). *José Narváez, The Forgotten Explorer: Including his narrative of a Voyage on the Northwest Coast in 1788*. Spokane, Washington: Arthur H. Clark Company.

———. (2011). *The Story of Sidney Island's Three Names*. Richmond, B.C.: JEM Publications.

———. (2012). *Father August Brabant: Saviour or Scourge?* Vancouver, B.C.: Ronsdale Press.

———. (Summer 2014). "Who Were These Two Mowachaht Men?" *British Columbia History* 47 (2): 12–15.

McMillan, Alan D. (1999). *Since the Time of the Transformers: The Ancient Heritage of the Nuu-chah-nulth, Ditidaht, and Makah*. Vancouver, B.C.: UBC Press.

Marmolejo, Luis. (2015). "Quantitative and Qualitative Analysis of the Cartography of José María Narváez, including the Pacific Northwest (Alta California and Vancouver Island to Alaska), Mexico and the Philippines." Online at groups.google.com/forum/#!forum/josemarianarvaez-cartographysanblas.

Mathes, W. Michael. (April 1992). "The Province of Anian and its Strait: Myth, Reality and Exploration of the Pacific Northwest, 1542–1792." Paper delivered at the Vancouver Conference on Exploration and Discovery, Vancouver. B.C.

Mathews, James Skitt. (1941). *Pilot Commander Don José Maria Narvaez, 1791: 150th Anniversary Sequcentennial of the Arrival of First European on Pacific Mainland Shore of Canada at English Bay, Vancouver*. Vancouver, B.C.: Special Collections, Vancouver Public Library, Vancouver, B.C.

———. (1955). "Conversations with Khahtsahlano, 1932–1954." Vancouver, B.C.: City of Vancouver Archives.

———. (1961). "Narváez 1791; Discoverer of the Boca de Floridablanca," *Vancouver Historical Journal* 4:1, 4–109.

Meillón, Edelmira Trejo de. (July 8, 1935). "La Fundacion de Manzanillo," *Ecos de la Costa*. Colima, México, 8–19.

Miller, Gordon. (2011). *Voyages to the New World and Beyond*. Vancouver/ Toronto: Douglas & McIntyre.

Mills, John E. and Robert F. Heizer. (1952). *The Four Ages of Tsurai: A Documentary History of the Indian Village on Trinidad Bay*. Berkeley, California: University of California Press.

Murià, José María. (1991). "Comentario sobre los documentos de carácter histórico aportados por la comisión de límites de Estado de Colima" and "Los mapas falseados de Colima," in an insert titled "Límites entre Jalisco y Colima," *El Informador, Diario Independiente*. Guadaljara, Jalisco, México, February 26, 1991, 7-E and 8-E respectively.

Neering, Rosemary. (2014). *The Spanish on the Northwest Coast: for Glory, God, and Gain*. Victoria: Heritage House.

Orozco y Berra, Manuel. (1856). *Apéndice al Diccionario Universal de Historia y de Geografía*. México: J.M. Audrade and F. Escalante, Vol. 3, 7–9.

———. (1881). *Apuntes para la Historia de la Geografía en México*. México: Imprenta de Francisco Díaz de León.

Otero, Mariano. (1850). *Obras del Señor Licenciado Mariano Otero*. Edited by his son Ignacio Otero. México: Tipografía de Nabor Chave, 62–63.

Palau-Baquero, Mercedes, et al., eds. (1998). *Nutka 1792: Viaje a la Costa Noroeste de la América Septentrional por Juan Francisco de la Bodega y Quadra, del orden de Santiago, Capitán de Navío de la Real Armada y Comandante del Departamento de San Blas, en las fragatas de su mando Santa Gerrudis, Aránzazu, Princesa y goleta Activa, Año de 1792*. Madrid: Ministerio de Asuntos Exteriores de España, Dirección General de Relaciones Culturales y Científicas.

Pezuela, Jacobo de la. (1863). *Diccionario Geográfico, Estadístico e Histórico de la Isla de Cuba*, Tomo Tercero. Madrid: Imprenta del Establecimiento de Mellado.

Regional District of Nanaimo, Recreation and Parks. (2010). *Little Qualicum River Estuary Regional Conservation Area 2010–2019 Management Plan*, Appendix B: "Estuary History," A23.

Rolfsen, Catherine. (2008). "Spain gives city historic drawing," *Vancouver Sun*, June 7, B2.

Sheridan, Thomas E. (1999). *Empire of Sand: the Seri Indians and the Struggle for Spanish Sonora, 1645–1803*. Tucson: University of Arizona Press.

Smith, Marian W. (1941). "The Coast Salish of Puget Sound," *American Anthropologist* Vol. 43: 197–211.

Smyth, William Henry, et al. (1867). *The Sailor's Word-Book: An Alphabetical Digest of Nautical Terms, including some More Especially Military and Scientific, but Useful to Seamen; as well as Archaisms of Early Voyagers, etc.* London: Blackie and Son.

Suttles, Wayne Prescott. (1974). "Economic Life of the Coast Salish in Haro and Rosario Straits," *Coast Salish and Western Washington Indians*, Vol. 1. New York: Garland Publishing.

———. (1990). "Central Coast Salish," *Handbook of North American Indians, Northwest Coast*, Vol. 7. Washington, D.C.: Smithsonian Institution Press.

——— and Barbara Lane. (1990). "Southern Coast Salish," *Handbook of North American Indians, Northwest Coast*, Vol. 7. Washington, D.C.: Smithsonian Institution Press.

Szewczyk, David. (1990). *The Viceroyalty of New Spain and Early Independent Mexico: A Guide to Original Manuscripts in the Collections of the Rosenbach*

Museum and Library. Philadelphia: Rosenbach Museum and Library.

Taylor, Alexander S. (September, October 1859). "Memorials of Juan de Fuca, Discoverer of Oregon," *Hutchings' California Magazine* 4 (39): 116–122; 4 (40): 161–167.

Thelander, Carl G. (1994). *Life on the Edge: A Guide to California's Endangered National Resources*. Santa Cruz, California: Biosystems Books.

Thurman, Michael E. (1967). *The Naval Department of San Blas: New Spain's Bastion for Alta California and Nootka, 1767–1798*. Glendale, California: Arthur H. Clark Company.

Tovell, Freeman M. (2008). *At the Far Reaches of Empire: The Life of Juan Francisco de la Bodega y Quadra*. Vancouver, B.C.: UBC Press.

Twigg, Alan. (Winter 2013). "Finding Juan de Fuca in Kefalonia," *British Columbia History* 46 (4): 36–39.

Wagner, Henry R. (1929). *Spanish Voyages to the Northwest Coast of America in the Sixteenth Century*. San Francisco: California Historical Society.

———. (1933). *Spanish Explorations in the Strait of Juan de Fuca*. New York: Fine Arts Press.

———. (1937). *Cartography of the Northwest Coast of America*. Berkeley, California: Arthur H. Clark Company.

Walbran, John T. (1909). *British Columbia Place Names, 1592–1906*. Ottawa: Government Printing Bureau. Reprint, Vancouver, B.C.: J.J. Douglas, 1971.

Watrous, Stephen. (2001). "Russian Expansion to America," *Fort Ross*. Jenner, California: Fort Ross Interpretive Association.

Wheat, Carl I. (1942). *The Maps of the California Gold Regions 1848–57*. San Francisco: Grabhern Press.

Williams, Glyndwr. (April 1992). "Myth and Reality: The Theoretical Geography of Northwest America from Cook to Vancouver." Paper delivered at the Vancouver Conference on Exploration and Discovery, Vancouver, B.C.

Williams, Maria Shaa Tláa. (2009). *The Alaska Native Reader: History, Culture, Politics*. Durham: Duke University Press.

ABOUT THE AUTHOR

Jim McDowell is an independent British Columbia historian who majored in history at Stanford University. His first career was teaching: he taught elementary school in California and Washington, worked as an inner-city education consultant in Harlem and Brooklyn, and educated teachers at Simon Fraser University. In Vancouver, McDowell also served as the first director of the Carnegie Centre — Canada's largest urban-core community centre.

After working for about twenty years as a freelance writer and independent reporter, McDowell combined his journalistic skills with a long-standing interest in history to write the following books:

Peace Conspiracy: The Story of Warrior-Businessman Yoshiro Fujimura (1993) — a partial biography of a once obscure Japanese naval commander who conspired with a handful of other realistic loyalists in the spring of 1945 to plot Japan's early exit from World War II. *Hamatsa: The Enigma of Cannibalism on the Pacific Northwest Coast* (1997) — a comprehensive, interdisciplinary investigation of the alleged existence of cannibalism among early Indigenous peoples versus the actual significance of ritual cannibalism among some Aboriginal communities. *Father August Brabant: Saviour or Scourge?* (2013) — a biography of the first Roman Catholic missionary to work among Indigenous peoples on the west coast of Vancouver Island during a period of dramatic change for First Nations cultures.

Uncharted Waters offers a full-scale biography of the mariner José María Narváez, which develops from his earlier work, *José María Narváez: The Forgotten Explorer* (1998). McDowell has also published three booklets about local history: *Warpings along the Sunshine Coast in June 1792* (1992); *Tyee: The Last Wild Salmon* (1995); *The History of Sidney Island's Names* (2006).

Currently, McDowell is working on two books: one that probes the possible psychological significance of bird songs for human beings, and another about British Columbia's first public school teacher. He practices Iyengar yoga, paints in watercolour, and co-leads a sixty-member, multi-ethnic walking group for seniors. He lives in Steveston, B.C.

INDEX